INTERNATIONAL BUSINESS HISTORY

INTERNATIONAL BUSINESS HISTORY

A Contextual and Case Approach

Dennis M. P. McCarthy

Westport, Connecticut
London

Library of Congress Cataloging-in-Publication Data

McCarthy, D.M.P. (Dennis Michael Patrick).
   International business history : a contextual and case approach /
Dennis M. P. McCarthy.
      p.   cm.
   Includes bibliographical references and index.
   ISBN 0-275-94413-1 (alk. paper).—ISBN 0-275-94414-X (pbk. :
alk. paper)
   1. International business enterprises—History.   2. International
business enterprises—Case studies.   I. Title.
   HD2755.5.M39   1994
   338.8'8'09—dc20   92-31844

British Library Cataloguing in Publication Data is available.

Library of Congress Catalog Card Number: 92-31844
ISBN: 0-275-94413-1
      0-275-94414-X (pbk.)

First published in 1994

Praeger Publishers, 88 Post Road West, Westport, CT 06881
An imprint of Greenwood Publishing Group, Inc.

Printed in the United States of America

The paper used in this book complies with the
Permanent Paper Standard issued by the National
Information Standards Organization (Z39.48-1984).

10 9 8 7 6 5 4 3 2 1

To Brandon, Sampson, Shane, Steve, and Heike: kindred spirits all

Contents

Contents

Preface

This book has grown out of a course I started at Iowa State University in 1982. In 1985 I began writing what I had originally planned as an introductory textbook for an upper-division undergraduate course in international business business history. In its initial in-house edition, which we first used in 1987, the work reflected the structure of the course as it had evolved since 1982. With no global approach to international business history in print, my students and I improvised our way through those early years. I used whatever sources I could find. These included scholarly monographs, general business texts, theses, dissertations, journal articles, special reports that my students had prepared, and the financial press, especially the *Financial Times* and *The Economist*.

As I gained more classroom experience with my book and as I studied the observations of those who had read it, I concluded that I did not have a real textbook but rather a case studies book. I decided to make numerous changes that would make the work accessible to more readers. I cut the manuscript substantially. I remembered one student's advice: students prefer more short chapters over fewer long ones. I incorporated introductions to each geographical region, more background material at the beginning of each case study, and suggestions for further reading all in response to student suggestions. I added a series of vignettes on international business and economic integration, a topic that is central to the contemporary internationalization of business and the current subject of my own scholarly research.

The command decision to write a case studies book rather than an introductory textbook is an effort to build on the strengths of my course. This book considers many of the themes that make up international business history: the long-term origins of business internationalization, the various types of international businesses over the centuries, and the interplay between the internal and external contexts of business. The organizing principle of this book is geographical because what is greatly needed are global and historical panoramas. I have also road tested the material in this format and believe that the book has relevance for a number of courses.

My case studies book could function as a substitute for a text in international business history, although it is designed as a supplementary work. It could enhance the range of material considered in courses in comparative management, economic development, economic history, international relations, political economy, and other courses that cluster around the global or world economy.

Many people have helped me along the way. I want to thank my first chairman, Louis Geiger, for urging me to teach international business history, Fred Carstensen and Wayne Broehl for their long-term encouragement, Ed Perkins, R. Douglas Hurt, Clair Keller, Wayne Osborn, James Whitaker, George McJimsey, and Adrian A. Bennett III for their advice, Mira Wilkins for her bibliography, Lew Bateman for his early interest in the book, Frank Webb and Zakariya Goshit for research assistance, a number of referees for their constructive suggestions, James Dunton, William Neenan, and Mark Kane of the Greenwood Publishing Group for their great patience, the excellent customer support personnel of the WordPerfect Corporation, Audrey Burton and Carole Kennedy for help in preparing the manuscript, and colleagues in an Iowa State history seminar ("Vigilantes") for critical analysis of several sections in the book. I owe my students at Iowa State special thanks. Since 1982 hundreds of them have taken my course, and some of the most useful suggestions for revision have come from their critiques. I have really enjoyed working with them and wish them all the very best of luck and fortune in the international business arena.

Introduction:
International Business
and Context

The central focus of this book is international business and its many contexts in the past. Emphasis on context is crucial for several reasons. Business history as a subject must continue to broaden its horizons in order to speak more effectively to generations already in or about to enter the "brave new world" of economic globalism at whose creation we are all present. Broader horizons include the multiple contexts in which businesses of all kinds have operated in the past.

A second reason for highlighting context pertains to what some call contextual thinking and its companion contextual decision making. There are some innovators in business education who have been promoting elements of contextual analysis in recent years. Juan Rada, former director general of the IMD international business school in Lausanne, Switzerland, has been stressing how business schools should be encouraging managers to think about the social and political contexts in which they operate. Managers, he argues, have to become more adept at anticipating trends, rather than simply reacting to them (Rada 1989: 28). Harold Leavitt of the Stanford Business School has been urging business schools to broaden their curricula in order to expose students to a variety of viewpoints that might nurture in them leadership and vision. "In the 1960s," he writes, "we brought on psychologists and mathematicians. This time, let's bring on the historians and philosophers and humanists" (Leavitt 1989: 50).

One way to speak to the concerns of Professors Rada and Leavitt and others is to offer a history book that takes as comprehensive an approach to the contexts of business as possible. The book would contain material on social, cultural, political, and economic matters that some conventional purists of business history might regard as extraneous or irrelevant to the subject. The business and business people are the core of business history. But how one presents them and what information and analysis one needs to best understand and appreciate their behavior are matters of interpretation. I strongly believe that businesses and business people are best understood in their multiple contexts. The fate of a business is often linked to how well or poorly its personnel grasped the spirit of the times and acted on its realities. An approach that concentrates on contexts internal to a business and does not sufficiently analyze those external to it is too narrow, especially for an era of multicultural business globalism.

In fact, the very distinction between internal and external contexts is artificial. As a point of departure one can group certain items in each of these two categories. Internal matters for a business are its structures, procedures, and personnel. *Structures* encompass how a business is organized. These include its tables of organization, the designs of its buildings, the locations of its offices or outlets, and relations between a home or parent company and its foreign branches or subsidiaries. *Procedures* embrace both the official and unofficial ways a business functions. *Personnel* are the people dealing with those structures and undertaking those procedures.

External matters for a business arise from outside its own structures. They are sometimes identified with an external environment. They involve such aspects as politics, social relations, and the economy. All of these can have local, national, and international dimensions. The external category also includes the cultures and other resources of the people in those areas where a business has operations. All these factors—both internal and external—have a history that can bear on present-day decision making.

In practice there is considerable overlap between external and internal contexts. Structures and procedures give order and direction to a business but also have strong connections with the external environment. For instance, how an overseas branch develops is influenced by its local environment. Personnel illustrate the meshing of internal and external contexts with special force. They live and work in business and private worlds simultaneously.

A comprehensive view of context considers the distinction between internal and external factors as a way to begin rather than end discussion. It systematically defines all aspects of those internal and external contexts as these pertain to a particular business under analysis. It proceeds to study the relations between and among these aspects. Such an approach will enhance analysis of some basic definitions and concepts in international business history. The definitions involve what an international business was or is. The concepts include centralization, decentralization, interdependence, policy, strategy, and business culture. It is worthwhile to lay out here the essentials of these definitions and concepts. Later chapters present case studies that enrich them.

Today international business has become closely identified with the multinational corporation (MNC). Some business historians regard the multinational corporation—its origins, emergence, and impact—as the central focus of international business history. MNCs are crucial: they are significant today and it is important to study them historically. But there were and are other types of international business that deserve attention. These include partnerships of various kinds, chartered companies, cooperatives, other types of associations, and single-person firms. When they conduct business across international boundaries, they legitimately become part of international business history. An open-minded attitude toward what an international business was or is underlies this book.

Certain concepts constitute an analytical core of international business history. Centralization, decentralization, and interdependence make up a trio of kinship notions. These concepts are reflected in structures and procedures and deeply involve personnel. *Centralization* refers to how much control the headquarters or center of an organization exerts over its local units. It also designates the ways in which that control is maintained and enforced. *Decentralization* highlights the contrary forces. It points to the degree of control that those local units have over their own affairs. A companion concept to decentralization is local autonomy. *Autonomy* means the ability and capacity to act independenly. So local autonomy is the degree of operational freedom of those local units.

Interdependence is a concept that has become familiar in recent years. It refers to the ways in which headquarters and local units relate. In general, the center and those local units rely or depend upon one another. This interdependence exists even though the organizational relationship is hierarchical: the center is on the top and the local units are on the bottom. Another way to define interdependence is to combine the concepts of centralization and decentralization. Interdependence is a particular mix of centralization and decentralization. The ways in which the center and local units depend upon one another all exhibit degrees of centralization and decentralization. Interdependence is thus a blend of centralization and decentralization.

Policy, strategy, and business culture touch upon the multiple contexts of a business as well as the aforementioned trio of concepts. Policy and strategy should be closely related. A *policy* is a framework that guides action. A policy can be a *strategy* when it is systematically linked to the pursuit of clearly defined goals in a short, middle, or long term. Policy and strategy influence and sometimes define structures, procedures, and personnel. But the interaction is mutual: structures, procedures, and personnel can greatly affect the formulation and implementation of policy and strategy.

Policy and strategy should incorporate information from the external environment. A business has to decide which aspects from politics, social relations, the economy, local cultures and other resources are relevant for it. This task is not easy, but it must be attempted. Profitability and sometimes survival depend upon an acute awareness of the possibilities and risks in one's external environment.

Business culture is a concept that, like interdependence, has received more attention in recent years. Each business has its own distinctive culture. It embodies the character or ethos of the business as reflected in the ways its personnel think and act. A business culture is the product of a continuing interaction between the internal and external contexts of a business. When a business operates in an environment of increasingly diverse local cultures, it is important for that business to study the impact of the environment on its own business culture.

These definitions and concepts do not exhaust all those that are useful for international business history. The structure of this work permits the introduction where appropriate of additional definitions and concepts. A sketch of this structure and an explanation of its rationale follows.

Our focus on international business and context takes us to many locations in the world. So the book has five parts. Each contains case studies from a region of the globe: Europe; North America; Central, South America and the Caribbean; Africa; and Asia and the western Pacific. Each part has its own introduction which discusses the overall significance of the material in that part. Case studies include background information and summaries of main points. Suggestions for further reading appear at the end of the book. Each part of the book features a vignette on international business and economic integration.

This case study approach is designed to acquaint the reader with the essentials of international business history, which derive from the previous discussion of contexts, definitions, and concepts. My hope is that after immersion in this book readers will systematically analyze a business in its multiple contexts. This process involves defining those essentials, which are worthwhile memorizing. One must consider a business in relation to its structures, procedures, personnel, policies, strategies, centralization-decentralization mix, business culture, and the dimensions of its external environment. These include politics, social relations, the economy, local cultures, and other resources. The history of all these internal and external items is important, as is their interplay.

One may not be able to find information on every essential for a particular business. Our case studies strive for comprehensiveness, but some businesses are more fully analyzed than others. Still, the goal is to consider as many dimensions of context as possible, with emphasis on the interaction between internal and external environments.

While the presentation is introductory, the horizon of the book is global. Its five-part panorama provides a crucial global perspective. This vision is greatly needed in a single-volume work aimed at beginning students and others interested in international business history. I am acutely aware that a less sweeping geographical approach would facilitate the more detailed development of fewer topics. However, my goal is to introduce international business in all its contexts, and a global approach increases the diversity of those contexts and makes the introductory nature of the book more complete.

Readers deserve that diversity presented in as many ways as possible. This job requires not only that global panorama. It also demands going back far enough in time to convey a sense of the long-term origins of the contemporary globalization of business. Different parts of the book reach back centuries in order to communicate that long-term perspective.

There are other reasons for insisting on a long-term approach to the past. One comes from historical method. The discipline of history addresses the past not as mere chronology but as the living record of changes in human beings and their environments. These involve many factors. One concerns changes in the meanings of words through space and time. It is not wise to take a current vocabulary of business terms, read it back into the past, and assume that all words necessarily keep their present meaning. The farther back into the past one goes, the more one is reminded of the transformation that words as well as other aspects of the human condition can undergo.

This very long-term perspective, which helps us better understand the secular origins of business globalization and related human and environmental phenomena, may also have another benefit. There is considerable talk of the need to take a longer view. This point has become a common recommendation of what United States business must acquire in order to compete more effectively in the global arena. It does seem as if too many U.S. business people are preoccupied with a financial short term of six months to a year. This focus may be appropriate for some business people, such as comptrollers and auditors. But every business and every business person needs a strategy for the short, medium, and long term. One component of that strategy is defining what those different time frames mean and what activities belong in each.

This exercise requires a depth of analysis that can be assisted by mental habits of thinking about the past in the long term. I am not suggesting that this book will automatically impart such long-term thinking skills to those who peruse it. But careful consideration of a variety of case studies that treat changes for business in short, medium, and long terms may help. The ability to put things in perspective greatly strengthens one's capacity to cope with change from day to day. Projecting systematically back into the past should fortify one's ability to think forward with some method. Please keep in mind those essentials as we travel around the world.

PART I. EUROPE

The following case studies present some facts of business life in Europe over seven centuries. The first set portrays three famous European financial families—the Medicis, Fuggers, and Rothschilds—against the background of their times. The second set considers multinational corporations from the United Kingdom, France, Germany, and Sweden in the context of a comparative emergence model.

The three families together offer a panorama that sweeps from fourteenth into the twentieth centuries. They were (and the Rothschilds still are) intensely involved in the major events of their times. Their experiences provide an opportunity to witness watershed phenomena in European history. These include the Renaissance in the fourteenth and fifteenth centuries, the overseas expansion of Europe from the fifteenth, the spread of industrialization from the eighteenth, and various wars and revolutions.

Besides the historical panorama, the families offer insights into the benefits and difficulties of moving money and goods across international borders during different time periods. Their stories also have a human interest that has made them popular reading for the author's own students.

The multinational case study introduces a *comparative emergence model*. This model, which is explained in the introduction to the case study, seeks to explain the appearance of multinational corporations from various countries in a comparative framework. The model considers the roles of five elements in the emergence of multinational corporations: (1) the role of government or the state; (2) export markets and external sources of supply; (3) technological change: invention and innovation; (4) relative factor scarcities and qualities of land, labor, capital, entrepreneurial ability, and opportunity; and (5) the internationalist nature of a country's and corporation's business culture.

Comparisons and contrasts are part of the historian's method. Because discerning similarities and differences among the multinational experiences of variety of countries is useful, a framework of comparison and contrast is essential. The comparative emergence model provides just this infrastructure.

The case studies in Chapters 1 and 2, along with the vignette on international business and the economic integration of Europe in Chapter 3, furnish concentrated looks from a European perspective at many of the essentials needed to study international business history.

1

Family Businesses Expanding Across Borders and Generations: The Medicis, Fuggers, Rothschilds

These families share certain traits. All were deeply connected with the politics and economics of their times. All were financial pioneers. All had to accept the consequences of the genetic "roll of the dice." That is, their offspring may or may not have been up to the demands of continuing the family business. These studies suggest a critical genetic divide around the third generation or thereafter for the Medicis and Fuggers but not the Rothschilds. At this time the person or people who should have led the business into the future turned out unwilling or unable.

All families had close relationships with political leaders. These ties presented great opportunities for enrichment but contained traps for the unwary. How each family dealt with political leaders holds a major key to understanding that family's financial fate.

All families faced continuing problems with their business structures, procedures, personnel, policies, and strategies. Readers should try to imagine what they might have done differently, if they had been the family leader at the time.

These essays also address another core issue. The question is the transfer of income and wealth from one generation to the next. The intergenerational transmission of wealth and income involves its own structures, procedures, and strategies. If the strategy is the very long-term survival of the business through many generations, the more the business has a life of its own, the greater is the likelihood of its enduring the problems of any one generation. The life of a business pertains not only to its legal identity but also to the flexibility and adaptability of its own structures, procedures, and personnel.

Family businesses must follow prudent business practices. The hallmark of a healthy business of whatever kind is a balance sheet showing equity cherished and debt disciplined. The business should not be consuming its assets, the basis of its wealth, in order to generate a short-term cash flow. The business should have a strategy of debt assumption designed to promote, not strangle, its own future.

The Medicis and Fuggers illustrate the perils of cutting too deeply into the equity (net worth) of a business in order to meet short-term financial demands. As they ate their seed corn, the survivability of their businesses deteriorated. Of the three only the Rothschilds have managed the continuous intergenerational transmission of their business but in a manner that has involved more key personnel from outside the family. The lesson here may be that sooner or later every family enterprise must grapple with the need to incorporate outsiders in ways that strengthen it but do not dilute its distinctive family business culture.

THE MEDICIS: BANK, BOOM, BUST

The Medici family has a long history of social and financial involvement on the European continent. It makes a cameo appearance here in connection with the Medici Bank, which lasted from 1397 to 1494. To understand the Medici Bank some basic facts about Renaissance politics and economics are needed. Europe was divided into numerous political jurisdictions at the time. Many had their own money, which created problems for most business people but opportunities for those skilled at exchanging currencies. The Roman Catholic church influenced business procedures. The church prohibited *any interest on any loan;* this was the usury doctrine.

To circumvent the interest prohibition the Medici and others popularized the *bill of exchange.* The essence of this procedure was to negotiate bills payable in another place and usually in another currency. A lender (creditor) would give a borrower (debtor) a document (bill of exchange) that required the holder to pay back a specified sum at some future date in another location and another currency. The introduction of three types of transformation—*space, time* and the *medium of remission*—facilitated the assessment of interest. It was included in the price of the bill, called a bill of exchange or letter of payment.

While the Medicis were evading the church in one way, they helped it in another. The church, as a continental organization with global aspirations, greatly needed the services of competent financiers. It received revenues in many currencies and wanted to take advantage of differentials in exchange rates in order to maximize cash flow. Capitalizing on these differences is one of the oldest versions of arbitrage.

Among those who provided these services was the Medici Bank, headquartered in Florence, one of city-states that then dominated an Italy that was not politically united until the 1860s. The Medici Bank piggybacked on the church to become a premier financial institution in Western Europe. To an analysis of that organization we now turn.

In 1397 Giovanni di Bicci de' Medici moved his headquarters to Florence from Rome, where he had been managing a bank. In so doing he founded the Medici Bank. This institution had its own life cycle. There were the antecedents and early years under Giovanni di Bicci (1397–1429). The second period was the heyday of the Bank with Cosimo at the helm (1429–1464). The last phase was the decline (1464–1494). The bank almost made it to 100, falling short at about 97.

The rise of the bank, from its beginnings up to several years before Cosimo died in 1464, can be analyzed within our framework of essentials (see introduction). As to personnel, the family benefited from the genetic roll of the dice in the cases of both Giovanni and Cosimo. Both should be appreciated in their own terms. Historians could not explain, according to Raymond de Roover, what seemed to be the sudden appearance of a major banking house at the outset of the fifteenth century until more was learned about the Medici family tree. None of Giovanni's direct ancestors is recorded as a banker or otherwise associated with finance.

Two related questions arise. How did Giovanni and the bank get started? It turns out that a distant cousin played a crucial part in the origins of the Medici Bank. That cousin was Messer Vieri di Cambio (or Cambiozzo) de' Medici, who lived from 1323 to 1395 and after 1370 was one of the leading bankers in Florence. Both Giovanni and his older brother Francesco worked for Messer Vieri's banking house. They rose from apprentices to factors (a facilitator or originator of exchange) and then to partners in the bank.

Several important connections stand out from this tale. The Medici Bank was an institutional "offshoot" of the distant cousin's banking house (de Roover 1968: 35). The brothers' experiences with their cousin's bank can be placed in other contexts. There was, as economists say, much "learning by doing." Giovanni gained the expertise needed to become a financial entrepreneur in his own right. In the language of anthropology, the nuclear family of Giovanni and his brother was using the extended Medici family to engage in the first stages of its own capital accumulation.

Without someone to build on the foundation laid by Giovanni, the bank would have had a short run. The Medici family was fortunate through another generation. Cosimo had the right stuff, the right approach, and was head of the bank at the right time. He had great aptitudes for both leadership and administration. Some people can lead well; some can administer well; very few people can do both. Cosimo had not only the aptitudes but also the strength and savvy to put them into practice. He was successful as a leader and administrator in both politics and business.

Cosimo's approach deserves study. He had just the right amount of indirection in his style, which was made possible by an uncanny knack of selecting the right person for a particular job. In the sphere of formal politics he preferred to stay behind the scenes and rule Florence through "front men." In Florence no important decision was ever taken against his will or advice and he inspired such awe that his power went unchallenged and no plots were hatched to overthrow his rule. In business, he was known and respected in Italy, throughout the rest of Europe, and outside the continent as well, although the Medici Bank operated mainly in Western Europe (de Roover 1968: 75).

As a business person his methods have received intense scrutiny. He had the capacity to distinguish generalization from detail and to establish priorities in both. He knew how to manage: he delegated power but never to the extent that devolution undermined his powers. He generated both policies and strategies and saw to it that his instructions were obeyed to the letter. Because of slow communications, managers of the bank's branches had considerable autonomy, subject to reversal from above. Contemporary communications and the structure of the bank itself, to be discussed shortly, made his ability to pick the right person for a post all the more valuable. Nowhere was this aptitude for personnel demonstrated more vividly or the importance of having the right people in certain jobs spotlighted so graphically than in the case of Giovanni Benci. He was Cosimo de Medici's general manager from 1435 to 1455, two decades of continuous expansion for a bank that had become the largest banking house of its time. He was an outsider to the family. Benci's death was an irreparable loss for the Medici Bank. Even the best never do it by themselves and usually have others, best in their own fields, working for them. Cosimo may have been a demanding boss, but the record shows that he could be generous in sharing profits with some of his managers. His real problems faced him toward the end, when his health was deteriorating from gout (de Roover 1968: 75).

The Medicis then encountered the intergenerational question again. This time their luck began to run out. Cosimo decided to replace the deceased general manager Benci with a member of the Medici family, Giovanni, Cosimo's own son. This move was unwise. Giovanni was not up to the demands of the general managership. In trying to correct one mistake Cosimo made another (de Roover 1968: 76). He summoned Francesco di Tommaso Sassetti, a key operative in Geneva, back to Florence to assist Giovanni. The combination proved a double difficulty. Piero, the Cosimo son who might have carried on his father's legacy, died shortly after his own father did. And Cosimo's grandson, Lorenzo (sometimes called the Magnificent), never demonstrated an aptitude for business, although he was an accomplished statesman. Cosimo's double gifts for both politics and business were a once in a lifetime occurrence for the Medicis. That legacy, which Piero and Lorenzo might have preserved, consisted of *structures* that made the Medici Bank one of the central antecedents of contemporary international business.

The Medici Bank was, in essence, not a single unit but a *combination* of *partnerships* (de Roover 1968: 78). There were reasons for this arrangement. In the thirteenth and fourteenth centuries such major companies as the Bardi, Peruzzi, and Acciaiuoli preferred a more centralized form of organization. Centralization was carried too far, however, as all three companies exhibited rigidity in crisis and failed around 1345. Approaches promising more flexibility became essential. Two variations of partnership emerged. There were combinations of autonomous partnerships controlled either by an individual person or by another partnership at the top of the whole edifice. The crux of both arrangements features two layers, which can be expressed in different sets of terms. At the apex of the table of organization was the controlling partnership or individual person; underneath were a number of tributary partnerships. Some designate the controlling partnership or individual as the *parent* and the tributary partnerships as the *subsidiaries*. These terms, especially the latter set, have been used to designate relations between headquarters and branches, or center and offshoots, of varieties of international enterprise.

For the Medici Bank these terms meant the following. The controlling partnership or parent included as partners the Medici family members and one or two outsiders. Among the latter were Benci and Salutati from 1435 to 1443. Besides the majority Medici–minority outsider mix at the center, there was a host of branches, including manufacturing establishments, underneath that apex. The bank, in fact, consisted of three major product divisions at its zenith in the mid-fifteenth century. These were silk manufacturing (one partnership), cloth manufacturing (two partnerships), and international banking and foreign trade (numerous partnerships) (de Roover 1968: 83).

The term bank can have many meanings. The Medici Bank was an authentic bank in one of the generic senses of that term: it was in the business of originating, facilitating, and promoting exchange through the extension of credit as some bills of exchange were loans. It also exhibited a degree of diversification that was distinctive through its involvement in silk and cloth manufacturing, as well as other Medici ventures as dealers in iron and in alum, a substance used in medicine, dyeing, and many technical processes.

Some have remarked on how closely the Medici Bank foreshadowed if not resembled the modern holding company (de Roover 1968: 81). But not all holding companies are exactly alike nor were their antecedents. Here are important details concerning relationships between the controlling Medici partnership and its tributaries. As in any arrangement of devolution, there were elements of both decentralization and centralization.

Decentralization was evident in the following facts. Each branch was a separate legal entity. It had its own style, capital, books, and management. The branches dealt with one another as if they were outsiders: one charged commission to another as if it were another business (de Roover 1968: 78). These arrangements worked to establish a distinctive identity for each branch.

Separate legal identity was important for the Medici Bank. Contemporary litigation seemed to establish the fact that one branch could not be held responsible for the actions of another (de Roover 1968: 82 and 84). Whether the Medici experience in this regard has any precedential value for recent liability litigation is a complex matter that is analyzed in the Bhopal case study (Chapter 16). For the Medici Bank legal protection was essential. The bank was not a combination of corporations or joint stock companies but of partnerships. As such it did not enjoy the limited liability that distinguishes the corporate form. Limited liability means that one's financial liability is limited to the extent of one's involvement in the corporation and does not include all one's assets. Nor did the bank enjoy the potential audience of financial supporters that a joint-stock company had. So practical acceptance of the legal notion of separate identity, a linchpin of decentralization, gave some means of defending against attack on the financial integrity of the overall Medici administrative structure.

This structure was maintained and strengthened by elements that promoted centralization. The parent in Florence controlled the subsidiary partnerships by owning more than 50 percent of the capital of each tributary. If he or she who owns the capital has ultimate influence, then the 50 plus percent rule was a start in that direction. If there were any misunderstandings as to where the power to make and enforce command decisions was located, the articles of association for each subsidiary gave the senior partners in Florence the powers to "determine policy" and implement it, with the attendant rights to inspect and supervise. They had, in short, "the power to lay down the law," according to Raymond de Roover (de Roover 1968: 81).

The presence within the same organization of legal principles promoting decentralization and centralization is intriguing on several counts. In terms of structural resilience, which the Bardi, Peruzzi, Acciaiuoli, and other companies too tightly organized did not possess, the tension between centralization and decentralization promoted flexibility and, in turn, institutional longevity. As far as questions of legal liability are concerned, judgments are not so readily pronounced. Establishing what separate legal identity means is crucial. Does separate mean unique or just distinctive, divorced or only detached? Any organization can benefit from being able to exhibit multiple legal personalities in different jurisdictions. Does this capacity establish the degree of separation necessary to insulate legally one part of a company from the consequences of the actions of another? To the extent that recorded litigation survives, the courts contemporary with the bank thought so. But the answer might be different at another time.

The bank's boom was a product of more than fate. It was blessed with able personnel in all its ranks. Its structures were not only well tuned internally but also consonant with the requirements of the times. The Medici Bank was on the financial frontiers as it refined the bill of exchange and a number of accounting procedures. The bank's bust resulted not only from the weakening of Cosimo's powers, the inaptitudes or unfortunate demises of his possible successors, and the loss of Giovanni Benci, but also from a convergence of external forces. The Medicis faced both a growing political opposition in Florence and elsewhere as well as a more general economic decline in many European locations that accelerated in the last several decades of the fifteenth century. The Pazzi conspiracy of 1478, which tried to bring down both the bank and Medici political rule, failed. But one Medici was murdered. This frightening episode indicated worse things to come. The official end did come in 1494 when the Medicis were expelled from Florence. The bank was then perhaps not technically bankrupt but on its financial death bed.

During those worsening economic times, the Medicis cut into their equity—residual value—in order to make ends meet. They ate their seed corn. This approach got the bank through the short run but was a sure prescription for long-run financial contraction and disintegration. As the saying goes, the short run got shorter and the long run got nearer. There are understandable differences of opinion on whether stronger, more expert leadership in its last several decades might have saved the bank. The challenges confronting it were formidable, crushing as it turned out, but someone else might have preserved the bank in a different location and in a down-sized fashion. That did not happen and one of the world's most interesting financial institutions died.

THE FUGGERS: THE REWARDS OF FINANCE,
THE PERILS OF POLITICS

The Fugger family was a central European financial dynasty with continental connections. While the Medici Bank was a creation of the fourteenth and fifteenth centuries, the Fuggers began their climb in the fifteenth, crested in the sixteenth, and started to decline in the seventeenth century. Theirs is also a story of able and farsighted leadership through the first several generations, leadership that seized, even defined, opportunities for amassing wealth. Theirs is, more so than the saga of the Medici Bank, the tale of escalating involvement with numerous political leaders that turned financially negative and then self-destructive.

The central contribution of the Fuggers to our study may be as negative role models. Their experiences demonstrate the perils of excessive political involvement. Some degree of involvement with political leaders was a necessary cost of doing business, and these relationships were sometimes financially rewarding, especially at the start. But they all eventually soured. What these relationships were and how and why they went wrong are themes of this story.

Their first significant entrepreneur was Hans Fugger, who came from the village of Graben to Augsburg, Germany, in 1367. He was a weaver and trader. He left an estate of 3,000 florins, which was considered to be a substantial fortune in those days. He fathered a number of sons, including Andreas and Jakob I. Andreas became the richer son, but he had sons who squandered his fortune (this is a male chauvinist financial world). Jakob I, a modest man, gained some recognition as a master of the Guild of Weavers in Augsburg, but he was looked down upon by his brother Andreas. History would treat him differently. He fathered Jakob II, who showed a real genius for business, and it is almost entirely to him, Richard Ehrenberg notes, that the Fugger owe their importance in world history (Ehrenberg 1928: 64-65).

This "genius" might not have flourished, had not another series of unforeseen events occurred. These concerned the sons of Jakob I. When Jakob I died, Ulrich, George, and Peter attempted to carry on the business; Jakob I had been a mint master in the growing Tyrolese mining district. This was an alpine region in western Austria and northern Italy, and Jakob I had given the Fugger family their first connections with this important mining industry. There were four more sons in addition to those three who took over the business after their father died. Two of them had died before their father did, and two more, Marcus and Jakob, were supposed to enter religious occupations. Then in 1473 Peter died. Ulrich and George asked Jakob to give up his clerical career and become a merchant. These were the decisive circumstances for the beginnings of the Fugger family as a continental financial dynasty: Peter's death, Ulrich's and George's request to Jakob, and Jakob's assent. Who knows what kind of a cleric Jakob would have become, but as a business person he found himself. These events occurred early in Jakob's life and gave him a chance to grow up as a merchant. He was only fourteen when he became a merchant in 1473. As the Medici Bank was experiencing greater strains, the Fugger family, though perhaps not knowing it, had reason for enormous hope.

Jakob II's early business years were marked by several key experiences. His most valuable period of "learning by doing" came in the Fondaco dei Tedeschi, the famous German business house in Venice, where other young south Germans of that day also worked. His elder brothers had a permanent warehouse also in Venice, and Jakob II eventually became a partner in that enterprise, and the three sons together operated the business for some time. As this trio guided the institutional antecedent of the Fugger fortune, they made an agreement that proved central to the transmission over generations of the Fugger business. They compacted that their male heirs and descendants should leave their property in common in the business. The daughters would be given money in dowries. The objective of this agreement was to ensure that the Fugger business would remain in every way undivided (Ehrenberg 1928: 65). This principle guided the Fuggers during the good times; when they hit bad times, it was abandoned, unwisely. But that happened much later. For now Jakob II had knowledge, experience, and a base on which to build.

When Jakob II entered the business, the Fuggers were still trading in their established patterns. Major products were spices, silks, and woolens. In 1487, fourteen years after he became a merchant, Jakob II made a decisive departure from those customary practices. He entered undertakings of greater profit, such as bills of exchange and mines (Ehrenberg 1928: 66). "Old" Jakob, as Jakob I is sometimes called, had laid the groundwork for this move in the middle of the fifteenth century. But it was his son who made these practices standard operating procedure.

Two episodes started the Fugger business in a grander direction. In 1487 Jakob II, in an informal banking consortium with Antonio de Cavallis of Genoa, lent 23,627 florins to Siegmund, the Archduke of Tyrol, the area where Jakob I had been a mint master. The archduke owned rich silver mines, but always had a liquidity problem: he constantly needed money. He was asset rich but cash poor. As collateral or security for the loan, Jakob II and Antonio de Cavallis received a mortgage on the best of the Schwatz silver mines and the whole province of Tyrol. According to the terms of the loan, if the money were not punctually repaid, the silver due from the mines to the archduke would be handed over. One year later, in 1488, Ulrich, George, and Jakob II lent the archduke 150,000 florins. The terms of the second loan revised those of the first and were more favorable to the Fuggers in the near term. Until the archduke paid back 150,000 florins, the Fuggers were to receive the entire silver production of the Schwatz mines at very low prices (Ehrenberg 1928: 66).

There are ominous elements in the archduke episodes. The Fuggers made a bundle from these transactions and others to come. But lending substantial sums of money to political leaders or underemployed nobility has inherent risks. The moneylender to the stars becomes involved in relationships not so easily turned off, develops expectations that he or she will have more money to lend when called upon, and may pass the point of safe financial return without fully realizing it. When all this went wrong may not be possible to answer nor may it even be the right question. Getting involved in such commercial behavior brought about factors that worked to create future problems. Not every political leader had assets as readily distrainable or repossessable as the archduke's silver mines. A monarch may offer his or her country as collateral for a loan, but how does one take possession of Austria or France or Spain when its ruler(s) default or lag behind debt repayment schedules? Such risks were present in Fugger operating procedure from the beginning, but did not become financially threatening until later.

Jakob II increased the family's wealth at an outstanding pace. The available numbers for various asset and expenditure categories are not reported in a standardized fashion from one time period to another. But it appears that from 1511 through 1527, two years after Jakob II's death, Fugger capital in land, houses, goods, book debts, and the intriguing "etc." category increased from 196,791 to 2,021,202 florins. During these seventeen years Fugger capital multiplied over nine times: it went up 927 percent, an average annual growth rate of 54.5 percent (Ehrenberg 1928: 85 and 87).

The inclusion of book debts, estimated at 1,650,000 florins at the end of 1527, indicates the high degree of intangibility that this definition of capital exhibits. Book debts are definitely assets not in hand, with varying probabilities depending on the particular loan that they will never be in or on hand. So this estimate of Fugger fortune growth, the 54.5 annual percentage rate (APR), must be used with caution. The Fuggers did own hundreds of thousands of florins worth of goods, mines and mining shares, and other real estate. Insofar as these were designated assets that one could touch and see, the Fuggers had a significant percentage of their fortune in tangible capital. But the ratio in a portfolio between tangible and intangible assets, particularly book debts, is crucial to appraising underlying financial strength in the present and prospects for future stability and growth. In 1527 the immediate future seemed bright, but the potential for more serious problems in the longer term was already embedded in the Fugger portfolio.

Jakob II had achieved this substantial increase in the book value of the Fugger fortune partly through connections with some of Europe's major political leaders. Relations with the Hapsburgs were central to the intertwined processes of asset and influence accumulation by the Fuggers. In their earlier phases these involvements were financially prudent and sometimes produced spectacular political results. Fugger business with Emperor Maximilian I in the early 1490s was judicious. Maximilian, the worst manager of all the Hapsburgs, received control over the government of Tyrol in 1490 from Archduke Siegmund of the insatiable liquidity habit. One money junkie succeeded another. The Fuggers during the first half of the 1490s were wary about giving Maximilian everything he wanted. When they did make a loan, they were careful to link it to a distrainable asset, in this case the silver and then copper mines of the Tyrol district. The influence and name recognition that these creditor associations with major political leaders produced only intensified the Fuggers' own desires for more. The most telling sequence of events demonstrating the power of money and justifying the description of this time as "The Age of the Fugger" surrounded the election of Charles V as Holy Roman Emperor during 1518 and 1519 (Ehrenberg 1928: 74). The Holy Roman Empire was a Germanic empire of central European states considered as beginning with either Charlemagne in 800 or Otto the Great in 962 and lasting until 1806.

The election of its emperor provided the greatest opportunity for demonstrating who had the strongest financial and political clout. The extended electoral process tested the determination and endurance of all its participants. Whoever wielded decisive influence was perceived, rightly or wrongly, as having the financial resources to underpin that staying power. This is a classic instance of the means, the electoral process, having perhaps more symbolism than the end, the titular perpetuation of the Holy Roman Empire itself. The election had enormous public relations value. Enter the Fuggers.

Charles, a Hapsburg, ruled only the Netherlands when he first dealt with the

Fuggers. Wolff Haller, the Fuggers' agent in Antwerp, a seaport in what is now northern Belgium, performed important services for Charles then and when he assumed control of the government in Spain in 1517. Haller continued to play an important intermediary role between the Fuggers and Charles through the electoral process for the leadership of the Holy Roman Empire. Being elected emperor involved buying off the German electors who did the voting. Prospective candidates and their agents had to deal with each elector as an individual. One had to fashion a series of bilateral "arrangements" with the electors, which involved quid pro quos: my vote in return for cash and/or credit. Each elector had various "requirements" in these matters.

What made this bargaining difficult for Charles and his agents was the presence of a competitor, King Francis, who sat on the French throne. This election had its share of continental competition and intrigue. Francis was from the House of Valois, another major European dynasty with high aspirations. On one level, the contest pitted the Houses of Hapsburg and Valois; on another, the nationalisms of France, Spain, and the Netherlands; and on still another, the strengths of the House of Fugger and their financial rivals. There were conflicts within these alliances as well. The camps of the Fugger dynasty and Charles did not get on perfectly. The Fuggers were still prudent in their financial dealings with nobility and continued to drive hard bargains for extending their support. At one time during the electoral process, Charles found the Fuggers' terms too hard and entered into relations with other merchants. In the end he needed the Fuggers because no others could deliver as effectively.

In early 1519 Charles seemed to be winning out over Francis, but the French king increased his financial efforts. He upped the ante, which caused the electors to escalate their demands on Charles. His representative reported that the electors would only sell their votes for cash or the Fuggers' promises to pay. The stakes rose a number of times during these purified proceedings. Charles, who still deemed the Fugger terms too exacting, continued to apply to them for new loans. As this process climaxed, the Fuggers were by far the most important participants in a consortium of financiers that lent over 850,000 florins to Charles. The Fugger share was 543,000 florins. There were eleventh-hour activities in finally fixing each person's bribe, but Charles won. And so did the Fugger family, again.

During this marathon there were portents. Jakob II complained over and over that as he was asked to lend new sums of money, comparatively small old payments due to him remained in arrears (Ehrenberg 1928: 77). The components of "book debt" in the Fugger portfolio, including time or maturation and scale or amount, were shifting dramatically in a way that boded ill. Jakob found that his past loans that were behind in their payment schedules (in arrears) were minor in contrast to his much larger new debt, the repayment capacity of which had yet to be tested.

Such after-the-fact technical analysis of the changing structure of Fugger loans should not diminish appreciation of the family's ascent under Jakob's leadership. In 1525, when he died, the Fuggers were, beyond dispute, the most influential financiers of their time. Unlike the Medici Bank, the domain of which was primarily Western Europe, the Fuggers were more continental. Their relations reached from Hungary and Poland in eastern Europe, through their home base in central Europe, southward into the Italian city-states, and westward into Spain and the Low Countries.

As befits the prominent, their name evoked both praise and scorn. According to Richard Ehrenberg, the Fuggers in many countries were hated by some people. "In popular language their name was used as a generic term for a great monopolist. The Fucker, Fokker, Fucar, and so forth, have ever since become in many different countries the name for the financiers which the people held responsible for every evil" (Ehrenberg 1928: 83-84).

Call them what you will, the Fuggers could have the last laugh for several decades after Jakob's death in 1525. Anton Fugger, one of the nephews already involved in the business as Jakob was childless, was empowered by his uncle's will to manage affairs with the same authority as Jakob had exerted. This choice was excellent. Anton presided over the Fugger heyday, which lasted from 1525 to Anton's death in 1560. This period fulfilled promise but also presaged more problems. The Fuggers continued as the most influential lenders to the political stars of their times. The Hapsburg connection became more financially demanding. Their rulers on several European thrones, including that of the Holy Roman Empire, required financing that escalated with each loan request.

Meeting those demands required more delicate acts of portfolio management. The Fuggers needed some basis on which to continue to make loans. As time went by, their ability to honor their new commitments depended more and more on their receiving repayments of old loans. The Fugger portfolio still consisted of such tangible assets as mines and other types of property, but these generated sometimes irregular cash flows. Playing the creditor game successfully requires that one preserve tangible assets, particularly when these represent equity, and lend on the basis of cash flow. The Fuggers found it harder and harder to operate on these principles. While public perceptions of the Fugger as financiers extraordinaire remained strong well into the sixteenth century, the basis for these views was eroding at an accelerating rate. The Fugger fortune became more fragile.

A significant alteration in internal structures also occurred that threatened the intergenerational integrity of the family money. Raymund died in 1535, Hieronymus in 1538, and Anton then felt the need to take his nephews into the business. The aftermath of this decision was not as favorable as Jakob II's willing of control to his nephew Anton. The compact that Jakob II and his brothers forged—that their male heirs and descendants should leave their property in common to the business—began to unravel. Requiring that descendants will their property to the business did not guarantee its survival.

The men had to have something to will in the first place. This was, however, usually the case. Relaxing the compact promoted estate fragmentation and undermined the capacity of the business to survive generational changes.

The Fuggers dreaded the prospect of default by monarchs. They became as desperate for the repayment of those larger new loans as some of their creditors were in their approaches to them. Maintaining a threshold cash flow was becoming more difficult. Then the dreaded happened. Their first major financial crisis occurred in 1557, three years before Anton died. King Philip, a Hapsburg running both Spain and the Netherlands, ordered that no further repayments be made to his creditors in either of those countries. He also confiscated silver valued at 570,000 ducats supposedly destined for the Fugger in Flanders. Anton Fugger was furious and nervous. Philip had seriously damaged his cash flow and placed the family fortune in jeopardy. In 1558 the Fugger claims against Philip in Spain, excluding those incurred in the Netherlands, amounted to a total of 1,660,809 ducats (100 crowns = about 94 Spanish ducats of 11 reals). Add to that the confiscated silver. The king reneged on his apparent promise to repay. The Fuggers' own capital at this time supposedly was about 2 million gulden (3 ducats = 4 gulden). They also had outstanding claims in the Netherlands amounting to 1.5 million gulden (Ehrenberg 1928: 114-16).

In this reckoning Fugger capital was not separated into its parts, perhaps because such information was not available. So one does not know to what extent, if at all, this estimation of capital includes other "book debts." Simply demonstrating the size of some loans, much or all of which would turn out to be irrecoverable, and showing how these surpassed estimations of current capital do not in themselves constitute evidence of imminent Fugger collapse. Crucial factors are not only the size of external debt, but also its quality and the artistry with which it is managed. The Fuggers had already passed into the zone of a mega-debt, the quality of which varied. In those cases just cited the debt had approached zero quality and would achieve that dubious status because it was irrecoverable.

What saved the Fuggers for the moment was an artistry of debt management made possible by perceptions that they were still excellent credit risks. In the aftermath of the 1557 crisis, the Fuggers had to borrow more money and seek more lines of credit. They borrowed large sums in Antwerp, usually at 8 to 10 percent per year (Ehrenberg 1928: 116). This was the familiar technique of borrowing at a lower rate of interest in order to lend at a higher. It requires an exceptional artistry of debt management, particularly when one's portfolio is already unstable. The Fuggers were able to use the Antwerp money market to sustain their cash flow for several years, but this procedure proved unworkable after the death of Anton in 1560. Problems concerning his successors and other matters undermined public perceptions of the House of Fugger as a sound credit risk.

When Anton died, the Fuggers had arrived at the critical third generation in any family's long-term survival as a financial entity. For them it was fatal. Anton's successors were inadequate. Anton had willed that his nephew Hans Jakob was to take over the business along with with Marx Fugger, Anton's oldest son. This tandem disintegrated. Hans Jakob had little aptitude or interest in business. He was more a patron of the arts and learning; he was a passionate collector. He was also occupied with his personal relations with princes, especially the dukes of Bavaria. Marx Fugger at least had some aptitude and interest, but minimal competence is not what the Fugger business required at this crucial juncture. It needed a leader of vision. No such person appeared. The Fuggers' financial rivals were more aggressive. Business people from Genoa, an Italian city-state, had made major inroads into the Fugger domain in Spain. The Fuggers remained shackled to their past and did not take advantage of the fresh financial opportunities that were developing (Ehrenberg 1928: 119).

Internal problems intensified. Fugger balance sheets throughout the sixteenth century show an acceleration of several disturbing trends. Their tangible assets dwindled; the later reports do not mention any "Landed Property." The degree of portfolio diversification diminished dangerously; as the sixteenth century went on, the Fugger for all practical purposes ceased dealing in commodities. Loans became all consuming, while the domain of Fugger activity contracted. In the latter part of the century Fugger efforts were focused mainly on Spain and Antwerp, all other continental business connections having ceased or become unimportant (Ehrenberg 1928: 120-23).

There were debilitating dissensions among the partners. The rift between Hans Jakob and other members of the family grew worse after he withdrew from the firm. His death in 1575 was not the opportunity for reconciliation it might have been. Management changes were frequent, but none arrested the firm's downward slide. The Fuggers endured the adverse consequences of several more Spanish bankruptcies and defaults from 1575 through 1607. All the while, their financial portfolio was hemorrhaging. The Hapsburg connection sapped their strength. The total loss the Fuggers sustained on their claims against the Hapsburgs up to 1650 may have approximated 8 million Rhenish gulden. The Fuggers lost the greater part of their earnings over a hundred years in this way (Ehrenberg 1928: 131).

Let us put the impact of irrecoverable loans in a final perspective on the family fortune. Even at their zenith, about the middle of the sixteenth century, the Fuggers never owned more than 5 or 6 millions of the money of that day, including the private fortunes of their individual members. What the Fuggers owned varied considerably in composition as the years went by. The amount in tangible assets declined, while the sum in book loans, reckoned as assets but really "phantom capital," increased dramatically. What remained of the Fugger fortune about 1650 was only some landed property, which had been laid waste in wars and was heavily mortgaged (Ehrenberg 1928: 131-32).

The perils of loan overextensions to people who defaulted are clear in retrospect. To be fair to the Fuggers, there was no science of country or leadership risk during their times. That is, there was no organized body of knowledge to help assign probabilities to the likelihood that a country or its leaders would repay their debts. Even today country risk is a young field of inquiry. One senses that even if the Fuggers had known the probabilities of default, they would still have done what they did. They considered loaning and debt managing more of an art than a science. They thought they had the magic touch, and for a long time they did. Even after that first threatening crisis in 1557 involving Philip of Spain, which required the Fuggers to borrow considerable sums of money, they undertook new loan business. The Fuggers illustrate the dangers of excessive debt and how the thrill of political involvement can corrode financial prudence.

ROTHSCHILD: A HOUSE FOR ALL TIME?

If the name Fugger meant finance to an earlier era, Rothschild has set the family standard for *haute finance* (high finance) in recent times. Both the Medicis and the Fuggers began to sputter around their third generations. But the Rothschilds have managed to carry on through at least eight generations. This impressive record for elegant survival in the major leagues of finance gives them added significance. What are the secrets to sustained intergenerational financial life? The simple answer is that there were and are no secrets. The techniques that the Rothschilds have used to increase their wealth over time are not mysterious. The "roll of the genetic dice" played an important part. But four sometimes related methods also helped them amass their fortune: (1) reaching across national boundaries and currencies; (2) being very loyal agents; (3) relying strategically on the prestige and integrity of their name; and (4) using wisely various methods of transferring their wealth to younger generations (Powers 1982: 1).

The founding father of this great financial dynasty, Meyer Anselm Rothschild, was born about 1743. Living in a ghetto for Jews in what is now Frankfort, Germany, he began as an exchange merchant. His specialties included currency exchanges and bills of exchange. Because Germany was not unified until the 1860s and 1870s, during Meyer's time (c. 1743–1812) its many jurisdictions with their moneys provided an enormous opportunity for someone skilled in currency transactions. Meyer was that person. He was not the only highly competent currency specialist in central Europe, but he had vision and wanted to be on the cutting edge of high finance.

As his business grew, Meyer searched for other money-making ventures. This quest for higher rates of return took him, as it did the Fuggers, into politics. However, the outcome was more favorable for Meyer and the Rothschild dynasty. Meyer had already made a major start in crossing boundaries and currencies in his monetary transactions. What made his business more continental was his association with politicians who had themselves already fashioned an extensive network of business contacts throughout Europe. Meyer piggybacked on their connections to build up his own international network.

Playing a major role in this process was Prince William of Hesse, an important German political figure. Prince William was one of Europe's wealthiest men. He had extensive business dealings throughout Europe and in England. He had many investments and provided mercenaries to those who could pay his prices. He was reimbursed through bills of exchange. These had to be discounted to reflect various factors: rates of exchange, distance, time, risk, and interest. Meyer began business with Prince William modestly. He received a small share of those bills of exchange for discounting. He astutely increased his share of the prince's business. Meyer got more bills by operating at a loss in order to give the prince higher profits. In time Meyer Rothschild became the prince's principal banker.

The prince's contacts were decisive in obtaining for Meyer something else of great value. Through the prince, an elector of the Holy Roman Empire and influential in its complex politics, Meyer received the title of Imperial Crown Agent of the Holy Roman Empire. To represent a Christian entity was a great achievement for a Jew in the often anti-Semitic climate of the times. Becoming Imperial Crown Agent was like getting a special passport. The title enabled him to travel on business anywhere in south central Europe and greatly accelerated the development of the Rothschilds as a continental organization.

The House of Rothschild had an exceptionally able second generation. Meyer and his wife had five sons, all of whom proved business apt. Each became a full partner when he reached 21. Four of the five moved to other major European financial centers, while Amshel, the eldest, remained in Frankfort with his father. Carl opened a branch in Naples; Solomon, in Vienna; James, in Paris; and Nathan, in London. This family operation facilitated capital accumulation. The Rothschilds, with their family branches, were positioned to perform with great efficiency.

Meyer had been involved with bills of exchange for a long time. But the dispersion of four keen family members to key European business centers was a financial bonanza. With the origin and destination of a particular bill of exchange the same family, some of the discount factors could be eliminated or reduced. The Rothschilds were able to make larger profits on long-distance transactions and work on building up their customer base by offering lower rates than competitors charged.

Some have made much about earning money the old-fashioned way through hard work. The Rothschilds energetically pursued their crafts but showed that the "old-fashioned way" consists of unwavering loyalty to one's clients. Their association with Prince William of Hesse provides a classic example of client loyalty. This episode occurred during the Napoleonic Wars. Exporting the French Revolution (1789–1815), Napoleon Bonaparte, French emperor from 1804 into 1815, led military campaigns that affected many parts of Europe and had repercussions worldwide. Napoleon's forces came to threaten Prince William, who had to flee so quickly that he did not have time to put his financial affairs in order. Most of Frankfort's bankers were not willing to take the risk of investing the prince's funds during a period of enemy rule.

But Meyer Rothschild rescued him. He got most of the prince's assets, managed them, and invested the profits. Napoleon's agents searched the Rothschild house many times in an effort to find the prince's books. The Rothschilds succeeded in concealing the prince's accounts by using various ruses. It is unlikely that even if records pertaining to Prince William's affairs had been uncovered, these would have contained enough information to give outsiders any lasting insights into his finances. In this respect, the House of Rothschild anticipated multinational corporate accounting with different sets of books. When Napoleon was defeated, the prince returned to power. Consummate business people, the Rothschilds gave the prince's vast funds back to him with interest. The man who was instrumental in Meyer's emergence as a continental force experienced what loyalty means.

The Rothschild conception of client loyalty also had ample room for patriotism. They showed how to balance family and local ties. As an international family the Rothschilds did view finance in ways that went beyond the concerns of any one country. But when his country faced a tough problem, the Rothschild on the spot promoted the welfare of that country. Some would say this behavior is only good public relations and does not necessarily indicate the presence of patriotic motives. On the second point, can one person disentangle the selfish from the selfless motivations in another? On the first, what is wrong with good public relations?

Perhaps the most famous episode of Rothschild assistance to any government took place in connection with events that led to the partitioning of Africa. During the 1880s and 1890s some European countries and King Leopold II of Belgium divided huge parts of the continent up among themselves. The boundaries of most contemporary African countries were drawn on maps by European officials during this process. The partition was a short-run acceleration of the long-term process of increasing European involvement on the coasts and then in the interior of the continent that began with the transatlantic slave trade in the fifteenth century.

The Suez Canal, which connects the Mediterranean and Red seas, was one of the "flash" points that focused the competition for Africa among European powers. The financial arrangements that supported the construction of the canal, which was completed in 1869, came together in the 1850s. The structures of canal financing made the government of Egypt guarantor of the debt instruments that the Suez Canal Company issued to raise capital to fund the construction.

Different countries jockeyed to obtain the upper hand in influencing the Suez Canal Company. The most direct way to ensure that influence was to get a majority of its outstanding shares. In the 1870s Chancellor Otto von Bismarck of Germany seemed to be making a move to acquire a substantial number of shares in the company.

This prospect greatly disturbed the British government in 1875. The British had special concern for the Suez Canal. It provided a shorter water route than transit around South Africa to their prized imperial possession, India. Matters became urgent during a frantic period of several days in 1875. To forestall Bismarck, the British government needed a substantial loan at very short notice, which would enable it to purchase the shares necessary to achieve a majority holding in the Suez Canal Company. Prime Minister Disraeli and members of his cabinet waited anxiously while an emissary visited the Rothschilds at one of their residences in England. It was a weekend; all the banks were closed; the government needed the money immediately. The Rothschilds were the only firm that could make the loan. The Rothschilds lent the British government 4 million pounds within hours, at the "patriotic" rate of 3 percent interest. The country itself was collateral for the loan. Patriotic client loyalty produced a rate of return below that obtainable from other loans. But this transaction generated great dividends in terms of enhanced prestige and reputation.

The Rothschilds could also manipulate political events for their own benefit. The episode of the "Waterloo coup" shows this behavior. When Napoleon attempted a comeback at the Battle of Waterloo in Belgium on 18 June, 1815, he lost. The "Waterloo coup" was made by Nathan Rothschild in how he benefitted from events surrounding the battle. Back in London Nathan received advanced word of the outcome. To many in England the defeat of Napoleon, one of their great archenemies of all time, would be great news. Instead of buying stocks in anticipation that Napoleon's loss would raise their prices, Nathan did the opposite. Before the news became public Nathan sold some of his shares. There had been rumor of a British defeat, and unsubstantiated stories have often proved as or more influential than facts in affecting trading on financial exchanges.

When a Rothschild acts, people listen. When word spread that "Rothschild is selling," the rumor of a British defeat was accepted as fact. A storm surge of panic selling engulfed the market and prices broke sharply. Nathan then ordered his agents to buy back shares at bargain prices, just before the accurate outcome at Waterloo became public. Stock prices then rose sharply, and Nathan gained greatly.

How the Rothschilds have held on through generations is an important part of their story. Before his death in 1812, Meyer split the bank into five partnerships, which gave each son an equal share in the business. None of Meyer's daughters was mentioned at all. This arrangement was legally binding. If a brother were to leave the bank, he would receive the legal value of his shares and no more. The legal value was that stated for tax purposes, far below actual value (Powers 1982: 6). This technique cemented the family business. As the family moved into the third generation and beyond, not all of their male offspring were as exceptional as the first five sons. Time brought Rothschilds who were not born to be bankers and had to be carried along. The House of Rothschild had the strength to take care of its own, even when some of its own did not take care of the House.

As the House moved through the twentieth century, its capacity to cushion its less able members diminished. The Rothschilds experienced an acute shortage of skilled family financiers. During the interwar period (1919–1939) the family's great problem was that the banks in London and Paris, traditionally run only by Rothschilds with no outsiders at the top, were short of able bankers. The shortage of Rothschild heirs able to fill command positions in the banks remains a problem.

Even among those male heirs with financial and administrative abilities, there was an increasing tendency to pursue other interests. One Rothschild became both a distinguished philanthropist and zoologist; another became fascinated with rare butterflies; still another was more intrigued with gardening than banking. The gardener's sister coauthored *Fleas, Flukes, and Cuckoos*. There is nothing wrong with embarking on other careers, and freedom to engage in such pursuits is one of the reasons for acquiring wealth, but the more often the family "rolled the genetic dice," the greater was the frequency of offspring not as financially apt or offspring with other interests. There is still a hard core of Rothschild kinship in the Rothschild enterprises, but the pool of Rothschild financial talent is such that recently only four of the seven major partners of N. M. Rothschild and Sons, a bare majority, were Rothschilds themselves.

The family has lasted so long as a major financial force for many reasons. One is intermarriage. Some claim that intermarriage is the main reason for the family's successful intergenerational transmission of wealth. Of the family's 59 weddings in the nineteenth century, half were between male and female Rothschilds. James, one of the five brother pillars of the business, married his cousin Betty. Of their five children four married Rothschilds. Nathan, another pillar, and his wife had seven children; four married Rothschilds.

Today in the partner's room of N. M. Rothschild and Sons Bank there hang ancestral portraits along with framed documents from the family's famous past. These include loan papers from the Suez Canal deal. Other families may amass more wealth, but it is hard to surpass the impact on the major events of their times that the House of Rothschild has had.

The family did follow a pattern of capital formation that many other banking families have pursued and others will attempt to imitate. But it was the extent of their reach across international borders, and the techniques employed to make that extension effective and influential, that ensure for the family a special place in international business history. The Rothschilds dealt with local political questions as opportunities for the exertion of power as finesse. Their careful eye on the future has enabled them to survive short-term setbacks. Such a track record, based on integrity, farsightedness, prestige, and multiple loyalties to clients and family members, now covers more than two centuries and eight generations. Nothing lasts forever, and no family will ever be absolutely the house for all time. But no other international family approaches the House of Rothschild as the leading contender for that distinction.

COMPARATIVE PORTRAIT

The stories of the Medicis, Fuggers, and Rothschilds reveal distinctive styles of intergenerational capital accumulation as all tried to cope with common problems. How to preserve wealth over time is a monumental task. How to deal with inescapable facts of the business world—politics and its practitioners—were other problems. Politics, sooner or later, proved poisonous to the Medicis and Fuggers but in different ways. The Medici Bank was already declining when family members had to deal with conspiracy in the 1470s and their ultimate expulsion from Florence in 1494.

Politics, which reinforced the disintegration of the Medici Bank, played a more causal role in the unraveling of the Fugger fortune. Excessive loans to leaders whose collateral did not exist or could not be repossessed corroded the Fugger financial foundation. The Fuggers were financial high rollers. After some initial loans to royalty who possessed physical and thus distrainable assets such as mines, the Fuggers embarked on more massive loan undertakings to the Hapsburgs, who were among the diplomatic and political high rollers of their times. These loans had no practical collateral. The combination of increasingly indebted debtors—the rulers—and increasingly indebted creditors—the Fuggers—was an earlier version of an international debt crisis. The Fuggers loved the fast financial life and relished the enjoyment they received from thinking they were manipulating the events of their times, whatever the costs. As the old saying goes, those who dance must pay the piper: the Fuggers' payment consisted of a severe shrinkage of their assets. But the Fuggers in miniature were the Fuggers no more.

The Rothschilds, for the most part, played matters just right. Perhaps the family most blessed with the greatest number of financially able heirs, even they had problems stemming from a shortage of qualified blood relations during the twentieth century. The second Rothschild generation was a five-brother cornucopia of business ability. One is hard pressed to produce another such instance from family business history. Appropriate legal arrangements girded kinship ties. This reinforcement safeguarded the intergenerational transmission and preservation of Rothschild wealth.

The Rothschilds were at their best in demonstrating the kinds of mutually beneficial links that can exist between government and business. The House of Rothschild was both international and patriotic at the same time. It has often been said that no one can serve two masters, but this fact does not rule out a person or business having multiple loyalties. The ways in which they have balanced their loyalties may be their strongest claim to be considered the financial house for all time.

2

Distinctive National Patterns of Multinational Emergence: The United Kingdom, France, Germany, and Sweden

These introductory notes address two topics. The first concerns the proper name for the multinational corporation and how to categorize it. The second is a comparative model for analyzing the emergence of multinational corporations from different countries.

MNCs: NAMES AND CATEGORIES

How the multinational corporation should be named is still debated. Some use transnational corporation. Transnational highlights the fact that a corporation has gone beyond the nationalities of its personnel and business locations. A transnational corporation is different, some suggest, from a multinational corporation, which reflects a mix of national cultures in its own business culture. Some use multidomestic corporation to indicate an mnc that has several homes.

Transnational has recently acquired a less vague meaning. This definition pivots on the degree to which a multinational corporation decentralizes power to its subsidiaries. Two business school professors, Christopher Bartlett of Harvard and Sumantra Ghoshal of Insead, have promoted this definition of transnational. The decentralization is so substantial that the multinational becomes polycentric or many centered (Bartlett and Ghoshal 1990: 215-55). In early 1991 Nestlé, the Swiss-based foods and coffee group, further decentralized its global structure by transferring its product management executives from corporate headquarters to its business units around the world (*FT* 8 February 1991: 12).

This decentralization should disperse power from the center to its most appropriate subsidiary. International Business Machines (IBM) and Hewlett-Packard (H-P) became transnationals, according to this definition, when they each announced relocation of the head office of one of their worldwide divisions from the United States to Europe (IBM to the United Kingdom and H-P to France). IBM and Hewlett-Packard join such already established transnationals as Unilever and Procter & Gamble (*FT* 8 February 1991: 12).

This definition of *transnational* has provoked criticism. Michael Porter of the Harvard Business School has dismissed it as old though of some merit. A more practical concept, he argues in *The Competitive Advantage of Nations* (1990), is that each business within a company should have its own home base.

Both proponents and critics of the transnational notion are arguing about what is the best mix of centralization and decentralization for a company; that is, how to optimize a corporation's interdependence (see introduction). About twenty years ago Jack Behrman pinpointed two core characteristics of a multinational corporation: policy centralization and integration of key operations among its affiliates (Behrman 1970: 2-3). Every international business must have some policy centralization and operational integration. Without these the business would lack coherence as an organization.

The transnational debate is probing these two characteristics in the context of interdependence but also raising difficult questions about the meanings of *headquarters* and *subsidiary*. In Behrman's definition policy centralization is associated with one headquarters. But is it possible and practical to have policy centralization coming from several locations that are serving as headquarters for different types of company business? Or is policy centralization in a polycentric organization a contradiction? How much policy centralization is necessary for a business? How much integration of key operations among subsidiaries is required for a business to maintain its coherence as an organization? It would seem that this integration, to the extent needed, could only be imposed and successfully managed by one location serving as the command headquarters in this regard. What are the relations between centralization and integration for an international business? If history has taught us anything in this area, it is that excessively centralized or decentralized businesses will eventually encounter serious, perhaps fatal, problems. All businesses need a mix of centralization and decentralization. The transnational debate may advance our understanding of how to define interdependence in practical terms.

Another issue, debated during the 1980s, was the global corporation. This enterprise was different, its theorists argued, from the multinational corporation. An mnc supposedly considered each country as a separate market. This approach, which entailed numerous local adjustments, led to high costs. The global corporation, to the contrary, saw the entire world as a single market. It sold the same things in the same way everywhere. It would not change its products to fit the preferences of consumers from one country. Instead it would make the best product it could sell at a competitive price (Levitt 1983: 20-49).

In the mid-1980s, when the concept of the global corporation was peaking, its theorists classified the following corporations as global. Japanese globals included Sony, Olympus, Seiko, and Toyota. United States globals featured Coca-Cola, McDonald's, General Foods, Procter & Gamble, and Revlon. The big oil companies, which come from a number of countries, were also global corporations (*Econ* 4 February 1984: 76).

The major theorist of the global corporation, Theodore Levitt of the Harvard Business School, has significantly modified his original analysis of the subject. One problem was a rigid distinction between corporations (mncs) that adjusted to local market conditions and those that did not (globals). The actual business behavior of globals upset that distinction. They did adapt to local conditions, although the manner and degree of those adjustments varied (Levitt 1986: xi-xix).

In this regard the notion of product standardization is crucial. A company may seem to sell the same product in many national markets. But that product can embody alterations designed to appeal to local consumer tastes. The same product may really be a set of similar items with important local modifications. Even in machine tooling, which strives for great precision, standardization is not a point but a range.

Another problem that undermined the distinction between global and multinational corporations came from assumptions about the ways each saw its markets. The market perceptions of mncs and globals were falsely stereotyped. Many multinationals and globals had more refined patterns than the two choices—the country or world as market—analysts of the global corporation maintained. Even though the original distinction between multinational and global corporation was not valid, surrounding debate has emphasized the fact that all multinational corporations are not the same.

A stimulating classification of multinationals comes from Michael Goold and John Campbell of the London Business School. They researched the management styles of sixteen large British multinationals and concluded that their approaches as of the mid-1980s fell into three broad categories: strategic planning, financial control, and strategic control.

Strategic planning companies emphasize the involvement of senior managers in the formulation of strategy, down to the lower managerial levels. These companies set targets for their individual businesses to reach. Achieving short-term goals is important. But it is crucial to move in the right direction in the long term; for example, winning a greater market share. Strategic planning companies included British Petroleum, Cadbury Schweppes, and United Biscuits (Goold and Campbell 1987: 47-85).

Financial control companies anchor their operations on financial targets. Their central managements are not as involved in detailed planning with their business units. Those financial targets are short term objectives, usually achieved within twelve months. Managers in financial control companies must therefore concentrate on annual results, not the pursuit of longer term strategies. Financial control companies included Hanson Trust, Ferranti, and Tarmac (Goold and Campbell 1987: 111-62).

Strategic control companies take elements of both strategic planning and financial control. They try to balance long- and short-term objectives. Managers face annual financial targets as well as strategic goals. The latter could include launching a new product or improving customer service. Strategic control companies included Courtaulds, the Imperial Group, and Vickers (Goold and Campbell 1987: 86-110).

This threefold classification touches upon the essentials for the historical study of international business (see introduction). All three types involve strategy. Even the financial control company, which deemphasizes longer-term strategic planning, is following a strategy in its concentration on annual financial goals. All approaches place personnel, procedures, and structures in relationships with one another. These make up centralization-decentralization mixes or varieties of interdependence.

The previous discussion of names and categories for the multinational corporation introduces important terms in the current vocabulary of international business. There is still a critical need to develop a comparative framework for analyzing the emergence and articulation of multinational corporations from countries around the world.

MNCs: COMPARATIVE EMERGENCE MODEL

There is no fixed historical formula for explaining the emergence of the multinational corporation in every context. Many thinkers have proposed theories concerning the rise of the multinational. These approaches often aspire to a universality that is more creative than factual. While theories that stipulate certain relationships between factors in every case have proved misleading, every national context does contain some common features though not necessarily in the same relationship with one another. These common features, which constitute the basis of a comparative framework, include (1) the role of government or the state, (2) export markets as well as external sources of supply, (3) technological change and its kinship notions of invention and innovation, (4) relative factor scarcities and qualities of land, labor, capital, entrepreneurial ability, and opportunity, and (5) the international mindedness of a country's business culture.

The Role of Government or the State

There is a wide spectrum of possible government action. A state can be more or less involved in a specific business environment in a number of areas, with a possible impact on the emergence of multinationals that must be determined on a country-by-country basis. Government can own something outright, which is a more prevalent mode of intervention in socialist than capitalist societies. Government can also invest in, promote, and regulate aspects of business activity. These concepts of investment, promotion, and regulation provide central organizing principles for any analysis of the role of government with respect to business and the economy. Investment consists of government giving money or other resources, such as land and tax breaks, to various agents and agencies. Promotion is investment linked to a goal. This objective should be more specific than just spurring growth and development. Regulation consists of rules imposed upon economic and business activity by legislatures, courts, and administrative agencies. Sometimes regulation is intertwined with taxation, as when taxes are levied to control certain enterprises. Tax policy can also intersect, as noted, with investment and promotion. Whether government acts in one or more of the above areas in a manner that affects the emergence, growth, and development of multinationals and if so how are topics of vital concern.

Export Markets and External Sources of Supply

Most economies throughout the world have historically had some degree of external contact, and all European countries had and have. Economic autarky, or total self-sufficiency, is rare worldwide and nonexistent in Europe on the national level. Since multinationals are cross-border creations, both the type and intensity of a country's external relationships may have influenced the emergence and evolution of its multinationals. Prior external government involvement is not a precondition for the emergence of multinationals. But there are connections between that and the rise of a country's multinationals that deserve investigation.

Technological Change: Invention and Innovation

Technological change has several aspects. It refers to innovation in the processes of production, distribution, and exchange, as well as to changes in how those processes are organized. Innovation, which some distinguish from invention, refers to any rearrangement of any aspect of the economic process; for example, extracting raw materials, manufacturing, distributing, and selling. It also pertains to ways in which economic processes are structured as institutions. Invention, which can be closely related to innovation, designates the creation of a new design, product, or process that can qualify for a patent. This is a legal document that recognizes the uniqueness of an item and creates intellectual property rights.

All of these concepts—technological change, innovation, and invention—are strongly connected. But they are kindred, not identical, notions. All raise the core idea of economic efficiency. Technological change and innovation deal with efficiency in practice. Invention, since it refers mainly to creativity on the drawing board or in testing before significant implementation, concerns prospective efficiency gains. Efficiency means getting a greater output with the same amount of inputs or the same output with fewer inputs. From this standpoint, technological change is a subset of innovation because gains in efficiency can result from innovations in processes or environments that some might not deem authentic technologies. Technological change and the related notions of innovation and invention have played crucial roles in the emergence and differing fortunes of multinationals in various parts of the world. As such these concepts represent key aspects of the dynamism that continues to power the further internationalization and globalization of business. This dynamism underpins product evolution, organizational refinement, and changing market perception.

Relative Factor Scarcities and Qualities of Land, Labor, Capital, Entrepreneurial Ability, and Opportunity

The transformation of a corporation largely focused on its home market into one with multinational divisions can involve one or more of the factors listed above in either the scarcity or quality dimension or some combination of the two. As an emerging multinational corporation surveys its domestic and foreign landscape, it confronts the following facts of life. The factors of land, labor, capital, entrepreneurial ability, and opportunity are all important to its survival. But the number of factors, their involvement under the quality or scarcity category or some hybrid of the two, and their exact mix will depend on particular circumstances. All multinationals need all of these factors at some time. Their precise requirements come from the nature of their product, organization, and market. A multinational involved in agriculture seems to need more land than an enterprise concerned with manufacturing and/or services, but this observation may not always apply. The demand for land pivots on quality, suitability, and technology. A crop mix and technology that economizes on land and labor should reduce the demand for land, but particular cases must be examined.

The economist's four factors of production are land, labor, capital, and entrepreneurial ability. Clustering them with opportunity under the dimensions of scarcity and quality gives flexibility to deal with many situations. Labor, for example, may be ample in one location for a corporation's needs measured quantitatively. But it may not meet a corporation's qualitative requirements. These attributes include industriousness, cooperativeness, and how local labor values its services in monetary terms. A multinational corporation can conclude, as many already have, that the labor force of its own domestic market monetarily overvalues its work in relation to its productivity or output per worker. The corporation will locate its operations where it can economize on wages. A qualitative evaluation of the demand for labor may lead to a quantitative increase in corporate returns.

Scarcity and quality are also useful concepts for treating other factors. Capital has several meanings. As physical capital it is such things as implements, machinery, and buildings. As liquid capital it is a wide range of financial instruments: different kinds of money, bonds, and stocks. As human capital it is people themselves. This concept emphasizes education in making people more productive economically. All three kinds of capital are related to the emergence and maturation of multinational corporations. But the mix of the three, and the extent to which considerations of scarcity and quality are compelling, will vary from one enterprise to another. The demand for capital, and the degree to which its fulfillment intensifies the foreign involvement of a multinational corporation, will depend on three crucial aspects of the enterprise: the nature of its product, organization, and market.

International Mindedness of a Country's Business Culture

The historical record of a country in the international business arena and how that past experience has molded a national business culture are important. The types and intensities of prior national involvement in international business can help explain the emergence of multinational corporations from that national context. The distinctive qualities of businesses and business people from a country are also useful in understanding the evolution of its multinationals. There are no automatic relationships between past involvement in international business by the nationals and government from a particular country and the emergence of multinationals from that nation. These connections must be explored case by case.

Some factors in the section on relative factor scarcities are related. Human capital includes labor and entrepreneurial ability. Human capital refers to people, regardless of their formal education and official position at work. Everyone can improve his or her standing as human capital but needs resources to do it. How a multinational corporation treats its human capital will affect not only the productivity of that capital but also prospects for corporate survival.

Opportunity touches the entire comparative framework. Businesses define and pursue opportunities for mixing land, labor, capital, and entrepreneurial ability. As businesses become multinational corporations, this process increasingly involves portions of factors outside their home borders. Opportunity can explain the role of the state in affecting the emergence of multinational corporations. Government as investor, promoter, and regulator can create, distort, or destroy opportunities for business. Opportunity relates to export markets and external sources of supply. In seeking these markets and supply sources business people use their own definitions of opportunity and one must try to understand them in their own terms.

Opportunity is central to technological change and its related notions of invention and innovation. Inventions and innovations result from people defining and then seizing opportunities to do something better. For multinational corporations technological change feeds a dynamism of product evolution, organizational refinement, and changing market perception. Finally, cross-border opportunity can influence the degree of international mindedness that the business cultures of countries and multinational corporations exhibit.

Against this comparative framework of government, markets, technology, factor scarcities and qualities, and international mindedness, four European patterns of multinational emergence and articulation are examined. These come from the experiences of the United Kingdom, France, Germany, and Sweden. At the same time, comparisons and contrasts within Europe as well as with the United States are featured. The evolution of multinationals is best understood in the contexts of the individual mnc. The first important context is domestic. As in the United States, the emergence and articulation of multinationals in Europe begins with what did or did not happen to the corporation at home and what it did or did not do there.

THE UNITED KINGDOM

British business culture has exhibited for centuries significant international mindedness in outlook and action. The distinction between domestic and international environments blurs in the British experience. Islands off the west coast of continental Europe, the United Kingdom could never afford to take an insular perspective on its own destiny. One of Europe's oldest nation-states, the United Kingdom always had to conduct business with outsiders—to obtain food, capital, and raw materials. Geography, size, and resource requirements led the United Kingdom to regard its foreign environment as integral to domestic survival and advancement.

The historical record of global British business involvement is extensive. The United Kingdom participated in the European expansion overseas that began with the voyages of discovery in the late fifteenth century. While the United Kingdom pioneered the factory industrialization that spread across Europe from the latter eighteenth century, it was not the pacesetter in overseas exploration. Portugal, led by Prince Henry the Navigator, and Spain, which sponsored the voyages of Christopher Columbus, were first. But once involved, the British participated with an energy, thoroughness, and sense of mission that would characterize their overseas activities throughout the centuries.

The chartered company played a major role in the British penetration of North America, Africa, Asia, and the Caribbean. The chartered company was an antecedent of the world-ranging multinational corporation, but it was more dedicated to one area of the globe. Its charter gave it presumed powers to conduct operations in a specific locale.

There were various kinds of British capital abroad in the centuries before British multinationals started to evolve in the 1860s and 1870s. Exports of British capital date back to the seventeenth century and beyond. Those exports included portfolio (securities, discount paper, etc.), merchant, and financial capital. These focused on the following areas. One was the primary sector. This term designates resource extraction and includes metals, minerals, and crops. A second sphere featured railways, utilities, and banking. A third domain was trade and commerce (Dunning and Archer 1987: 19).

Such substantial international activity prepared the way for the emergence of British multinationals. Their structural beginnings are traced to the 1860s and 1870s. During those decades market-seeking and resource-seeking international corporations started to emerge. These enterprises were already operating at home and then began to set up foreign value-added activities. This means that corporations based in the United Kingdom were positioning outside their home borders the means to process a product.

Processing, packaging, and handling add value to a product. These activities add value in that they usually increase costs or can be used to justify price increases. They may also add intrinsic value but this point is arguable.

Deploying value-added activities outside their home base gave British multinationals extra options with regard to product, organization, and market. Some of these choices, phrased as questions, follow. Which inputs should be processed where? How should external operations be structured in relation to domestic organization? And how can overseas outlets foster a more global marketing strategy?

Externalization placed those corporations on the road to becoming full-fledged multinationals. But neither the emergence of authentic multinationals nor the global strategies that are one of their hallmarks happened at once. British multinationals took almost one full century of growth and development to reach high levels of global operations in certain areas. Not until the late 1950s and early 1960s would British multinational enterprises seeking to pursue a global production strategy come on the scene.

Why this process took so long has no single answer. But a large part of the explanation lies in what did or did not happen to the corporation at home and what it did or did not do there. In the United Kingdom what did not happen to the corporation and what it did not do illuminate why British multinationals experienced formidable problems in their structural articulation. Consider the slow emergence of managerial hierarchies. These constitute the bureaucratic essence of the large-scale corporation. They express the operational chain of command, and the aptness of their formulation has much to do with the efficiency and effectiveness of an organization. So far no one has invented a table of organization for a large-scale organization that dispenses with hierarchy and still ensures that the command decisions essential for institutional security and advancement will occur on a regular and sustained basis.

The managerial hierarchy does not imply vertical or horizontal stagnation of thought and action nor an immobility of personnel. Every level or tier, no matter how many people are on it, must operate with a dynamism that strengthens the entire organization. Without energetic, creative, and purposeful management at all levels an organization will suffer. Horizontal management, pioneered by W. Edwards Deming, refined by the Japanese, and today imitated worldwide, does not abolish managerial hierarchies but tries to transform the chain of command into a kinship of cooperation. The essence of the hierarchy remains—the chain of command—but the unnecessary elevation of the few over the many is muted.

One British problem was the long-standing influence of the family firm on company organization. There is nothing wrong per se with family firms and they can be motivated expressions of entrepreneurship, but the ways in which family firms in the United Kingdom continued to play important business roles, in conjunction with key features of the British domestic market, retarded the emergence of managerial hierarchies. The principle of supply and demand applies to structural innovation. Where there is little or no demand for managerial hierarchies, they will not spread. Managerial hierarchies emerged in U.S. corporations in the latter decades of the nineteenth century in response to the need to supervise and implement the distribution of high volumes of goods over long distances. In the United States there was a crucial demand for a large infrastructure of distribution that existing retailers and jobbers (wholesale merchants) could not fill.

In the United Kingdom the situation was different. There extensive networks based on kinship, friendship, or long-term association developed over the centuries. These networks drew strength from distinctive features of the domestic environment. The home market was compact in physical size and dense in people clustered in strategic locations. A transport and communications infrastructure promoted market unification and integration. All these factors—market compactness, population density, and infrastructure effectiveness—made it possible for these networks to meet demands for distribution. But the workability of these networks reduced the demand for managerial hierarchies.

The slow emergence of managerial hierarchies had adverse consequences for the modern internationalization of British business. As Alfred Chandler, Jr., has noted, the slow articulation of managerial hierarchies may have deprived British industrialists of "some of the cost advantages and therefore market power of large-scale enterprise." British manufacturers, although adept in merchandising consumer goods, moved slowly into their mass production. Their tardiness came from the fact that mass production required new methods of organizing production and distribution. British delay in moving into mass production benefited U. S. corporations. These corporations, with less difficulty than if British businesses had effectively competed, gained a significant share of international markets, including the British home market itself in numerous commodities. The list of goods in which U.S. businesses achieved important market penetration abroad including the United Kingdom is long: canned goods, frozen meat, proprietary articles such as toothpaste and pills, and such durables as sewing machines, typewriters, cash registers, and other office machinery (Chandler 1980: 408).

A striking case of arrested structural development concerns British heavy-machinery firms. These enterprises had not developed marketing organizations in the United Kingdom. This omission made it easier for U.S. firms to take over the British market for numerous volume-produced standardized producers' goods. Producers' goods are commodities that play roles in the production process and facilitate the manufacture of goods that consumers purchase. In the United Kingdom U.S. businesses penetrated markets for such producers' goods as harvesters, electrical equipment, elevators, shoe manufacturing machinery, and printing presses (Chandler 1980: 408).

The slow emergence of managerial hierarchies in the United Kingdom had another major disadvantage for British businesses both at home and abroad. The British were not on the cutting edge in pioneering or adopting modern management methods. U. S. managers, from the latter nineteenth century on, "were perfecting the basic techniques of mass production and mass distribution." They were devising "new methods of inventory and quality control." They were working out "cost-accounting procedures based on standard volume and capacity" that enabled "middle managers to monitor systematically and continuously the work of the operating units under their command." And they were refining scheduling procedures essential to maintain a high and steady flow of material through the plants and various departments of an enterprise. Such accounting and control methods are crucial in improving the competitiveness of an enterprise by reducing its costs. British businesses only began adopting these techniques extensively in the 1930s, sometimes borrowing directly from the United States (Chandler 1980: 408-9).

The lagged appearance of managerial hierarchies hampered British business in other ways. There was an even longer and more internationally damaging delay in adopting top-management procedures. They had initially emerged in the United States in response to the needs of big corporations that were growing through mergers (combinations of businesses). Efficiency drove many U.S. mergers. But most U.K. mergers strove to maintain family control—that mixed entrepreneurial blessing of British industrial history.

U.S. business reorganization stimulated development of top-management procedures.   Senior executives developed organizational plans to promote institutional efficiency on a large scale. These plans "defined the functions of managerial positions, drew the lines of authority, responsibility, and communication," and distinguished "between line and staff activities." Those executives worked out accounting and budgetary procedures that helped top management to evaluate systematically the performance of its middle managers. These procedures facilitated the allocation of resources for the future activities of an enterprise. Business leaders also dealt with the necessity of forecasting in both the short and long term. They fostered the development of short-term forecasting of the conditions that would affect their attempts to coordinate flows of goods through their enterprises. They were keen on upgrading the long-term forecasting techniques that would assist in the evaluation of capital appropriations for facilities that would not come on line for several years or more. Sophisticated formulas were invented to determine the rate of return on total investment.   Even the largest British multinationals did not begin to make systematic use of these basic bureaucratic procedures until after World War II. Such methods, according to Alfred Chandler, Jr., were imported into the United Kingdom, largely by U.S. consultants, only in the 1950s and 1960s (Chandler 1980: 409).

British tardiness in articulating managerial hierarchies reinforced itself. Personnel—particularly the recruitment and training of managers—illustrates this process. During the 1880s and 1890s in the United States there was great demand for various specialists, especially from the machinery, electrical, and chemical firms that were in the vanguard of technological change. Established schools and those just getting started, like the Massachusetts Institute of Technology, responded to that demand and began to offer courses in mechanical, electrical, and chemical engineering. About the turn of the century in the United States some universities started to introduce new courses in business and even created business schools to fulfill the increasing need of growing U.S. enterprises for people with more specialized skills and professional training.

In the United Kingdom the situation was very different. For a long time "there was little such training."   In a family-dominated environment, top managers often include the owners themselves. What few middle managers who were needed could be recruited from within a company's ranks—from its travelers, buyers, or production supervisors. This managerial incest limited the pool of talent to the inside and reduced the need for outsiders. There was little demand for engineering courses and even less for business schools. This situation changed during the twentieth century. As managerial hierarchies multiplied and developed in the United Kingdom, especially after World War II, engineering schools expanded and business schools came into existence. When there was a significant demand for educational innovation, the academic establishment responded (Chandler 1980: 409-10).

Relationships between business and education in the United Kingdom offer another set of contrasts with the U.S. experience and also with the German pattern. In explaining the lagged response of British business to the demands of international markets from the later nineteenth century on, some claim a bias of British universities and British undergraduates against trade in general. To rely too much on the bias argument is as misleading as overemphasizing the structural factor of managerial hierarchies. While some British educators were concerned about associations with business and some undergraduates saw commerce as beneath them, there was no universal disdain for trade. In fact, when such large multinationals as Unilever began to recruit college graduates, they usually got the men they wanted (this is still a male chauvinist world) from Oxford, Cambridge, and other British universities (Chandler 1980: 409-10).

But there were certain characteristics about business-education relationships in the United Kingdom that hampered the cross-fertilization of ideas and experience that marked the U.S. and German situations. While universities provided highly educated personnel to British business, before World War II there was not much personal and structural interaction that might have assisted industry in its attempts to update itself. In the United States and Germany managers on both the production and distribution sides maintained ties with their universities. These contacts helped recruitment and the transmission of ideas. The information flow was a two-way street. There was a synergy between theoretical and applied science in the United States and Germany that helped those countries gain a substantial lead in many important new technological processes of the Second Industrial Revolution. This term refers to the surge of innovation in technologically intensive industries, such as those involving chemical, mechanical, and electrical engineering. The United Kingdom continued to educate its best minds in a dangerously compartmentalized way. There was insufficient contact between business and the educational establishment in the realm of those ideas with implications for the technological change that made the Second Industrial Revolution.

British industry entered the modern era with significant disadvantages. But the lagged development of managerial hierarchies, as well as the slower emergence of educational institutions and curricula that dealt with the realities of the Second Industrial Revolution, did not hamper every British industry. Producers and distributors of branded, packaged consumer goods, except possibly perishable products, were not fatally handicapped in either local or international markets (Chandler 1980: 410).

Those British industries in which technological changes crucial to the Second Industrial Revolution were occurring—those in chemicals, machinery, and electrical equipment—did experience problems. These were the industries in which managerial hierarchies proved essential and in time decisive. U.S. and German international businesses in these areas were able to capture markets in the United Kingdom and elsewhere. British industry lagged behind because the United Kingdom did not participate until much later in the managerial revolution that made possible and expedited the Second Industrial Revolution.

Why British multinationals took almost one full century to reach high levels of global production in certain areas has no single answer. The slow emergence of managerial hierarchies and its underlying causes, as well as the lack of synergy between education and business, are major parts of an explanation. Another key is the British Empire, which expanded from the 1600s and contracted greatly in the 1960s.

This global empire resembled the multinational corporation. It transcended national boundaries by generating its own supranational structure. This bureaucracy linked headquarters in London with many imperial territories worldwide—the subsidiaries. The British Empire acted as a substitute for some of the activities that multinational corporations perform in crossing borders and creating markets.

The existence of a British Empire puts the slower emergence of British multinationals in a different light. With so much of the globe painted British imperial red, some of the forces that promote the articulation of business multinationals were not as compelling. Potential markets for exports and external sources of supply were already under one's own national flag. And why abandon reliance on the family firm, when those much praised managerial hierarchies had long been developing in the structures of the empire itself? It is easy to criticize British business for articulating managerial hierarchies too slowly, if one forgets that the British Empire—a great institutional innovation in its time—had been refining tables of organization, chains of command, and management and control functions for centuries. The empire absorbed so much energy and creativity of the United Kingdom's best minds. Perhaps the human capital that could have spread managerial hierarchies in British industry more rapidly was occupied with preserving the Empire itself. In the context of total British international involvement over the centuries, delayed multinational emergence is more understandable.

FRANCE

The emergence of French multinationals is also anchored in what did or did not happen to the corporation at home and what it did or did not do there. Until well into the twentieth century, the large-scale corporation was not a dominant feature of the French landscape. Most businesses were small or medium sized in French terms. The slow development of large domestic corporations has received more refined attention from scholars. For a time some emphasized how France suffered from an excessive number of small businesses by contrast with firm configurations in Germany and the United Kingdom. Many small enterprises in France were family businesses. Some argued that heavy reliance on small-scale industrial firms constituted weakness: industrialization was hindered and the appearance of large-scale multinational enterprises delayed. Over the years a more accurate portrait has emerged. The vitality of French industrialization in the nineteenth century is striking. By 1914 both France and the United Kingdom, the pioneer of factory industrialization, had achieved comparable levels of economic growth per person.

Credible research also suggests that French firm size did not bring significant inefficiencies. To the contrary, French entrepreneurs were dealing rationally with their environment. The large number of small firms was not the result of managerial failure. The reasons lie in the environment. French entrepreneurs had to cope with excessive state intervention and inadequate infrastructure. This research shows that small size does not imply inefficiency, retard economic growth, or indict management (Nye 1987: 666-69).

There is a major difference, however, between smallness in relation to economic growth and smallness in relation to the emergence of large-scale multinational enterprise. French firm size has not constrained economic growth, but was that configuration so benign in its consequences for the emergence of large-scale multinationals? Consider next what did and did not happen to the French corporation and what it did and did not do.

The French experience reveals five important characteristics, according to Maurice Lévy-Leboyer. First, "the building of large firms in France was overdue." These emerged at least twenty years later than those in the United States and Germany. They did not develop a solid base in the years before World War I as they had in the United Kingdom (Lévy-Leboyer 1980: 153).

Second, emerging large firms were slow to diversify out of heavy industry. Typical products of modern large-scale French business enterprises included, first, capital equipment, then such intermediary products as energy, and lastly, automobiles and other consumer durables. This three-stage development, with phases that emphasized capital goods, intermediate products, and consumer durables, resulted from a crucial imbalance between supply and demand. Large-scale French businesses, which had the facilities and coordination necessary for high-volume, continuous-flow production, faced erratic domestic demand (Lévy-Leboyer 1980: 153).

Third, the market for volume-produced goods expanded discontinuously: growth was not steady, but periodically accelerated. The French market grew before 1914. Recovery from the great economic downswing of the late nineteenth century brought high domestic capital formation. A second phase of market growth occurred during World War I and postwar reconstruction. A third took place during the 1920s. Rising French exports and then strong domestic demand were the impetus that kept production and capital investment rising during the 1920s (Lévy-Leboyer 1980: 153).

Fourth, managerial training and attitudes slowed the emergence of mass production in France. Many managers, influenced by their education, concentrated on improving engineering and on developing a science-based technology (Lévy-Leboyer 1980: 153). They preferred quality production and disdained making unsophisticated articles suited for mass production. This is a classic expression of French business culture. As time went by, they would discover ways to produce what they perceived as sophisticated goods in greater quantities without perpetrating the grossness that they associated with mass production in other countries.

Fifth, inadequate domestic financial markets gave French business a special institutional concern with finance. Domestic capital markets could not meet the needs of growing French firms. French banks did play important roles in financing French industry, but some companies could not borrow substantial amounts of capital from banks, nor could they raise it in French capital markets. These markets were not developed enough to handle large corporate offerings in a timely manner. To whom or what could growing corporations turn for help? They formed business combinations to satisfy their large financial needs: big industrial groups were tied together by financial holding companies (Lévy-Leboyer 1980: 153).

The road to corporate largeness in France holds several keys to understanding the emergence of French multinational enterprise. The French holding company was set up to obtain capital and finance investment in new risk-taking ventures. It functioned as a "central financial unit" that provided capital to develop and expand industrial groups. Since it specialized in finance, it did not exercise the comprehensive functions that marked the evolution of large-scale U.S. multidivisional enterprises. This type of organization "tried to control economic performance, allocate resources, and open up new activities." Multidivisional organization was eminently more suited for orchestrating the aggressive overseas market expansion that highlighted the emergence of U.S. multinationals. Only after 1945 did the methods of organizing and operating big business in France resemble more closely those prevalent in the United States. In the last several decades French multinational enterprises finally developed a significant international presence (Lévy-Leboyer 1980: 154).

The lagged emergence of French multinationals has no single cause. Managerial structures, as they did in the United Kingdom, played a role in France. The evolution of French managerial structures occurred in two stages. The first was one of technological change and financial experimentation, the latter noticeable after World War I. The second stage unfolded during the 1930s. It featured the beginnings of concentration on marketing and organization, which prepared the way for the emergence of large-scale multidivisional corporations after World War II (Lévy-Leboyer 1980: 154-55).

Managerial enterprises were tested in France in the 1920s. Some favorable factors were then present: a new generation of engineers and ideologies oriented toward growth. But the diffusion of managerial enterprise encountered major obstacles that postponed the process until after World War II. These barriers were the Great Depression of the 1930s and deflationary policies that the government pursued too long (Lévy-Leboyer 1980: 152-53).

The financial nature of the French holding company is a factor in understanding the emergence of French multinational enterprises. The whys and wherefores governing the articulation of French managerial structures constitute a second. The distinctive ways in which French industrialists perceived market formation furnish a third.

For a long time French industrialists could take markets for granted. From the 1890s through the 1930s French entrepreneurs operated in an expanding domestic market. During World War I and postwar reconstruction, French businesses benefitted from state assistance in transportation and energy supplies (Lévy-Leboyer 1980: 154). When the compact domestic market was creating opportunities and when the state did some things that business might have to do, business did not have to work as hard to create markets. A reduced burden of market making was a short-term blessing, but in the long run French multinational enterprises had to face the consequences of this deceptive good fortune. In the United States the demands of market making confronted corporations on the road to largeness from the beginning. In France industrialists did not seriously face and act upon these necessities until after World War II.

Market making in the domestic economy can be an invaluable education for market making in the international economy. In the United States market making across a continent generated knowledge and experience about product, organization, and market formation that greatly assisted the transformation of U.S. corporations into multinationals. For that key period, from the latter nineteenth century well into the twentieth century when U.S. multinationals established a dominant position in many world markets, French industrialists were not receiving a comparable education in the "hard knocks" school of domestic and international market making.

The French Empire is a fourth key to understanding the emergence of French multinational enterprise. The formal French administrative empire, which at its peak included a large part of Africa and possessions in the Pacific and Caribbean, did not distinguish between domestic and foreign. Territories outside of France proper were for administrative purposes, and for some economic, political, and cultural matters, integral parts of France itself. Administrative assimilation, which blurred a distinction between domestic and foreign, had as its counterpart economic assimilation. This aimed to reduce the differences between national and international within the global French Empire. French business, operating outside of mainland France but within the French Empire, was, by the Gallic logic of assimilation, at the same time domestic and international, but not foreign. The French Empire, as did the British Empire, acted as a substitute for some of the activities that multinational corporations perform in crossing borders and creating markets.

Four key factors explain the lagged appearance of French multinationals: the financial nature of the French holding company, the whys and wherefores of developing managerial structures, perceptions of market formation and features of the domestic market, and the French Empire. These all show that the French experience in articulating their multinationals was, like that of the British, part of the changing structures of an already formidable French international presence.

GERMANY

The development of German multinationals is best understood in connection with what did or did not happen to the corporation at home and what it did or did not do there. The German corporation emerged in a nation-state that was itself a recent creation. Chancellor Otto von Bismarck, using his home state of Prussia as a base, gave Germany political and administrative unity in the 1860s and early 1870s.

An economic basis for unification had been in place since 1833. Then a treaty among the larger states of south Germany, except Austria, created the *Zollverein*. This customs union developed at the same time as pre-unification Germany was surging economically. The annual output of German coal, considered along with iron to be two essential ingredients of most European industrialization processes, increased from 5 million tons in 1850 to 36.4 million tons in 1873. Commerce was increasing; and factory industrialization was spreading.

A serious recession in the early 1870s broke the first major wave of German growth which had lasted several decades. Stagnation persisted until the mid-1890s. Then a strong and consistent expansion began which boosted the economy until 1914. During this cycle (1873-1914) a second wave of industrialization occurred.

Modern business enterprises in Germany emerged during the second wave of industrialization. Jürgen Kocka suggests five factors that promoted the emergence of the modern German firm: (1) the processes of expansion, diversification, and integration, (2) the rise of cartels and other associations, (3) changes in relationships between banks and industry, (4) the rise of managerial capitalism, and (5) the increasing importance of science and systems in production, distribution, and management (Kocka 1980: 78).

From the early 1870s until World War I significant industrial expansion took place. Average plant and firm size grew. In 1882 only 23 percent of all manufacturing and crafts workers were in operating units with more than fifty employees; by 1907 this proportion had reached 42 percent. Some areas of German industry experienced the clustering of their work force more than others. Mining, engineering (including electrical engineering), chemicals, and textiles were in the forefront of concentration. Less clustered areas included clothing manufacture, food, and wood and leather products (Kocka 1980: 79).

This expansion involved, as it did in the United States, product diversification and vertical integration. Product diversification was strongest in primary metals, electrical engineering, and machinery production. Vertical integration was most pronounced in chemicals, primary metals, and mining. Firms seeking vertical integration try to control all aspects of the economic process relevant to their products, organization, and market. The German firms approaching vertical integration during this period interconnected all stages of production from the mining of coal and iron ore, through pig iron and steel production, through the many phases of working the metal, sometimes even to heavy engineering. Activities of the integrating firms sometimes included the utilization of by-products and usually included wholesale marketing (Kocka 1980: 80-87).

Technological changes sometimes interwove diversification and integration in practice. In fact, integration sometimes meant diversification. For instance, the discovery that blast-furnace gases could be used as sources of energy induced foundries to establish or join with steel works and rolling mills. The same potential efficiencies created incentives in an opposite fashion. It was advantageous for rolling mills to merge with or establish foundries themselves. Combining stages of production to exploit technology and realize economies was at the same time both integration and diversification. More product lines were added, which constituted diversification; their combination under the control of one enterprise entailed vertical integration (Kocka 1980: 87).

Cartels became important during the economic sluggishness from 1873 to the mid-1890s. These are syndicates, combines, or trusts formed to regulate prices and output in some business field. German cartels were usually based on voluntary agreements among independent firms. Not every German cartel evolved in the same manner. The most successful cartels integrated decision making. They set prices and regulated the level of output and the conditions of its distribution for each member firm. They also established joint marketing organizations. German cartels with the most integration were often called syndicates. Unlike in the United States, with its tradition of marked if unevenly implemented antitrust legislation, in Germany cartels were both legal and generally popular (Kocka 1980: 88).

Cartels sometimes stimulated vertical integration and product diversification. Participation in a cartel fostered linkages between mines and foundries, for instance. This outcome demonstrates how membership could intensify the connections between participants. Sometimes cartel restrictions had a different result. A member firm, feeling hampered by those regulations, might diversify into a product line that was not subject to cartel oversight (Kocka 1980: 87).

As related processes, diversification and integration were especially powerful in the electrical engineering and chemicals industries. In these areas diversification meant the diffusion and utilization of technical expertise and state-of-the-art machinery across whole technical and industrial fields. The increasing complexity of finished products and associated services, itself connected with product diversification as well as product differentiation, accelerated vertical integration in these areas. By the mid-1880s, such large electrical engineering and chemicals firms as Siemens, AEG, and Bayer were taking over retailing through sales to the final consumer (Kocka 1980: 87-88).

Financial intermediaries, particularly banks, played key roles in the emergence of large-scale company and industrial organization in Germany. In France the holding company raised needed capital and to a critical degree substituted for imperfect capital markets and financial intermediaries unable to meet large-scale capital demands. In Germany the articulation of large firms, cartels, and syndicates was closely connected with the changing role of banks. Big corporate banks started to appear in the third quarter of the nineteenth century. These furnished essential capital to industry during the boom of the 1850s and in the years immediately preceding 1873. From the mid-1890s, when a second phase of economic expansion began, banks and industrial enterprises cooperated more closely (Kocka 1980: 89).

The major German banks, including the Deutsche Bank, the Commerzbank, and the Dresdner Bank, provided a mix of services that greatly facilitated the emergence of large-scale industrial organization in Germany. This mix changed over time in response to shifting needs and structures. From the outset the large banks provided short- and long-term loans and underwrote and marketed industrial securities. These banks were fulfilling a classic function associated with financial intermediaries: the mobilization of savings and their transformation into investment. They served as depositories for the sometimes modest savings of many people and made these funds available to their corporate clients as potential investments.

This function remained constant, but the mix of loan time frames changed as a result of an evolving corporate structure. Expansions either internally or through mergers became more frequent than the establishment of new enterprises. With a decrease in the demand for start-up funds that involved a significant short-term component, relationships between large-scale banking and large-scale industry became more long term. The provision of funds in arrangements structured over a longer term became the single most important service that those banks furnished their clients (Kocka 1980: 89-90).

The major German banks, in using the available capital markets for emerging large-scale corporations, were performing an essential task. During its formative period, from the early 1870s into the twentieth century, large-scale German industrial enterprise depended more heavily on external finance, particularly as represented by the capital markets, than did major industries in the United States and the United Kingdom. The emergence of largeness in banking, which made the utilization of those still developing German capital markets feasible, is a crucial factor in the articulation of large-scale company and industrial organization.

The interdependence of large-scale banks and large-scale industrial enterprises, reinforced by bank membership on the boards supervising those industries, diminished during the twentieth century. The key influence here, as it was in forging that relationship in the first place, was the need for external capital. Early in the twentieth century the rate of self-financing achieved by larger German manufacturing firms increased. Self-financing means that an enterprise is using retained earnings, money that it generated and did not spend, to pay for its projects. Complete self-financing eliminates the need for outside capital. As the rate of self-financing increased, industrial enterprises depended less on the capital markets and banks. Though the direct involvement of major German banks in large-scale industrialization declined, the links remained significant (Kocka 1980: 92).

The rise of managerial capitalism contributed to the articulation of large-scale corporate organization in Germany. Managerial capitalism refers to the growing significance of the salaried entrepreneur in managing the largest enterprises. A managerial enterprise is an organization in which managers who own little or no stock in the business itself make top-level as well as middle- and lower-level decisions. The managerial enterprise, to borrow Alfred Chandler's distinctions, differs from both the personal and entrepreneurial enterprise. An enterprise is personal when its owners manage it. An enterprise is entrepreneurial when its owners retain top-level decision-making ability but hire managers to deal with middle- and lower-level tasks (Chandler 1988: 361).

The emergence of managerial enterprises was a significant though deliberate phenomenon during the formative period of large-scale German industry. The number of managerial enterprises increased during the period from 1887 to 1907. In certain sectors their presence was noteworthy from the start. Mining firms were often managerial from their foundation. Managerial enterprises were strong in chemicals and made up a substantial minority of iron and steel firms. But managerial enterprise seems to have spread more rapidly through the ranks of middle-level firms than at either end of the scale spectrum. In 1907 most of the 100 largest corporations were still entrepreneurial, and managerial firms were rare among the smallest companies (Kocka 1980: 93).

The rise of the salaried entrepreneur or manager was a key element in the professionalization that accompanied the emergence of large-scale German industrial enterprises. As hierarchies and other aspects of large-scale corporate organization developed, management had to be more systematic. This approach required specialized knowledge and skills. The salaried manager needed those skills and in turn helped diffuse technical information and expertise to all levels of the corporate hierarchy.

Professionalization was related to an increasing emphasis on science and systems in production and distribution as well as management. People with substantial academic training, often of a technical and scientific nature, occupied many important jobs in German industry. The acquisition and dissemination of technical knowledge was supported by German technical colleges and industrial research laboratories. These institutions began to appear in the 1850s and flourished in the areas of metal production, chemical production, and electrical engineering. The combination of professional technical education and research laboratories made production, distribution, and management in German industry more scientific and systematic. The schools and laboraties cooperated on projects and maintained close contacts with one another (Kocka 1980: 94-95).

Some of the factors that promoted the emergence of the German corporation contributed to its internationalization from the late nineteenth century. Cartels provided an important bridge between national and international operations. The victorious Allied powers banned cartels in West Germany after 1945. But in the formative period of large-scale German enterprise, cartelization was sometimes integrally linked to internationalization. By 1914 German firms were involved in about 100 international cartels (Kocka 1980: 89).

Some firms acquired structures that enabled them to compete internationally. Product diversification, vertical integration, and scientific and systematic professionalization sometimes combined to produce the international corporation. Already before 1914 one outstanding example of such convergence had appeared in Germany. Siemens, headquartered in Berlin, was two interlocking enterprises that made electrical machinery: Siemens & Halske and Siemens Schuckertwerke. By 1914 these had become decentralized multidivisional structures, which later typified highly diversified German industrial concerns. Siemens had already developed an intricate mix of centralization and decentralization. To achieve that blend it had put in place a number of administrative mechanisms and internal price systems, as well as the needed management hierarchies, with their boards, committees, and chains of command (Kocka 1980: 98).

The emergence of national and multinational enterprises in Germany was fueled by factors that sometimes converged: diversification, integration, cartelization, bank capitalization, and a professionalization that became more scientific and systematic. Modern industrial enterprise in Germany was generic yet distinctive. The generic aspects include product diversification, vertical integration, and professionalization, as well as management hierarchies and multidivisional unit articulation.

Distinctive aspects are cartelization, a heavy reliance on bank financing in the formative period, as well as several features that pertain to the German environment, state, and market. Germany got a comparatively late start as a nation-state, but late political unification did not obstruct the emergence of German national and multinational enterprises. In fact, modern industrial organization had established a substantial presence by the start of the twentieth century. Central to this accomplishment was the appearance of a sufficient number of major banks with the right product and organization for a new market. These banks developed the product—financial services—and themselves had the organization—a large-scale firm that integrated those financial services. The banks diversified their product, but kept the design, formulation, and delivery of those services under their control. In these respects they practiced an integration of product and organization that greatly assisted emerging large-scale German industrial enterprises, which constituted their new market.

The German state was notably internationally minded in thought and deed from its inception. Bismarck was one of the premier diplomats of his day and one of the most analytically comprehensive of all time. He tried to make Germany a major force in Europe and the world. He made the command decisions that led to the creation of the German colonial empire, which lasted from the 1880s until Germany lost its colonies as a result of its defeat in World War I. Though short-lived, the German Empire had possessions in Africa and the Pacific and provided a framework in which German businesses could operate overseas. The empire, which rested on the support of key business interests at home, gave German enterprises opportunities abroad that they would not otherwise have had. In this sense the German Empire strengthened an internationally minded outlook among certain segments of the German business community.

SWEDEN

Sweden greatly intrigues because, as *The Economist* has noted, it has a disproportionate number of successful multinational companies. Sweden has a total population of more than 8 million people and a domestic economy that is still comparatively small. Its gross domestic product (GDP) is about 10 percent of Germany's GDP and 3 percent of that of the United States. Yet about 25 to 30 of the biggest 500 companies in the world outside of the United States are headquartered there (*Econ* 1 August 1987: 63-64). Why this is so can best be explained by examining the Swedish experience in light of the comparative emergence model.

Sweden demonstrates that size in itself is a superficial indicator of how well one can incubate large-scale multinational enterprises. More relevant considerations involve a country's environment and how people initiate and respond to opportunities. Sweden, which began an industrial transformation about the middle of the nineteenth century, was from the outset outward-looking. The area of technological change illustrates this outlook. As the Swedish industrial transformation unfolded, Swedes produced a great number of refinements of foreign inventions. The international awareness of Swedish inventors was matched by their own ingenuity. They developed many industrial inventions of their own. Inventions of both kinds accelerated around the turn of the century.

There was a synergy of invention and innovation in Sweden that involved not only product but also organization and market. Companies formed to implement advances in such fields as separators, electricity transmission technology, ball bearings, and foundry-steel processes (*Econ* 1 August 1987: 64). With a dynamism of product and organization, those Swedish companies needed markets. In this domain Swedes became even more outward-looking, as the sales of these firms quickly outgrew their modest domestic market. They needed external markets.

Technological change drove company formation, and industrial demand for markets that could not be met locally powered the internationalization of those businesses. However, it is the nature of the Swedish environment that stimulated the standards of production in certain areas that helped create world-class products; for example, motor vehicles. Volvo and Saab made cars and trucks to operate in difficult weather and over challenging terrain. Too many roads of poor quality (until recently) made domestic motor vehicle manufacturers fiercer competitors in the international marketplace. The durability of their products enabled both Volvo and Saab to become world market leaders in trucks of sixteen tons and more. Volvo increased sales of its automobiles in North America for ten consecutive years through the mid-1980s. In 1987 Volkswagen of Germany was the only European car maker to export more cars to the United States than Volvo (*Econ* 1 August 1987: 64).

The nature of the Swedish home market and the search for external markets energized an internationalization of Swedish business that was highly market-selective. Market selectivity means niche marketing or narrow casting. A business targets a product line for a segment of an intended market. The smallness of their domestic market contributed to the accumulating market expertise of Swedish businesses. Swedish vehicle manufacturers realized that they could not profitably offer a full range of models at home because the number of their potential customers would not economically support such diversification. This lesson had great transferability for Swedish businesses as they approached foreign markets. Niche marketing at home and abroad became an axiom of market identification and cultivation. This selectivity in both products and markets enabled Swedish automakers and other manufacturers to avoid serious mistakes made by other multinationals, such as British Leyland.

At the core of the internationalization of Swedish business is an international mindedness in thought and deed that ranks as one of the most intense anywhere in the world. As *The Economist* put it, "Swedes have to be linguists and have to have an international outlook" (*Econ* 1 August 1987: 64). Their geographical smallness and an historical apartness fostered by their location on the northern edge of Europe have required a cosmopolitanism of spirit and behavior to survive. Their multilingualism is shared by many other Europeans. Swedish business has been most effective in harnessing three attributes that many of its employees possess—an international outlook, multilingualism, and engineering training—as it has penetrated global markets. Many Swedish managers, according to *The Economist*, have an innate feeling of superiority in competing against corporate America. Harvard, Stanford, Wharton, and other U.S. business schools, Swedish managers supposedly say, turn out people trained to cope with one language, one culture, and one market (*Econ* 1 August 1987: 64). This criticism still has merit, but there are important exceptions to this characterization of provinciality: one quality U.S. business school with an international curriculum (the Thunderbird School in Arizona) and some course internationalization at other schools. In any event, if belief is what counts, the fact that many Swedish managers believe that they are better prepared internationally than their U.S. counterparts will give them a mental edge in the international marketplace.

The international mindedness of Swedish business used to stop at its equity doorstep. Swedish business historically had a share structure that protected it against foreign control. In this porcupine-like defense it shared a strong similarity with Japanese multinationals. Foreign nationals could only purchase shares of stock in a company that had considerably diluted voting power. But under pressure from a recession that hit hard in the late 1980s, Sweden moved to liberalize these regulations. It now allows foreign participation in banking. Sweden has applied to join the European Community (EC). If admitted, the country will have to dismantle the share barriers to conform with EC policy.

Foreign participation in Swedish business is increasing. In early 1990 General Motors acquired a 50 percent stake in and management control of Saab. General Motors is struggling to improve the efficiency of Saab's car operations. Its difficult decisions, including plant closings, may make Saab more competitive, but they threaten the fabric of worker friendly corporate behavior that is a Swedish hallmark (*FT* 11 February 1991: 12).

A center-right coalition goverment assumed power in 1991 from the Social Democratic Party. This party, alone or in coalition, had led the government of Sweden most of the time since 1945. They built a country that, as the *Financial Times* noted in 1987, combined the biggest public sector of any western country, the highest taxes, the narrowest wage differentials, and the most highly unionized workforce with one of the highest standards of living, and one of the most vigorous industrial sectors (*FT* 21 September 1987: 20). The new government announced in late 1991 its plans for a new era of enterprise, growth, and development. A major goal is to cut Sweden's high level of government spending and its tax burden as a proportion of gross domestic product—then at 55 percent, among the highest in the world—to around 40 percent. A 1992 financial crisis delayed the government's privatization program and led to a reduction in social spending (*FT* 11 May 1992: 19).

3

Vignette: International Business and Economic Integration: EC92

In every major region of the world today governments are pushing instruments of economic integration. These involve the concepts of free-trade area, customs union, common market, confederation, and federation. A *free-trade area* has no internal tariffs, but its members are free to set their own tariffs with the rest of the world. A *customs union* has a common external tariff and no internal tariffs. A *common market* is a customs union, but it also has a common system of commercial law permitting freedom of movement of goods, services, capital, and labor inside. A *confederation* is a group of sovereign states sharing some tasks. A *federation* has a central authority with real clout, although members retain specified and perhaps unspecified powers (*Econ* 9 November 1991: 60).

A common market is the ultimate in economic integration. Its members gain more than they lose from dismantling barriers to exchange among themselves. Economic synergy works here: the whole (the common market) is greater than the sum of its parts (economies of member states). Common markets can be powerful bargaining units in the global business arena. This bargaining can turn into economic warfare with other countries or common markets, which will reduce global economic welfare.

Common markets can promote political integration, a natural outcome for common markets are organizations of political economy that interweave politics and economics. Common markets originate in political cooperation, but the process of interlacing economic and political integration is not easy. As a common market evolves through phases of economic unification, one or more members may balk at going farther. This controversy can hamper political integration.

Common markets are not creations of the twentieth century. They go back centuries. The United States is a very successful common market. The U.S.

Constitution, written in 1787 and ratified in 1788, is a framework for the simultaneous economic and political integration of the states in a federation. The five vignettes in this book focus on economic groupings of more recent creation or discussion. These include the European Community, the U.S.-Canada Free Trade Agreement, a U.S.-Mexico Free Trade Agreement, South American alliances, economic integration in Africa, and greater economic cooperation in the western Pacific. These groupings present great opportunities for business.

The long-term outcome of this global push for larger economic blocs is anybody's guess. It could be a single common market for the entire globe: "one world, one common market." This would require a radical transformation in the politics and ideologies of many nation-states. The short-term consequences are likely to be more determined economic competition both within and between these mega-blocs. This accelerating competition raises the stakes for international business and makes the formulation of strategies for dealing with economic integration urgent. An integral part of strategy design is knowledge of the contexts in which the challenge is developing.

THE EUROPEAN ECONOMIC COMMUNITY: EC92 AND MARKET PENETRATION

The European Economic Community (EEC), now known as the European Community (EC), is the most successful common market to have begun in the twentieth century. This organization has deep roots. One is the dream of European unity, which has been alive for over 1000 years, dating to Charlemagne (A.D. 742-814) and the Roman emperors. Another is the manner in which Europe tried to come together after World War II (1939-1945) devastated huge portions of it.

A direct ancestor of the EC was the European Coal and Steel Community (ECSC), which began in 1952. It contained the Benelux countries (Belgium, the Netherlands, and Luxembourg), France, Italy, and West Germany. The ECSC provided for the elimination of tariffs and quotas on intracommunity trade in iron ore, coal, coke, and steel, a common external tariff wall on imports from outsiders, and controls on production and sales. The 1951 treaty creating the ECSC set up several agencies to run it. A High Authority had executive powers, a Council of Ministers safeguarded the interests of member states, a Common Assembly had advisory powers, and a Court of Justice settled disputes. All these bodies were supranational: member states surrendered elements of their sovereignty to the ECSC (Cameron 1989: 390).

The ECSC prepared the way for the EC. The European Economic Community or Common Market originated with a treaty signed in Rome in 1957, which took effect on 1 January 1958. The Common Market treaty stipulated a gradual elimination of import duties and quantitative restrictions on intracommunity trade over a transitional period of twelve to fifteen years. Members promised to permit the free movement of people and capital within the common market. They pledged to implement common policies in transportation, agriculture, social insurance, and other critical areas of economic policy (Cameron 1989: 390).

The Common Market treaty had other crucial provisions. It could not be renounced unilaterally. After a certain stage in the transitional period, further decisions were to be made by a qualified majority vote, not by unanimous consent. These provisions were essential to ensuring the long-term survival of the EC (Cameron 1989: 390).

The EC has made considerable progress. Its members shortened the transitional period. All tariffs between member states were completely eliminated by 1 July 1968, several years earlier than planned. It has added six new members: Great Britain (1973), Denmark (1973), Ireland (1973), Greece (1981), Portugal (1986), and Spain (1986). They joined the original six: Belgium, the Netherlands, Luxembourg, France, Italy, and West Germany. Turkey, Cyprus, and Malta are associates of the EC. On 21 November 1991 the European Community signed association agreements with Poland, Hungary, and Czechoslovakia, which give them access to the EC by the end of the century but stop short of full membership (*NYT* 10 December 1991: A6). Turkey has applied for full membership, but its application has been put on hold. Sweden and Norway have also applied for full membership.

The summit meeting of EC heads of government at Maastricht, The Netherlands, in December 1991, produced a watershed agreement in money and banking. They decided to create a single currency and regional central bank no later than 1999. The actual plan consists of three stages. The first, which began in July 1990, is limited to closer coordination of economic policies. The second, to begin on 1 January 1994, will include the creation of a European Monetary Institute, a forerunner of the central bank, and require minimal exchange-rate fluctuations. The first opportunity to create a single currency will come in 1996. But the economies of a majority of members must meet strict conditions. These include low rates of inflation and budget deficits that are a few percentage points of gross domestic product. If no such "critical mass" of countries exists, another set of rules goes into effect to produce a single currency and central bank by 1999 (*NYT* 12 December 1991: A8). This currency should be one of the world's strongest and will rival the U.S. dollar. Great Britain, with its historic ambivalence toward greater community integration in both economic and political senses, has chosen the right to "opt out" of any single currency agreement. The Maastricht Treaty encountered opposition. In 1992 referendums Denmark (6 June) rejected it, while Ireland (17 June) and France (20 September) approved it.

The Single European Act of 1986 set the goal of creating a single EC market for products and services by 1 January 1993. The EC abolished tariffs on intracommunity trade by 1 July 1968. But national borders remained customs frontiers and a number of non-tariff barriers stayed in place: paperwork, inspections, and licensing procedures. EC92 became shorthand for the EC becoming a single product and service market (*Econ* 7 December 1991: 63).

Economic integration involves not only products and services but also the factors of production themselves. Integration of some factor markets is proceeding, but full unification remains a long-term goal. Capital illustrates this process. By 1 July 1990, eight EC countries had removed all restrictions on capital movements. France and Italy eliminated foreign-exchange controls, while Belgium abolished a two-tier foreign-exchange system. A European financial marketplace is taking shape sooner than expected (*The Commerzbank Report on German Business and Finance*, No. 7/90, *Econ* 21 July 1990: 62).

But other actions are needed to create a single capital market. All members must give securities—stocks and bonds—from other EC countries the same status as domestic issues in various circumstances. These include a country's investment rules for insurance firms and pension funds. Another important area is fiscal or tax policy. A unified capital market would require that every member stop fiscal discrimination against foreign investment from other EC countries (*The Commerzbank Report on German Business and Finance*, No. 7/90, *Econ* 21 July 1990: 62).

Important developments are affecting the factors of labor and entrepreneurial ability. By December 1991, eight EC countries had signed an agreement to abolish all frontier controls on people passing between them. Belgium, the Netherlands, Luxembourg, Germany, France, Italy, Portugal, and Spain will, once all parliaments have ratified the agreement, become the free travel zone of Schengenland. This name comes from the place where five countries first signed the agreement on 19 June 1990, the village of Schengen in Luxembourg (*FT* 19 June 1990: 18). Schengen is where Luxembourg, Germany, and France converge on the Moselle River. Implementation is gradual. By December 1991 only the French parliament had ratified the treaty (*Econ* 23 November 1991: 58).

Into the late 1980s the EC was one of Europe's three main trading blocs. The other two were the European Free Trade Association (EFTA) and Comecon, an economic association of the Soviet Union and its satellites: Poland, East Germany, Czechoslovakia, Hungary, Romania, Bulgaria, Mongolia, Vietnam, and Cuba. The EFTA continues into the 1990s. Its members are Austria, Finland, Iceland, Liechtenstein, Norway, Sweden, and Switzerland. But tumultuous events in 1989 and 1990 led to the disintegration of the Soviet bloc in Eastern Europe. Comecon formally disbanded in early 1991. On 3 October 1990, East Germany, unified with West Germany, became part of the EC. Poland, Hungary, and Czechoslovakia have signed association agreements with the EC. Comecon is to be replaced by an association called the Organization for International

Economic Cooperation.   Its goal is to help members convert to market economies.

One of the most exciting prospects on the international economic scene is the possible joining together of the EC, EFTA, and some former members of Comecon.   The EFTA and the EC agreed in 1991 to create a European Economic Area (EEA).   The EEA is a potential common market of both the EC and EFTA, although many see it as a bridge that will allow many members of EFTA to join the EC.   After difficult negotiations the seven members of EFTA agreed to accept EC trading, financial, and labor rules.   EFTA members will also have to adopt EC laws on consumer protection, company law, environmental protection, competition, and social policy.   In return, EFTA, with its combined population of 40 million, will get broad access to the EC, with its total population of 345 million (*NYT* 23 October 1991: C18).   The EEA hit a legal roadblock in December 1991.   The European Court of Justice, the EC's supranational court, suspended it because the EEA called for a tribunal of judges from both the EC and EFTA, and the European Court believed that arrangement would abridge its own powers (*FT* 16 December 1991: 1).   A compromise was apparently worked out between the EC and EFTA that preserved the EEA as a bridge from the EFTA to EC (*FT* 4 February 1992: 2).

Even if the EC, EFTA, and former members of Comecon do not become one common market, the trends toward greater integration and possible unification of their economic activities are accelerating.   These prospects present outstanding business opportunities.   Many companies are already positioning themselves to take advantage of these events.

This positioning has taken a number of forms: mergers, acquisitions, takeovers, and joint ventures.   The first three represent structural integration of two formerly separate companies.   A merger is the joining of two or more enterprises into a single one.   An acquisition refers to one business obtaining another business or part of it.   A takeover is an acquisition marked by degrees of aggressiveness from the acquiring company.   Takeovers can be hostile from start to finish or proceed from an aggressive initiation into a transaction of compromise.   Joint venture is an umbrella term for various cooperative agreements between two organizations that keep their separate structural identities throughout their association.

A main goal of all these activities is for a company to grow bigger and more powerful.   Mergers, acquisitions, and takeovers create larger, more powerful companies.   Joint ventures use the principle of synergy to enhance the power of both partners without actually increasing the physical size of either.   These techniques have numerous variations, have appeared in combinations, and are used both by companies already headquartered in Europe and outsiders desiring to establish a base within an economic community.

The capital goods field furnishes a major example of "bigger is better."   A capital good is used to produce consumer goods or more capital goods. A capital good is sometimes called an intermediate good. This means it mediates or stands between the first phases of the production process—preparation of raw materials—and those toward the end—final consumption. Capital goods industries include mechanical engineering, computers, telecommunications equipment, and semiconductors.

Some companies already headquartered in the EC are determined to win a larger share of the international capital goods market, currently dominated by the United States and Japan. The strategy of these companies is to capitalize on the opportunities offered by their unifying community base. Their goals are to increase their share of the international market by building up their sales within the EC and to piggyback on this strength to penetrate the international capital goods market outside the EC. Their methods involve greater product specialization and a more international approach.

The activities of several EC companies illustrate various approaches to increasing their share of the international capital goods market. CGE, the French communications giant, took over ITT's telecommunications activities in what used to be West Germany. This takeover has increased CGE's clout in the capital goods market by focusing it on a few specialized products. Siemens A.G., a major German multinational, has already completed a number of moves to enhance its position in the capital goods industry. Among them is the acquisition of the Nixdorf Computer Company, another German enterprise. Siemens combined its own profitable computer and software activities with Nixdorf in a new company, Siemens-Nixdorf Informationssysteme. The result is Europe's largest indigenous computer company, significantly larger than Olivetti of Italy, Groupe Bull of France, and International Computers (part of STC) of the United Kingdom (*FT* 11 January 1990: 1).

The computer industry is central to the international capital goods industry. So many key business moves have concentrated on the computer industry in the EC and elsewhere. Japanese companies are leading the way in an outsider penetration of the EC capital goods market, especially in computers and related areas.

In 1990 Fujitsu Ltd. acquired 80 percent of ICL P.L.C., Great Britain's only manufacturer of mainframe computers. This acquisition pushed Fujitsu past the Digital Equipment Corporation into the number two spot worldwide behind the International Business Machines Corporation (IBM). IBM is also number one in Western Europe. ICL was the world's ninth largest manufacturer of mainframes and Western Europe's fifth largest computer company. It was also the most profitable computer company in Western Europe (*NYT* 31 July 1990: C1).

Fujitsu picked its acquisition well. Though not very well known outside of the United Kingdom, ICL was a well-managed enterprise with a healthy balance sheet and significant though not dominating market share. It had about 20 percent of the British computer market and 5 to 10 percent of the Western European market. Before the acquisition Fujitsu got about 5 percent of its revenues from sales of computers and data processing systems in Europe (*NYT* 31 July 1990: C1). ICL gave Fujitsu significant U.K. market share and an established beachhead in Western Europe.

The Fujitsu deal reflects the long-term strategy that most Japanese businesses follow worldwide, but it was punctuated with immediacy—EC92. Fujitsu's move raised fears about a possible Japanese domination of the global computer industry. It intensified doubts about the effectiveness of Europe's strategy of "national champions."

Throughout the 1980s Europe tried to create "national champions" in strategic technologies. These corporate champions were to form a group of computer telecommunications, and semiconductor makers to take on IBM and Japan. These companies were too slow to cooperate in research. With research and development costs spiraling in the computer industry, only the largest and best-financed companies can remain on the cutting edge of product innovation. With the exception of IBM, all the companies now on this list are Japanese. They include Hitachi, NEC, and now Fujitsu (*NYT* 31 July 1990: C1 and C5). In the early 1990s France is trying a new variation of "national champions." IBM and Groupe Bull are forming an alliance, but the clouded futures of both corporations make any predictions of success unwise (*FT* 29 January 1992: 1).

Some EC banks have been vigorously expanding their operations to meet several challenges simultaneously: EC92, the possible widening of the EC to include EFTA and former Comecon members, and Japanese domination of the major leagues of world banking in physical size.

The Deutsche Bank has a far-sighted strategy. It is Europe's largest bank by market capitalization; that is, what monetary value stock markets attach to a company's equity as represented by its publicly traded capital in stocks and other debt instruments. It is looking both east and west as it seeks to become a Pan-European financial institution without losing its German identity. To the West it launched a $1.48 billion takeover of Morgan Grenfell, the London merchant bank, in November 1989. This move was the Deutsche Bank's first into the merchant banking business and gave the bank a historic anchor in Great Britain (*FT* 28 November 1990: 1). To the East the bank has set up a joint venture universal bank with the East German Deutsche Kreditbank, the former state banking monopoly (*FT* 18 April 1990: 1).

This strategy rests in large measure on the work and legacy of Alfred Herrhausen, "speaker" or chief executive of the Deutsche Bank. He envisioned the Deutsche Bank as Europe's first authentic continental bank, one playing a more important role in global banking circles. This vision motivated his strategy of internationalization. As he himself said shortly after the Deutsche Bank had announced its biggest deal ever, the takeover of Morgan Grenfell, "Strategy begins with a vision." Herrhausen was brutally murdered in a bomb attack on his car outside Frankfurt, on 30 November 1989, supposedly by extreme left-wing terrorists of the Red Army Faction (*FT* 1 December 1989: 1).

During his tenure as "speaker" the bank used its considerable strength as a banking giant in Germany to reach across geographical boundaries and product lines. Already a powerful institutional shareholder in such companies as Daimler-Benz, the Deutsche Bank undertook bank acquisitions in Italy, Spain, Portugal, the Netherlands, Austria, and the United Kingdom. With Deutsche Bank Capital Markets, its established London-based debt issuing and trading operation, and Morgan Grenfell, the bank is a commanding player in Europe's largest financial center. The bank also has banking and security operations in New York and Tokyo. The product diversification under Alfred Herrhausen took the Deutsche Bank into management consultancy, insurance, and particularly investment banking (*NYT* 7 November 1989: 25; *FT* 1 December 1989: 41). Herrhausen's successor, Hilmar Kopper, has slowed the bank's globalization. In the early 1990s the bank was concentrating on expanding its home base in a unified Germany (*FT* 16 January 1991: 21).

Some U.S. businesses are responding to the challenges posed by a stronger EC with various strategies. One of the most creative approaches comes from General Electric (GE), the U.S. conglomerate with interests in power generation, medical systems, and financial services. Its acquisition in late 1989 of Tungsram, the Hungarian manufacturer of lighting equipment, hints at a bold and comprehensive strategy for penetrating the European market. A headline in the *Financial Times* aptly noted that "General Electric plans attack from the east" (*FT* 20 November 1989: 25). In 1992 GE, blaming rising costs, cut its investment in Tungsram, but insisted that the company's long-term promise remained strong (*FT* 26 March 1992: 19).

The key is to look at the emerging European market as a potential *whole*. This includes not only the EC but also EFTA and the former Eastern European members of Comecon. GE's Hungarian opening concentrates on the last component of this potential whole. This move is based on past ties. GE's links with Tungsram, which was founded in 1896, go back to 1913, when the Hungarian company was licensed to use a GE patent. The political changes in Eastern Europe revived and intensified long-standing connections between the two companies.

A wider Europe is on the horizon. Each business must define what this means for its own future and refine a long-term strategy for dealing with the opportunities that this wider Europe is bringing.

PART II. NORTH AMERICA

U.S. multinational corporations form the focus of the second part of this book. Their origins and development will be analyzed with reference to the comparative emergence model. Readers should recall the five factors—the role of government, export markets and external sources of supply, technological change, relative factor scarcities and qualities, and how international-minded a culture is—and highlight information in the rest of this introduction and following case studies that relates to each. Another vignette examines the United States-Canada free trade pact.

The United States had plentiful economic resources, a flexible legal framework, and the political support that nurtured the emergence of the corporation as a domestic, then international force. As with the experiences of the United Kingdom, France, Germany, and Sweden, multinational emergence begins with what did or did not happen to the corporation at home and what it did or did not do there. Two sections that complete this introduction analyze the U.S. national market and the corporation, as well as the emergence of U.S. multinationals.

These sections give a context for the case studies of part II. They concern three U.S. multinationals—International Harvester, Singer, and United Fruit—in late nineteenth- and early twentieth-century settings. International Harvester and Singer, two leading U.S. multinationals at the time, appear mainly in connection with their activities in Russia from about 1870 until the Russian Revolution of 1917. Harvester and Singer were dedicated to defining and developing a market in Russia for their products. They were market-oriented investors: putting in resources to build up markets.

United Fruit (UFC), by contrast, was a supply-oriented investor in its Central American activities. It wanted to extract a commodity—bananas—for export to overseas markets, so it put resources into constructing an infrastructure of extraction. It built a railroad, roads, and port that facilitated the removal of a country's output. This infrastructure of transport and communications fostered a dependence of the local economy upon outside forces. The core meaning of dependency is reliance on external interests in harmful ways. Using foreign resources and personnel to help a country develop is not in itself wrong. The harm comes from the nature and degree of these external connections. For Costa Rica and Guatemala dependency resulted when the company paid more attention to building an infrastructure of extraction than one that promoted internal exchange. Had the resulting economy been more integrative and less extractive, corporate behavior in these instances would be less tarnished.

These case studies together provide sharp contrasts in the impact of corporations upon their foreign environments. International Harvester and Singer produced many more benefits than harms for Russia. Their market-oriented behavior was, for the most part, constructive. Many Russian consumers purchased "big ticket" items—farm machinery and implements and sewing machines—that enabled them to economize greatly on their labor. Harvester and Singer both helped buyers by providing flexible credit arrangements that harmonized with local business needs.

United Fruit's record in Central America has a strong negative component. As a company focused so single-mindedly on supply-oriented investments, it did little to promote the economic autonomy of its workers or the economic independence of the countries in which it operated. It meddled in local politics when it felt threatened. The UFC played a role spotlighted here in the 1954 intervention by the Central Intelligence Agency of the United States government in Guatemalan politics.

There are other examples of U.S. business behavior abroad in this book. They appear elsewhere because they relate to events and processes that need treatment in their local contexts. The Cerro Corporation appears in Chapter 7, Exxon in Chapter 8, Wallace Groves and the Bahamian Port Authority in Chapter 9, the Tsumeb Corporation in Chapter 12, and Union Carbide in Chapter 16.

THE U.S. NATIONAL MARKET AND THE CORPORATION

As the East, South, and West specialized and traded more with one another and as a supportive infrastructure expanded, an authentic national market emerged in the United States during the nineteenth century. The growth and development of the corporation needed this national market. In turn, the expansion of the corporation boosted the development of the national market. The corporation has several advantages that partnerships do not possess, such as legal perpetuity and limited liability. It also has a great capacity for bureaucratic extension and refinement. Though registered in one legal jurisdiction, the corporation could operate nationally thanks to the Supreme Court. The court gave corporations key protections that ensured their potential national character. For instance, a state could not arbitrarily bar a corporation legally registered in another state from doing business within its own boundaries (*Bank of Augusta v. Earle*, 1839). After the U.S. Civil War (1861–1865) corporations constituted the administrative and entrepreneurial vanguard in the further articulation of a national market as the land frontier continued a movement westward that only officially stopped in 1890.

In a country that was growing and developing in so many ways, the corporation itself was undergoing significant transformations. Large corporations were not the only energizers of business and economic activity because small- to medium-sized incorporated businesses were critical to economic change and job generation then as they are now. In the latter third of the nineteenth century, though, the large-scale corporation did emerge as the preeminent vehicle of concentrated economic power in the United States. Largeness included quantitative growth and structural development. By 1900 most major U.S. industries were oligopolistic; that is, a few large companies dominated an industry. The concentration of power in U.S. industry resulted from technological change. There were significant innovations in production, distribution, and exchange. The benefits from many were scale biased: the larger the business unit, the greater the gain up to a point. The fact that gains from change were often scale biased accelerated the emergence of oligopoly.

Technological change also pertains to how production, distribution, and exchange are organized. Many corporations tried to control as much of the economic process as possible, from sources of supply, to transport to manufacturing centers, to manufacturing, through distribution and sales, right up to the final consumer. A company seeking this control is striving for *vertical integration*. Vertical integration, a crucial structural change, can and often does represent concentrated economic power.

Corporations became more bureaucratic but not necessarily more coherent. The large-scale corporations that emerged in the United States in the latter nineteenth century were hierarchically organized, multiunit administrative bureaucracies. Raymond Vernon has suggested that as large corporations articulate their separate manufacturing, marketing, and financial sub-bureaucracies, they become sets of "cooperating semi-independent forces with distinguishably different goals" (Vernon 1969: 131). These objectives include those other than profit maximization and can conflict with each other. The preeminent vehicle of concentrated economic power and a major force powering the national market, the large-scale corporation had also become by 1900 more difficult to analyze.

THE EMERGENCE OF U.S. MULTINATIONALS

Large-scale U.S. corporations were especially well suited, if not uniquely poised, to become multinationals from the later nineteenth century on. They had already developed, and were refining, products and structures that were appropriate for the conditions that characterized their home market. These included relatively high per capita incomes, labor scarcity, and channels of distribution that were not adequate to handle the enormous volume of output that resulted from the implementation of continuous-process production (manufacturing) technology.

The first feature is straightforward. As incomes rise, so can effective demand for a product. Income translates demand into practice: effective demand. The second and third, which are related, need more explanation. Throughout the nineteenth century and as far back as colonial times, labor in the United States was relatively scarce in relation to land and sometimes to capital. Skilled labor was the perennially scarce factor. This shortage motivated innovators to develop processes that economized on the scarce factor. The result was technological change that was labor saving and capital using. Continuous-process production technology needed human labor but tried to use it as efficiently as possible.

The central consequence of this multiple adaptation to their home market was that U.S. corporations had the products, the organizational knowledge, and the large, integrated administrative structures which they could export to other countries when they deemed conditions there suitable. U.S. companies later in the nineteenth century made numerous market-oriented investments in Europe and elsewhere. A market-oriented investment aims to develop a market in the host country for a company's product(s). This investment considers such factors as per capita income.

A supply-oriented investment affects resource extraction within a foreign country. Companies wish to improve their capacity to extract and export raw materials, metals, or minerals. Supply-oriented investments bolster a company's ability to take from a country, not improve the domestic economies that surround the enclaves in which those extractive enterprises operate. U.S. business abroad made both types of investments. There are examples of supply-oriented investments in chapters 5, 7, 8, and 12. U.S. supply-oriented investments predominated in areas sometimes stereotyped as the "Third World." But as U.S. business penetrated Europe and its environs, market-oriented investments were more important than those concerned with enhancing extraction.

The reasons for treating the Old World differently from the Third World lie in the ways large-scale U.S. corporations were positioned to become multinationals with worldwide connections in the latter nineteenth century. These companies were producing high volumes of goods; they needed foreign territories with significant consumer potential for those commodities; they perceived Old World countries as more attractive markets because per capita money incomes there were rising or could increase. Estimates of income, actual or potential, are central to ranking market potential. The Third World, as seen at that time and today, does not seem to present as alluring opportunities in sales. Per capita money incomes, stated as official government statistics, often seem low and sometimes very low.

But it is misleading to rely on available per capita income statistics as the major determinant of market potential. Monetized income, especially in the "developing world," omits significant resources that might contribute to market punch. These include commodities that may be barter goods or local money that is not legal tender of the government. Monetized income, as reported in official statistics, is everywhere subject to the limitations of the agencies collecting, compiling, and interpreting raw data. These constraints apply with special force to governments in the developing world.

While the Old World was then perceived as a greater source of demand than supply, the reverse was true for the Third World at the time. The Old World may have had more clustered numbers of consumers with money incomes perceived as rising, but the Third World had the raw materials, metals, and minerals. Since business perceptions of the Third World fixated on commodities and not people, it is understandable why companies did not devote more time to devising marketing strategies for selling goods to the people who lived on the land that held all that wealth or produced all those crops.

Market-oriented U.S. businesses from the later nineteenth century intensified their activities in European countries, including Russia. Such U.S. firms as Singer, McCormick Reaper (predecessor of International Harvester, now Navistar), Kodak, Otis Elevator, and others made numerous market-oriented investments in Old World locations. These investments represented transfers, and to some extent extensions, to those foreign markets of the procedures and structures that those companies used in their mature domestic marketing organizations.

Why U.S. business activity abroad intensified significantly from the 1890s can only be sketched here. The foundation for acceleration was already in place before that decade. In the 1890s an ominous sequence of events occurred that convinced key U.S. decision makers in business and government that a substantial expansion of the U.S. economic presence abroad was necessary. In 1890 Western Europe entered a severe recession, caused by widespread crop failures and the collapse of one of the world's premier financial institutions, Baring Brothers banking house headquartered in Great Britain. In a North Atlantic region that was becoming more interlinked, the United States escaped the fate of Western Europe by exporting unusually large amounts of agricultural products. Earnings from these exports provided critical support for the U.S. economy because, in the rippling nervousness of the times, about 70 million dollars worth of gold had left the United States in the first half of 1891. In 1892 part of the scenario that triggered recession in Western Europe in 1890 repeated itself. European crops in many areas failed again and triggered another wave of anxiety that precipitated another run on gold in the United States by concerned foreigners. What worked for the United States in 1890 and 1891 proved effective again. The United States exported more agricultural products to Europe and again reversed the outflow of gold (LaFeber 1963: 151).

During the first half of 1893, U.S. exports dropped below their 1892 levels and imports into the United States soared. At the same time, European investments, a pillar of U.S. economic strength in the nineteenth century, declined as investors reacted to the increasing strain on the U.S. Treasury's gold reserves. In the calculus of an international balance of payments that then assigned to gold a major stabilizing role, an excess in value of imports over exports could be paid for with gold, among other techniques. That is what was happening in 1893: gold was leaving the United States to pay for that excess. It was essential to reverse that outflow again, if the United States were to sidestep the spreading effects of recession overseas. Many people hoped that what had already succeeded twice in the 1890s might succeed one more time. An increase in agricultural exports, some still believed, could shield the United States from recession. But supply needs demand. In 1893 European crops proved sufficient (LaFeber 1963: 151-52). There was no special demand for more U.S. agricultural exports. In retrospect, it is clear that an approach to prosperity that relies on the distress of others is faulty: the distressed may not always be so. At the time, the abrupt removal of the economy's agricultural export shield devastated confidence.

There were other events in 1893 that assaulted notions of business as usual. In the United States the Philadelphia and Reading Railroad collapsed in February. The company was overextended and underfunded. Because railroads were still the bellwether of the economy, not being able to "take a ride on the Reading" so shook financiers that the Panic of 1893 ignited in the United States. A financial panic results when depositors, fearing for the safety of their money, "run" to their banks, and those institutions, unable to meet all the demands on their reserves, suspend payments to those claimants. A panic, an up-front financial event that commands public attention, is usually part of an underlying business cycle that is not so easy to understand at any time but especially when one is living through it. The Panic of 1893, as did so many others, signaled the end of an upside and the beginning of a downside.

Some panics and their downturns were more painful than others in U.S. history. In the nineteenth century only the aftermath of the Panic of 1837, particularly the turbulence from 1839 into 1843, compares with the years from 1893 to about 1898. Some regard the downside of the 1890s as more severe than that of the late 1830s and early 1840s. The 1890s descent featured, in acute form, a problem for capital. In the summer of 1893 outlets for surplus capital that could be invested or loaned largely disappeared. Loan rates dropped, demand diminished, and a severe recession followed the panic. The home market had collapsed (LaFeber 1963: 152-53).

While the severity of the post-1893 recession was not singular in the nineteenth century, the soul searching that intensified during the contraction was distinctive. Some people began to fear for the future of a U.S. capitalism that remained land based and locked in continentally. Two features of the 1890s experience prompted the rethinking of what had been traditional cures for U.S. recessions. Capital could not rejuvenate the situation if it were forced to stay idle. Agricultural exports, as a revitalization strategy, would not work when foreign demand for food, which the United States did not control, was not sufficiently vibrant. U.S. decision makers in the 1890s were wrestling with an aspect of capitalism that has long intrigued scholars. They decided, as have most scholars, that to survive capitalism must expand. A stagnant or stationary capitalism was heading for destruction.

The way in which decision makers of the 1890s decided U.S. capitalism was to expand had great implications for future U.S. business behavior abroad. Most influential people then agreed that it was essential to find foreign markets for U.S. industrial goods. Agricultural exports did not lose their importance. Far from it. But businesses also had to seek foreign markets for industrial goods in order to keep capitalism at home vigorous. To borrow a phrase from President Theodore Roosevelt, U.S. capitalism had to lead the "strenuous life" abroad in order to stay healthy at home. U.S. capitalism, to maintain its dynamism, had to compete for more foreign markets for more kinds of goods and, once in them, had to fight to stay there.

This seeming consensus on the necessity for a reinvigorated and expanded U.S. foreign business presence had enormous consequences for the conduct of both government and business. The drive for more markets for more kinds of goods played an important, though not total, role in the expansion of U.S. power westward across the Pacific. The United States acquired Hawaii (7 July 1898), Guam (10 December 1898), the Philippines (10 December 1898), and Samoa (7 November 1899) for geopolitical and geo-economic reasons. Geopolitics studies politics in relation to geography; geo-economics, economics and geography. The United States had been emerging during the last decades of the nineteenth century as a world power and needed bases in the major oceans of the world. This aspect of great power identity would have received emphasis in any event. What made bases crucial at the time was the central role accorded by some strategists, especially Alfred Thayer Mahan (1840-1914), to sea power in preserving and enhancing the security of great powers.

There was the related question of interoceanic canals. For the United States this meant land across Central America where a canal connecting the Pacific and Caribbean/Atlantic oceans might be built. The Panama Canal, for which the United States seized territory, occupied a central position in the geopolitical strategies of the U.S. government. With the canal some believed that the United States could more effectively fight a two-ocean war or two wars in two oceans. Oceanic bases and canals had critical geo-economic functions. The islands and archipelagoes that the United States acquired in 1898 and 1899 were stepping-stones to the Asian market. The Panama Canal enabled the U.S. Navy to protect trade routes across the Pacific with less difficulty. In general, the canal gave the U.S. military more options in positioning its forces throughout the world.

The 1890s were an important decade in the history of U.S. capitalism abroad. Whether they were a watershed decade for both government and business is a matter of definition and perspective. From the standpoint of federal land acquisition overseas for strategic purposes, the 1890s were memorable. From the perspective of business, the problem is more complicated. There were many U.S. corporations already involved in marketing industrial goods overseas before the 1890s and so there are multiple perspectives on the 1890s. For a significant number of large-scale U.S. corporations the 1890s were a time when their activities abroad accelerated. But how each corporation viewed its growth and development abroad in this larger picture of the 1890s as a crisis decade can only be answered in specific cases.

4

Singer and International Harvester in Late Imperial Russia

Dennis M. P. McCarthy with Fred V. Carstensen

Singer and International Harvester were the two leading U.S. multinationals in the late nineteenth and early twentieth centuries. Their activities provide valuable evidence for understanding how U.S. businesses made the transformation from national to multinational corporations. The westward expansion of the continental U.S. market during the nineteenth century compelled corporations to develop structures that would enable them to operate over longer distances. These structures involved hierarchies that became more refined as companies discovered the strengths and limitations of their then current arrangements. The essential hierarchy was managerial. Levels of management gave the corporation the coherence it needed to function. The articulation of managerial hierarchies skilled in the requirements of long-distance transport and communications gave U.S. businesses a tremendous asset when the time came for overseas expansion.

The problems of a national corporation intensify as it becomes multinational. Some of the most difficult involve personnel. Local managers have always had minds of their own and sometimes operate on or beyond the fringes of what headquarters wants. As a corporation establishes branches overseas, managerial problems can prove especially difficult to resolve. In late Imperial Russia (from the 1860s until the Russian Revolution in 1917), Singer and Harvester were trying to develop their subsidiaries in an era of slower communications, which worked against centralization. Strong-minded and strong-willed local managers, with visions of their own as to what the company should do, could use lags in communication with headquarters to pursue their own agendas. Managerial hierarchies, essential to the development of large-scale, multiproduct, multiunit businesses, brought their own problems of implementation. These difficulties could multiply, as a business became more far flung and dealt with people from more culturally diverse backgrounds.

Singer and International Harvester had other problems. The policies of the Tsarist or Russian government toward foreign business constituted, at different times and in different ways, both an opportunity for and a hindrance to business. How to define the segments of a Russian market that was not homogeneous and deal with customers in varying circumstances posed other challenges.

While both corporations confronted similar problems in building a market for their products in Russia, their initiatives and responses present intricate portraits of comparison and contrast. Toward the following interwoven sketch of their activities readers might wish to take a comparative approach based on our essentials for the historical study of international business (see introduction).

SINGER AND HARVESTER MOVE INTO RUSSIA

As to the expansion of U.S. business and its timing, both companies had come to Russia in the 1860s and 1870s as they searched for a new market for their products. International Harvester manufactured a line of farming equipment, while Singer made sewing machines. They both developed their Russian operations slowly for at least two reasons. Russian demand at the time of their market exploration and initial establishment was weak. There were attractive opportunities to cultivate markets in other locations, especially in the United States and Western Europe. But from the middle of the 1890s Russia provided the primary growth market for each company. From that time until 1914, Kompaniya Singer and International Harvester in Russia, subsidiaries wholly owned by their U.S. parents, achieved remarkable success. The Russian market for their products, measured in total sales, was to become not just the largest among all foreign markets but almost as large as the U.S. market itself. In general, the experience of both Harvester and Singer confirms the rough outlines of the 1890s crisis scenario presented earlier. There was a major acceleration in foreign sales, principally from a developing Russian market from the mid-1890s on. Both Singer and Harvester had been preparing the groundwork for decades.

The importance of the Russian market came from several factors. Both Harvester and Singer knew that the U.S. market for their products had limits. Harvester experienced a flattening of domestic sales around the turn of the century. They, along with other U.S. companies, had been making market-oriented investments in Western Europe in a successful attempt to create and strengthen overseas markets for their products. But these newer markets also had ceilings. The severe recession of the 1890s undermined consumer demand throughout the entire North Atlantic region. Both U.S. and Western European markets for the goods of Harvester, Singer, and other companies weakened.

Meanwhile, in Russia changes were occurring that would build a growing market for the commodities Harvester and Singer sold. The Russian government made pivotal investments in the infrastructure, especially in railroad construction that spanned the country.   During the last several decades of the nineteenth century outlines of a national market appeared.   The emergence of a national market facilitated the operations of both U.S. multinationals.   As Singer, Harvester, and other foreign companies expanded their businesses in Russia, they all promoted the articulation of that national market.

Rising personal income in Russia made that surge in sales from the mid-1890s possible.   Increasing prices for key farm commodities, especially in the first part of the twentieth century, boosted the incomes of Russian farmers and greatly benefitted the overall economic environment, as the country was still heavily dependent on agriculture.   Harvester, Singer, and other market-oriented U.S. multinationals specialized in products for which demand was highly income elastic: demand was very sensitive to discretionary (after-tax) consumer income. In economics elasticity applies to situations in which demand rises or falls in some proportion to increases or declines in income.   The exact increment is the degree of elasticity.   For Harvester and Singer as incomes rose in Russia, so did their sales.   There is more to the story than just rising income and the availability of market structures to translate that income into effective consumer demand. Both Singer and Harvester had to have their organizations in the right places, with the right personnel, the right resources, and the right strategies.

Singer came to Russia with remarkable strengths.   It was large and experienced.   It had developed structures and procedures that gave it one of the business world's most sophisticated and effective systems for accurate information flows.   These are the lifeblood of any integrated, multiunit, and hierarchical enterprise.   These flows had a great impact on both short- and long-term operations.   In the near term management was able to coordinate and control production, distribution, and sales.   In the longer term it could develop adequate manufacturing capability to satisfy the demands of its sales organization.   Supervision was divided along functional lines.   In Russia manufacturing under Walter Dixon and sales under Albert Flohr reported to higher offices with worldwide responsibility.   Singer's long experience in intensive marketing and foreign manufacturing gave it an international track record that Harvester in some respects could not match.   Singer had a richer endowment of direct company experience in foreign environments and of individual people skilled in international operations.   The success of Singer in Russia reflects the quality of leadership that Dixon, Flohr, and others provided and the general maturity of Singer's worldwide experience and approach to organization.   It also testifies to the efficiency of administrative hierarchies in producing, distributing, and marketing a large volume of certain types of goods and services.

Singer's experience illuminates what happens to corporate hierarchies as they become more intricate, extended, and involved in foreign environments. Raymond Vernon is right: as corporations enlarge, they become coalitions of interest groups, which can share goals but have specific objectives that differ and sometimes conflict with one another. The Singer organization did not have a single goal of profit maximization. Dixon strove to maximize the efficiency of his factory in Russia, even if that endeavor denied to the sales organization the models it most wanted. He tried to create on the micro level part of what Singer had already achieved on the macro level: a largely independent, vertically integrated manufacturing operation. The completion of this enterprise would have given him both a larger administrative domain and a relative freedom from other Singer factories for components. Flohr wanted to maximize growth and market share, even at the expense of profits of not only the Russian subsidiary but also Singer worldwide. He successfully resisted testing the limits of Singer's market power, a process that would have required promoting older models and raising their prices.

While Singer showed the internal tension and conflict that can increase with scale, it managed to strike a balance between standardization and flexibility in its daily operating procedures. This stance is crucial to successful business performance in any environment, but especially in new market situations. Singer was able, in large part because of its superb information flows and quality personnel, to permit flexibility while it retained standardized procedures to insure adequate performance. Dixon changed the structure of supervision in the factory to reflect the skill and experience of the available workers. Sales was an area of exceptionally creative adaptation. Here George Neidlinger and Albert Flohr made numerous adjustments in traditional company operating procedures. As far as personnel went, they combined what had been the separate functions of canvasser and collector. As to repayment periods, they stretched the usual time allowed under the prevailing lease/purchase contracts to twice its usual length. With respect to mode of payment, they accepted what appeared to them to be barter installments, even though those paying may have viewed what they offered as money. None of their adaptations compromised the critical functions of maintaining financial control and generating the standardized reports from which the managers calculated the all-important operating ratios.

Although hierarchies are useful for many extended business operations, they have limits. Singer's history suggests the limitations of hierarchies in competing with simple market transactions. Throughout the period of 1865 to 1914, Singer faced numerous competitors in Russia. In 1914, despite high tariffs imposed by the Russian government, three dozen firms still sent their machines to Russia, where together they held a significant share of the cash trade. In Poland some retailers were even capable of using Singer's own techniques successfully in the credit trade.

The persistence of Singer's competition resulted from several factors. One deals with the economics of the sewing machine industry. Here the scale economies in the available process (manufacturing) technology were not decisive in eliminating small manufacturers, as was happening in numerous other industries. A second reason resides in Singer's organization. It had developed a fully integrated marketing organization, a marvelous example of product technology, but this organization was expensive to operate. It could function successfully only with a large volume of sales. To insure such volume, Singer insisted on using its own stores and employees. In creating its own distribution network Singer did not preempt the existing marketing infrastructure. It left numerous marketing intermediaries that could sell the sewing machines of other manufacturers. As a result, Singer's combined manufacturing and distribution hierarchy did not command a decisive cost advantage over low-volume market transactions. The two distribution systems coexisted. No firm could challenge Singer in volume, but Singer could not drive out the small producer and retailer, who continued to nip (and ultimately bite) at the leader's heels.

This situation, which existed in other countries besides Russia, foreshadowed Singer's vulnerability. The company began to lose market share after World War II and then suffered sharp reverses in the 1970s. Forces gathered that eventually undermined what had been the basis for Singer's competitiveness for nearly one hundred years. After 1950 service skill diffused widely and the interest in home sewing declined. When one hitches one's wagon to a single star or product, one will rise and fall with it.

In 1914 Singer was still evolving and developing its administrative techniques. It had not yet begun to use systematic budgeting to allocate capital expenditure internally. It did not make careful calculations of comparative costs on a regular basis, although it gave Walter Dixon's request to purchase forest lands unusually close scrutiny. Singer gave no serious consideration to diversification. It was totally a sewing machine manufacturer and marketer. So long as that market could absorb the energies and resources of the company, it apparently gave no serious consideration to whether other products, services, or investments might generate higher returns or enhance the performance of its existing organization.

There is a lesson here. Every organization has some inertia. It is often setback or failure that forces owners or managers to change a firm's strategy and/or structure. Singer suffered no reversals before 1914 and thus stuck with its proven approach. One is not advocating courting crisis for the sake of promoting stronger long-term performance. But the fact that Singer encountered no challenges that provoked a more comprehensive consideration of future corporate possibilities was, as it turned out, an unhealthy entrenchment of business as usual.

But knowledge of what happened in the long term does not diminish the extent of the Singer achievement in Russia and elsewhere. Singer was a pioneering U.S. multinational in several respects. Its experience provides an early example of the ways in which multinational enterprises handled the problem of internal pricing and transfer payments both to minimize taxation and to allocate total overhead costs. Its balance sheet reflected more the demands of the Russian tax environment than the realities of its investments. Such balance sheet entries are usually a poor basis for analyzing the timing or size of actual investments in any case. An official source listed Singer's total Russian investment as 50 million rubles. It was actually nearly 118 million rubles, which equaled the entire investment normally attributed to the United States in Russia.

The distribution of this investment shows that Singer knew its environment in a way that every business should emulate. The overriding need of Kompaniya Singer was for working capital. In 1914 almost 100 million rubles were needed to finance inventories and installment credit. Only 18 million rubles were tied up in the physical plant and land. Most Russians, with rising but still modest incomes, had to rely on credit for a wide range of purchases. Singer was a relatively self-contained operation, providing virtually every service, including credit, necessary for a customer to purchase its product. An approach of total service required great amounts of working capital, as Singer's investments demonstrate.

International Harvester was also a relatively self-contained company in the total service mode. It too needed large amounts of capital in its Russian operations. It, like Singer, was a pioneering U.S. multinational in several ways. Its record in Russia, unlike Singer's, was before 1914 more complex and one of only qualified success. A final vignette analyzes the reasons for that more checkered record.

Harvester's preparation for entering foreign markets in a major way was comparatively limited. McCormick, its principal predecessor company, had long used foreign exhibitions and trials to promote U.S. sales but had devoted minimal resources to developing foreign markets. Market-oriented investments in the 1860s and 1870s were sparse. It was only in the 1890s that foreign markets became a primary interest for the McCormick company. International Harvester did not come to Russia with the fully articulated marketing structure and mature sales strategy that Singer brought.

Nor did it take years of careful expansion to build its Russian organization. Singer constructed its Russian subsidiary at a pace and in a pattern determined primarily by the internal logic of maintaining corporate growth. Harvester operated abroad less on a detailed internal plan and more in response to external events. The threat of significant local competitors emerging in each European market, the danger of higher tariff barriers, and the absence of an adequate commercial infrastructure in Russian Siberia all forced Harvester to take a series of steps that were essentially defensive. The first step was to articulate a large European marketing organization. The second was to support it with manufacturing facilities. When it was time to develop its Russian organization, Harvester was not fully focused on the tasks involved in this endeavor. Internal management tensions had become oppressive, and U.S. anti-trust action against the company diverted attention and resources from the Russian organization when it most needed them.

Cyrus McCormick had a great desire to show his creation, the mechanical reaper, to the world. He presented it at every major international fair from the first exhibition at the Crystal Palace in London in 1851 until he died in 1884. His company, however, was unwilling to use in Europe any of the marketing techniques that it had perfected in the United States. The McCormick company, unlike Singer, did not dominate its industry and found that growth in the U.S. market absorbed all its energies and resources until the 1880s. Then Cyrus McCormick, Jr., appointed a salaried European manager headquartered in London and began a systematic process of building a European marketing organization. France was the first target, then Germany, and only in 1894 did the potentialities of the Russian market come under scrutiny. Even after this work McCormick still had no hierarchy in place to supervise and develop these foreign markets. The company had only a small number of foreign employees. It sold its machines to established dealers it could interest in handling its product and provided limited credit to those merchants. Other U.S. harvester manufacturers followed a similar pattern. After the crisis of 1893 they, too, began to establish salaried agents in Europe.

Between 1900 and 1905 U.S. demand for harvesting equipment passed its peak and began a gradual, steady decline. As a result, International Harvester needed to develop foreign markets just to maintain the same level of sales in those lines. At the same time, the company tried to develop a broad line of implements, both to occupy its extensive manufacturing facilities and to utilize its large marketing organization. But as conditions in the U.S. market made European markets more important, competitors began to emerge in those markets and bring pressure to bear on their respective governments to raise trade barriers against imported farm machinery. If Harvester wished to preserve its already established position and to develop those markets further, it had to act. It had to extend its administrative hierarchy and intensify its marketing efforts. Management systematically expanded Harvester's branch house system in order to cut out wholesalers and improve the supervision of and support for retailers.

These responses, defensive and limited, were not enough. Harvester needed a more intensive marketing technique, not just an acceleration of existing efforts, and, most important for long-term survival in foreign situations, local manufacturing capability. First in Sweden, then in France, Germany, and Russia, Harvester bought or built factories. It introduced the long-standing U.S. procedure of using commission contracts and extending credit directly to the final consumer.

As did Singer in a more deliberate fashion, so did Harvester, under pressure from external factors, adapt to the Russian environment. Faced with reaching customers where there were virtually no satisfactory commercial institutions, Harvester established its own retail stores. Even when it adapted, Harvester did it in a less than totally integrated manner. The retail stores were not deemed intrinsic to marketing strategy. Nor were they intended to be a permanent part of the corporate structure, as were Singer's. Management saw them as ways to demonstrate the viability of a retail implement business. The hope was that they might attract Russian enterprise to undertake such work. The company also relied on them as insurance against the established market power of large merchant houses.

International Harvester confronted a more complex problem in developing its foreign hierarchy than did Singer. In one way Harvester did not need the same large and elaborate bureaucracy because it supervised dramatically fewer transactions. Singer had to maintain contact with at least ten times as many customers on a more regular basis. Its collections were weekly or monthly; Harvester's were annually, after the harvest. Singer's product was the same, unchanged from office to office. The nature of its business permitted standardized rules and procedures, virtually identical performance standards for each office, and a consistent set of triggers and thresholds for alerting management to problems within the organization. International Harvester faced more complex markets, with many small but significant product variations needed for each area. It slowly developed procedures for collecting technical data and for field-testing improvements between 1910 and 1914. It also began to generate a more detailed set of performance statistics with which to improve supervision and control of the branch houses. Even so, in 1914 it had, contrasted with Singer, a significantly looser organization in structural terms, less sophisticated standards for information collection, and mainly ad hoc rules to guide management attention.

Harvester encountered difficult problems in developing Russian manufacturing. U.S. marketing lessons transferred more easily than the manufacturing technology, which had to take into account the skills and attitudes of Russian workers. Singer recognized this fact because it pursued a policy of deliberate development at its Podolsk factory. When Harvester found conditions similar to those in the United States and could transfer experienced workers out of its U.S. plants and work on a limited scale with one or two lines of machines, as it did in Sweden, France, and Germany, its manufacturing operations were a success. In Russia, however, where development was done at a forced pace, largely without experienced U.S. workers or foremen, and on a large scale with several types of machines, Harvester did not have the experience or organization to carry out the work smoothly or efficiently.

This outcome suggests that the rate of expansion of a hierarchical, multiunit enterprise may be limited by the administrative and supervisory skills that the enterprise commands. Singer had a larger reservoir of talent and recruited broadly in Europe for people who could, it seems, mediate between U.S. entrepreneurial drive and Russian economic realities. International Harvester presumed knowledge of the business itself was more important than cultural awareness or linguistic skill. It believed that skill was industry or even firm specific and refused to recruit outside of its own ranks. As a result, it had insufficient personnel to supervise its Russian manufacturing operations. It was also persistently ignorant of and insensitive to the process of policy formation inside the Russian government.

In some ways Harvester's experiences echoed those of Singer. The operations of both revealed tensions and differing goals within their corporate hierarchies. In Harvester's case the factory organization and branch managers wanted to have as many resources within their control as possible. This resembles the thrust for local autonomy in Singer's Russian organization. Harvester's factory in Russia caused constant problems. Management in the United States seemed unable to stop it from producing air brakes until that part of the business was sold. Worse, stateside managers could neither get the Russian engine department to confine itself to what they considered a "rational" building program nor convince the engine sales force to sell engines within the horsepower range that they wanted the factory at Lubertzy to manufacture. And, astonishingly, the company was unable to develop a reliable crude-oil engine, despite the presence of numerous successful competitors. These problems were far more serious than those with which Singer stateside grappled, such as Dixon's desire to run the Podolsk factory on his own terms and expand his domain to include the large Troitskaya forest tract.

While Harvester's factory brought more problems than Singer's, the sales organizations of each were independent minded though in different ways. The International Harvester sales group, like Singer's, had its own objective of controlling the entire trade in harvesters. But contrary to Flohr's efforts to push higher quality sewing machines, Harvester's branch managers wanted to move to the lowest end of the market with the production of the *lobogreika*, essentially a hand-rake reaper. This down scaling was a typically defensive posture for Harvester, consistent with management's cautious and sometimes indecisive development of its European and Russian organizations.

In yet other ways Harvester's experience parallels Singer's. Both firms lubricated the wheels of commerce with large investments in operating capital. But they did more. On the one hand, their extensive sales organizations, which employed perhaps 60,000 workers, were creating a commercial cadre up to date in its skill, procedures, and discipline. This process generated significant entrepreneurial spin-offs. Particularly among the nearly 2,000 International Harvester retailers who were in business because of the commission contract, a new group of potential business people for other areas was emerging. Many of those Harvester retailers, like Otto Tuemmel, did build their own businesses from the base that the company had provided. On the other hand, both U.S. firms, through their extensive, aggressive sales organizations brought to Russia a new awareness of consumption opportunities and a new capacity through generous credit to consume. They provided the desire and means for entrepreneurial activity. As an economist might write, they enabled the individual person to adjust his or her factor utilization to make use of those opportunities.

Singer and International Harvester created the two largest coordinated commercial organizations in Russia. Singer probably reached deeper into the stretches of the Russian empire than any other organization, except perhaps the government itself. But it probably had a greater impact on people's perceptions of the world around them. The sewing machine facilitated the acquisition of more and better clothing in less time and saved labor which could be devoted to other tasks. The opportunity to buy such a machine conceivably led many small-scale farmers, including nomads in central Asia, to husband their resources, to use them in new, more productive ways, and to save toward those regular monthly payments on the outstanding debt. International Harvester offered a reprieve from backbreaking labor and provided a chance to cultivate and harvest much more than any family could have done without modern farm machinery. This result created the opportunity to increase income, which would permit the consumption of a new range of goods, perhaps a sewing machine.

On the commercial front, then, these foreign enterprises became agents for stimulating a pervasive entrepreneurial response. By changing perceptions of consumption opportunities, they induced individuals, whether city dweller or country dweller, to reorder their use of available productive factors and employ new, additional resources to achieve higher incomes. These would permit the realization of those consumption opportunities and/or investment in further entrepreneurial activities. Singer and International Harvester in late Imperial Russia were agents for economic development in the widest sense.

5

United Fruit Company
in Costa Rica and Guatemala

The operations of the United Fruit Company (UFC) in Costa Rica and Guatemala present a mixed record. The company's involvement in Guatemala is a classic case of business as an insensitive and meddling corporate guest. It intervened directly and ineptly in local politics. The company won in the short run. In 1954 the Central Intelligence Agency (CIA) of the U.S. government orchestrated the ouster of President Jacobo Arbenz Guzmán, whose policies of land reform threatened UFC's interests in Guatemala. Arbenz, his plans for Guatemala, their projected impact on the UFC, and the CIA's psychological dismantling of his regime—all these are detailed in the following case study.

Both the UFC and the CIA prevailed in the near term in Guatemala. But both the U.S. government and U.S. business lost in the long run in Central America, South America, and elsewhere. The government's loss came in Cuba. The easy success of the CIA operation against Arbenz in Guatemala in 1954 lulled that agency into thinking it could repeat similar plans elsewhere. The infamous Bay of Pigs disaster in Cuba in 1961 can be traced directly back to a CIA mind-set that received unfortunate confirmation in Guatemala in 1954. The Bay of Pigs is the location in Cuba where a small band of Cuban exiles tried to establish a beachhead against the government of President Fidel Castro. The CIA had used a small invading force on the ground in Guatemala in conjunction with intimidating air sorties and unnerving radio broadcasts. The agency pinned its hopes on a small landing force in Cuba that was to ignite an internal uprising against Castro. But President John F. Kennedy decided not to commit U.S. air support. It is unlikely that even with sufficient air support, the invading force would have succeeded in catalyzing the ouster of Castro. So the swift removal of Arbenz led to action that only reinforced the power of President Castro.

The tradition of heavy-handed business intervention in local politics seemed to work in Guatemala in 1954. This outcome entrenched the notion that U.S.

business could take gross steps in a foreign country to counter what it perceived as hostile intent or action against its interests. The stereotypes of the "Ugly Corporate American" and "Yankee Business Imperalist," never accurate labels for every U.S. business and business person, did find support in the later actions of some corporations. These moves eventually backfired and the businesses faced more than just public relations disasters. The perception, widespread south of the border, that U.S. business would stop at nothing to protect its capacity to "exploit" strengthened.

A striking instance of corporate intervention came in Chile in the early 1970s. International Telephone and Telegraph (ITT), a major U.S. multinational, blatantly intervened in Chilean politics in an effort to damage the career of Salvador Allende Gossens. A member of the Chilean Communist party, he was democratically elected president of his country in 1970 with 35 percent of the popular vote. In September 1973, he was murdered in a military coup d'état, which began sixteen years of dictatorial rule by Augusto Pinochet. ITT was upset by Allende's plans to nationalize its holdings in Chile and outraged when he did it.

ITT tried to engage the CIA in a secret plan to manipulate the outcome of the 1970 presidential election in Chile. This plan called for U.S. corporations in Chile to cooperate in economic disruption. The disorder that resulted could be used to justify a military coup. Jack Anderson, a newspaper columnist, disclosed the plan. ITT reacted by maintaining that the money involved was for improving housing and agriculture in Chile. In his book *Managing* (1984) Harold Geneen, chief executive officer of ITT at the time, does not mention his company's intervention in Chilean politics.

While UFC's political behavior in Guatemala has received history's tar brush, its operations in Costa Rica present a more complicated portrait of entwined harms and benefits. The Costa Rican case provides an opportunity to debate the merits and demerits of a foreign company creating a commodity-based export economy and opening up economic opportunities for local citizens that might otherwise have not existed. To be fair, UFC did the same thing in Guatemala, but its involvement in events surrounding the removal of Arbenz has overshadowed discussion of its economic role there.

The facts of UFC's economic role in Costa Rica are presented here to stimulate discussion. Is Costa Rica as a country better or worse off as a result of UFC's operations there? What does better off and worse off mean in this context? When does reliance on outside sources for help become dependency? Which generations of Costa Ricans benefitted most and least from the UFC presence in their country? What should the UFC have paid its workers in Costa Rica and why? What constitues a fair or just wage for workers in these circumstances? Was there a better way to build the infrastructure to promote both exports and internal economic exchange? These are some questions that arise in the following case studies and throughout similar studies of foreign corporate involvement elsewhere in the book.

UNITED STATES PENETRATION: UNITED FRUIT IN COSTA RICA

In Central America the United Fruit Company established a presence in Costa Rica that illustrates a controversial penetration of U.S. capital south of the border. The United Fruit Company resulted from a merger between the Boston Fruit Company and the Keith interests. Incorporated in 1899 with an authorized capital of $20 million, UFC was one of the companies that emerged during a period of heavy merger activity in the United States from 1898 to 1902. Other companies had their reasons for merging at that time. The Boston Fruit Company and the Keith interests to reduce risk by diversifying the production base. Both "realized that a more constant and reliable flow of fruit from the tropics could only be obtained by spreading their production base to a number of areas so that any local disaster" might be offset "by a good crop elsewhere. Both had been the victims of floods, droughts, blowdowns, and poltiical upheavals" (May and Plaza 1958: 6).

The UFC did not lack incentives for expanding its corporate presence in Costa Rica, which lies to the south of Nicaragua and to the north of Panama. The government of Costa Rica was eager, as were others south of the border, to open up large tracts of land for development. This usually meant producing, rarely processing, crops that generated jobs for the "locals" and revenue from taxes on those crops and the businesses that exported them. To attract business governments offered many lures, which included cheap and/or free land, low taxes in some cases and exemptions from others, and a favorable operating climate. This featured labor that was not organized and worked long hours for low wages. In return a business was to build an infrastructure that would bring about "development," build all necessary operating facilities, and be a good guest in every sense, from paying what taxes were levied on it to providing for the welfare of its workers.

The UFC got land in abundance. At one time earlier in the twentieth century, before economic nationalism surged, the UFC claimed ownership of 1.7 million acres of land in Central America, of which 497,000 acres were in Costa Rica (May and Plaza 1958: 80-81). Critics of the UFC argued that its large landholdings prevented agricultural enterprise by others: the company held so much choice land backed by its economic power that it chilled the entrepreneurial instincts of others or derprived them of the means to start.

While not a very large corporation by U.S. standards, the UFC did possess considerable power in Central America. In Costa Rica the company at one time accounted for 98 percent of banana exports, which made up about 46 percent of Costa Rica's total export receipts (May and Plaza 1958: 150). Defenders of the company's presence point out that its overall landholdings amounted to about .5 percent of all cropland in Central America; its Costa Rican possessions allegedly represented about 10 percent of the total cropland in that country. This argument does not deny that the company was a large landlord with a substantial share (45.08 percent = 98 percent of 46 percent) of Costa Rica's export trade. Company defenders maintain that in each of the Central American countries in which the UFC was involved there were still incomparably larger tracts of rain forest as good or better than the company's holdings available for general agricultural purposes. Besides, they argue, most of the company's land was purchased as virgin rain forest, mainly in "undeveloped" areas, which at the time had few or no linkages to human settlements (May and Plaza 1958: 81 and 150).

The UFC also got abundant tax concessions. The early contracts between the company and its host governments typically fixed low export taxes on bananas for a specified period of years and granted certain tax exemptions. The company did not have to pay any import duties on heavy equipment or materials needed for the construction, operation, and maintenance of railroads, wharves, and ports (May and Plaza 1958: 20).

What governement gives it can take away. The pattern of initial generosity was replaced, under the force of economic nationalism that accelerated in the 1960s, by one of greater corporate tax accountability. The government of Costa Rica took the initiative and deserves major credit for bargaining through the pattern that now applies throughout the Central American region. This change has greatly increased the revenues of tropical countries from UFC operations. Existing contracts between the UFC and host governments were amended in a crucial way: the company accepted liability to income taxes in the countries in which it functions (May and Plaza 1958: 20). In 1966, the UFC had a net profit before taxes of $3,374,000 in Costa Rica, of which it paid to the government $1,983,000, about 59 percent (Villanueva 1969: 42 and 46).

The UFC also got a labor force it paid controversially. Critics assert that the company "exploited labor" and that its "cheap labor policy" has harmed economic development. The UFC has usually paid its workers more than they could have earned in other local agricultural enterprises. But whether this difference means sufficient fairness is for the reader to decide. In 1967 the UFC paid, on the average, $5.00 a day (including fringe benefits) to its workers; in other local businesses the total package was about $3.23 (Villanueva 1969: 67). The organization of labor unions, where successful, has exerted upward pressure on wages. But still the total wage seems too low to many people.

Defenders of the UFC respond that the money wage does not adequately reflect everything the company has given its workers. They point to the housing, hospitals, schools, and labor clubs the company has constructed for its workers, the use of which is in many cases free. Nor do company critics, they maintain, take into account the prices of food and other goods available at company commissaries. The UFC allegedly worked to hold food prices down and make other commodities accessible at below prevailing retail levels. Nor do company critics, its defenders contend, consider other aspects of the "social wage." This consists of the money wage and how far its purchasing power can be stretched by such policies as low-cost food. It also includes improvements in the general environment that enhance the value of the money wage. Company defenders here take into account everything the company has done to promote health. It has carried out extensive programs of sanitation and clean water delivery to reduce the incidence of disease. Swamps were drained; sewer and potable water systems were built.

The UFC was deeply involved from the beginning in human and commodity transport. This dimension of its infrastructure activity is more controversial than its sanitation and potable water projects. The issues here hinge on the design and impact of the railroads it constructed. The UFC was interested in building railroads to service its banana operations as economically as possible. The specific lines would follow the shortest good route from the port or connecting link to the banana plantation (May and Plaza 1958: 9).

What is good business for the company may not be good economics for the country. Much of the railroad mileage in Costa Rica and other Central American countries is on the coastal plains. There bananas are grown and the banana industry has been most closely involved in the siting, construction, and operation of railroads in that area. The railroads were designed to create a banana version of an export economy and they did. Transport in general, since so many roads serviced the railroads rather than competed with them, facilitated far more the export of commodities than internal commerce. There is nothing wrong with exports, but it was excessive reliance on export-led economic growth, with its neglect of internal commerce as an equal source of stimulation, that entrenched dependency.

The UFC was involved in many controversies in Central America. It was not the model corporate guest in every aspect of its behavior. While cases can be made for and against UFC's economic activity, it is impossible to defend its interventions in local politics. These were ill-considered and heavy-handed maneuvers. The company was not alone in its meddlesome approaches to foreign governments. Other U.S. businesses, and the U.S. government itself, were similarly inclined. Crudeness loves company, but collectivity does not lessen the historical indictment of gross inappropriateness. The infamous Guatemala episode in the 1950s is a classic instance of grossly inappropriate business and government intervention.

U.S. INTERVENTION: THE UFC IN GUATEMALA

To understand why the U.S. government intervened directly in Guatemalan politics in 1954 one needs some facts about that country and how Washington would come to analyze them. Jacobo Arbenz Guzmán was elected president of Guatemala in 1950. His far-reaching plans aimed at a profound transformation of the country's entire economy. He and his followers advocated the construction of factories, the improved acquisition of minerals and raw materials, the building of communications and transport networks, the development of modern banking systems, the conversion of land to growing staple foods for local consumption rather than producing export crops, and the systematic application of technology to increase agricultural yields (Immerman 1982: 64). The central thrust of this program was to reduce the types of dependency that enslaved his country; that is, on external capital goods, finance, food, information, and expertise.

To implement part of his program Arbenz announced Decree 900, or the Agrarian Reform Bill, in June 1952. Some provisions were not controversial: the institution of new credit facilities, the careful monitoring of prices, the adjustment of tariff regulations, the provision of tax incentives, and the expansion of research programs. One major item was destined to provoke a major collision with already entrenched large-scale interests. This feature concerned land and plans for its expropriation and redistribution in specified circumstances. The Ministry of Agriculture planned to expropriate and distribute the idle land of those plantations with more than 223 acres, but proprietors with holdings between 223 and 669 acres were permitted to keep one-third of their fallow. Permanent pastures and woods that were in economic use, as well as those fields with a slope in excess of 30 degrees, were exempted (Immerman 1982: 64-65). The controversy associated with the implementation of this agrarian reform program, particularly its impact on the UFC, brought the Guatemalan Revolution dramatically to the attention of the U.S. public. Any remaining skeptics in the Eisenhower administration back in Washington became convinced that the programs of the Arbenz government were communist inspired.

The United States had first associated communism with Guatemala in the administration prior to Arbenz's. President Juan José Arévalo, Arbenz's predecessor, had made the Truman administration uneasy by his doctrine of spiritual socialism, by his enactment of such sweeping reforms as the 1947 Labor Code, and by his identification with increased labor union agitation against major enterprises, including the UFC. The F.B.I., under the direction of J. Edgar Hoover, investigated and compiled dossiers on Arévalo and many other prominent Guatemalans. The fear of communism in Guatemala escalated among many people in the Washington establishment into belief that communists were active in all of the Guatemalan government propaganda outlets, including the information offices, the official newspapers, and the government-owned radio stations.

The evidence used to substantiate this belief is revealing. The most widely cited indications of communist penetration in Guatemala were the hardships allegedly encountered by the UFC. These difficulties first surfaced in the late

1940s, when Guatemalan workers, newly organized, struck several UFC operations. Real problems came in the aftermath of Arbenz's 1952 Reform Bill, which expropriated close to 400,000 acres of UFC property. According to that law, the UFC was to receive compensation in the form of bonds and in an amount determined by the property's declared tax value. As it worked out, the UFC was supposed to get $1,185,000 in twenty-five year, guaranteed, 3 percent bonds. The company had a valuation of its properties prepared for tax purposes. The government employed the company's own declaration as the basis for compensation (Immerman 1982: 81). The expropriation and the modest compensation horrified UFC and U.S. government officials: communists had to be behind it.

To his credit, President Eisenhower did not endorse this argument coming from the State Department in every particular. Expropriation, Eisenhower maintained, was not in itself full proof of communism (Eisenhower 1963: 421). To his discredit, Eisenhower then employed an argument from association that was logically flawed but emotionally compelling. He cited the stance which the government of Guatemala had taken with respect to the Korean War, fought on the Korean peninsula in the early 1950s between communists and forces of the United Nations. Eisenhower argued that the Guatemalan government must have been in league with the Soviets and the Chinese because it "accepted the ridiculous Communist contention that the United States had conducted bacteriological warfare in Korea" (Eisenhower 1963: 422). In the climate of the times, when communists seemed to be everywhere, it is understandable that those who sided with the enemy on an issue would be automatically classified as one of them, even if such an equation grossly over-simplified the situation.

Fostering the perception of a linkage between the Arbenz government and the specter of global communism was essential to the UFC's strategy. Its people were active on a number of fronts. They got prominent statespeople to lobby among their influential friends in Washington, and public relations counsel sponsored trips to Guatemala for leading newspaper and magazine reporters and publishers. A goal of the UFC approach was to emphasize the alleged international conspiracy and to use this fear of communist involvement to win the support of the U.S. government and people.

It was not hard to succeed in this endeavor, since many officials and private citizens were already receptive to the prevailing reasoning. Communism threatened the American way of life; foreign investment was essential to this way of life; any threat to this investment jeopardized national security; and any threat to national security was necessarily the result of communist activity. On 13 March 1954, *The New York Times*, in an article that purported to be straight news reporting, referred to "the Communist situation in Guatemala" (*NYT* 14 March 1954: 27). In a televised press statement, 8 June 1954, Secretary of State John Foster Dulles explained to the U.S. public the relationship between economic interests and national security. The expropriations were only the beginning of greater danger. Dulles said, "If the United Fruit matter were settled, if they gave a gold piece for every banana, the problem would remain just as it is today as far as the presence of Communist infiltration in Guatemala is concerned. That is the problem, not the United Fruit Company" (Dulles 1957: 1310). With such straightforward premises, the die was cast for intervention.

The events that led to the resignation and flight into exile of President Arbenz on 27 June 1954 are summarized here. The White House gave the Central Intelligence Agency the go-ahead to develop a plan for intervention. The CIA, following its own guidelines, ruled out direct U.S. military intervention. A puppet was needed, and a CIA task force selected Castillo Armas to be the next leader of Guatemala. He had graduated from Guatemala's version of West Point and the U.S. Army Staff School at Fort Leavenworth, Kansas. He received from a unit of the CIA, headquartered at Opa Locka, Florida, near Miami, everything needed for an invasion: ample funds, war material, and an army. Shipments of money, rifles and other small arms, machine guns, and ammunition reached rebel centers in Honduras and Nicaragua. One of these was located on a personal estate of General Somoza, the late dictator of Nicaragua. The army contained many mercenaries.

While preparation for intervention had crucial military components, an even greater role was assigned to the psychological. CIA operatives transmitted anti-Arbenz, pro-Castillo broadcasts from station(s) in the surrounding areas. This source, called the "Voice of Liberation," sounded so authentic that many foreign correspondents, including those from the *New York Times* and *Life* magazine, believed it to be accurate in key respects (Phillips 1977: 40-49). The CIA arranged for propaganda leaflets to be dropped from aircraft throughout the countryside. These criticized the Arbenz government and prepared rural citizens for invasion. The CIA persuaded Guatemalan Catholic leaders to hold meetings with their church members. It disguised one of its German operatives as a European businessman who tried to bribe high officers of the armed forces. It planted news stories throughout the hemisphere that proposed an anti-communist resolution for the Tenth Inter-American Conference held in Caracas, Venezuela.

Arbenz sensed what was coming and, in preparing for it, made it a certainty. The United States had traditionally supplied Guatemala with most of its armaments. But in the late 1940s, unnerved by activities under President Arévalo, the United States had embargoed arms shipments to Guatemala. President Arbenz appealed again and again to the State Department to lift the embargo. His requests met rejection. He then sought assistance from behind the "Iron Curtain." Soviet leaders seized what they thought would be an opportunity to embarrass the United States. But the shipment of arms and artillery was intercepted by U.S. officials who, having learned through clever intelligence work about the mission, were waiting on the docks of Puerto Barrios when the

Swedish freighter *Alfhem* arrived. Listed on the ship's manifest as optical supplies and other goods, the cargo really consisted of some 2,000 tons of small arms and light artillery pieces from the Skoda factory in Czechoslovakia (Immerman 1982: 155).

This discovery sealed Arbenz's fate, though he himself still had much to do with what eventually happened to him. Washington was in an uproar; the shipment was viewed there as evidence of the global communist conspiracy. The Soviet Union was accused of disregarding the Monroe Doctrine, which since its proclamation in the 1820s had given the United States an ideological shield to ward off intrusions that it deemed hostile by "outside interests" into the western hemisphere. From this perspective, the weapons shipment was overwhelming evidence that the Soviet Union was using Guatemala to establish itself firmly and actively in the hemisphere. The *Alfhem*'s arrival determined the date for Castillo Armas's invasion.

The actual military penetration was not great and demonstrated how important psychology and information were in these proceedings. On 18 June 1954, the forces of Castillo Armas crossed the Honduran border to invade Guatemala. The forces were only about 150 troops, most of whom had no military experience. The rebels settled down in the Church of the Black Christ, the country's major religious shrine, just six miles inside the border. There they awaited the regime's collapse.   And unravel it did.   The CIA jammed Guatemalan radio communications so that the inhabitants of Guatemala City had little or no idea as to what was actually happening at the "front." Wild rumors circulated, which reported major government defeats and the arrival of well-equipped divisions of rebel troops.

Arbenz aggravated the situation when, in an effort to silence the "Voice of Liberation," he ordered a total blackout of the capital and other large cities. This silence increased the tension by making the threat seem more real. The blackout was not entirely effective. Many people in the poorer urban areas, not connected to the official electrical supply, obtained their power from batteries or gasoline generators and continued to receive the antigovernment transmissions. These people became sources of "accurate news" for the rest of the population.

Police sirens and curfew bells added to the crisis atmosphere, along with the arrival of wounded soldiers and civilians, no matter how small the number. Airplanes circled Guatemala City and dropped anything that caused a loud noise, such as blocks of dynamite attached to hand grenades. In return, the only sounds coming from the government defenses were bursts of machine gun fire. Hundreds fled the capital for the mountains and created a scene of mass confusion (Immerman 1982: 166-67).

Arbenz never did know the actual size of the invading force and supposedly believed that the United States might even send its own troops. But there never was a U.S. plan to increase assistance. When a Guatemalan pilot defected, CIA agents "elevated his mood" through alcohol and put him on the "Voice of Liberation" to appeal to his fellow citizens. Former operative David Phillips remembers the situation: "From that moment the Guatemalan air force was grounded. Arbenz, fearing his pilots would defect with their planes, did not permit the flight of a single military aircraft during the duration of the conflict" (Phillips 1977: 44). On 27 June 1954, ten years after the Guatemalan Revolution had begun, Jacobo Arbenz Guzmán resigned and fled into exile.

Most members of the media at the time treated the coup as a successful anti-communist uprising. The precise role that the U.S. government had played in destabilizing the elected Arbenz administration remained secret. Only a few journalists easily labeled as left-wing raised questions that were not answered until years later. The swiftness with which Arbenz conceded defeat, the apparent ease with which the United States succeeded, and the ideological orientation of those critics strongly worked against any broadly based contemporary investigation into the real "liberation" of Guatemala by Castillo Armas and associates. Many people in the United States genuinely believed that the Guatemalan people had recognized communist infiltration for what it was and expelled it. Within a few years the victory of Castillo Armas became for the U.S. public a vague memory. Some even forgot the communist issue and remembered the coup only as, in the condescending vocabulary of imperialism, just another "banana revolt" (Wemhoff 1984: 8).

6

Vignette: International Business and Economic Integration: The U.S.-Canada Free Trade Act

While the twelve members of the European Community constitute a market of about 345 million consumers, a North American free trade area of the United States (250 million) and Canada (26 million) would have about 276 million participants. Setting up this area took a giant step forward with the birth of the U.S.-Canada Free Trade Agreement on 1 January 1989. This agreement will eliminate over a ten-year period all tariffs and duties on all trade between Canada and the United States.

This pact, negotiated for years and ratified easily by the U.S. Congress, provoked a firestorm of political controversy in Canada. It was the central issue in the Canadian general election of 21 November 1988. During the election campaign the government of Prime Minister Brian Mulroney and his Progressive Conservatives vigorously defended the agreement that they sponsored. Eliminating all tariffs between the United States and Canada, they argued, would bring Canada much more than it would lose from this process. Canada's two other major political parties, the Liberals and New Democrats, largely opposed the pact. John Turner, the Liberal leader, and Ed Broadbent, the New Democratic chief, raised numerous objections. Canada would lose much more than it would gain from free trade, they contended. Canada's farmers would be hurt by unrestricted U.S. competition. Key Canadian industries would be in jeopardy without some protection. Canada's distinctively generous social programs might be regarded under the agreement as "unfair competition." The United States would so dominate the arrangement that Canada's national identity would be threatened.

The Progressive Conservatives decisively won the 1988 general election, only the second time in the last century that the Conservative party had won back-to-back terms in Canada. Faced with that outcome, the Liberal party relaxed its opposition to the pact in the non-elected Canadian Senate. It held a majority there and was blocking approval of the agreement, which the Canadian House of Commons had already passed. This move guaranteed Canadian ratification of the Free Trade Act, as it is known in Canada, after the general election.

Since it creates a free trade area not a common market, the Free Trade Act does not provide for the kind of supranational agencies that run the European Community. But it does set up dispute settlement mechanisms. Bilateral panels are to review most trade disputes. The ultimate stage of appeal involves an extraordinary challenge committee.

Five-member binational boards will hear appeals of several sets of cases: where government agencies determine that there has been dumping or approve a countervailing duty on what they consider an unfairly subsidized import. Dumping is sending large quantities of commodities into a country and pricing them below the cost of production. A countervailing duty is placed on an import to countervail or offset what is believed to be some unfair government help that its manufacturers received. Dumping and countervailing duties are difficult issues in trade relations and talks worldwide. Countervailing duties are an especially acrimonious subject in Canadian-U.S. trade relations. Canada has experienced a steady stream of countervailing duties imposed by the United States on such products as pork and stretch limousines (*NYT* 8 October 1989: F4).

The dispute settlement mechanisms evoked contrary reactions. Some believe that they will encourage fairer reviews and quicker disposal of frivolous claims. Others are not so optimistic and point to the limited powers that these bilateral and binational panels have. All they can do is determine whether a country violated its own laws. They have no enforcement powers other than persuasion. Lacking a supranational character, they will prove ineffective over the long haul, skeptics contend (*NYT* 8 October 1989: F4).

These mechanisms and some disputes to be reported later should not cloud the enormous opportunities the free trade area brings to both countries and their international businesses. Canada and the United States greatly need each other. More than $200 billion (US) in trade flows across the border each year, by far the world's largest bilateral economic relationship. The United States trades more with Canada's Ontario province than with Japan. In 1988, 72 percent of Canada's exports by value went to the United States, while 66 percent of its imports came from the United States. In 1988 Canada accounted for 22 percent of all U.S. exports and 19 percent of its imports (*NYT* 8 October 1989: F4). In trade dollars Canada needs the United States more than it needs Canada, but to leave the question of reciprocal dependence there is wrong. Canada has crucial resources to sell to the United States, like energy. Canada has proven to be a secure and dependable source of natural gas for the United States. The existence of an important supplier so close and friendly is a major asset that makes

Canada-U.S. ties more reciprocal than trade figures suggest.

Building on this long-standing basis of economic interdependence is what the Free Trade Act is all about. The potential for increased reciprocity—mutual exchange—between the two nations is great. The advantages extend far beyond increasing each country's gross domestic product by one or two percentage points. Another major benefit is educational. Companies need to know how to compete more globally and to learn by doing in regional venues. Just as companies from the EC are becoming more international as they prepare themselves to compete in their own single product and service market, so can U.S. and Canadian companies use a North American free trade area as launching and testing grounds for internationalizing themselves. Both economic groupings can be stepping-stones for companies desiring a more global role.

By early 1990, 80 percent of Canada-U.S. trade was duty free. On 1 January 1989, tariffs were eliminated on $3 billion worth of goods, such as computers, leather, pork, fur, skis, and motorcycles. A second group of goods, including paper, furniture, and chemicals, had tariffs reduced by 40 percent initially and will have all tariffs eliminated in five years. A third group, including plywood, steel, and textiles, had tariffs cut by 20 percent. In ten years all tariffs on this group will end as well. Over half of the trade on which there is now duty (the remaining 20 percent) may be tariff free by 1993 (*CSM* 13 February 1990: 8-9). Many companies have already seized opportunities offered by a Canada-U.S. free trade area.

Opportunities exist in various areas. Demand for legal services has risen. Canadians are doing business with U.S. law firms that have set up branches across the border. Typical is Kavinocky and Cook, a Buffalo-based firm that opened a Toronto office in 1989. That office reported inquiries from clients on how best to apply the Free Trade Act for their benefit. Of special interest is a provision that allows Canadians greater immigration access to the United States to oversee their operations (*CSM* 13 February 1990: 8).

Other examples come from the banking, food, and manufacturing sectors. Canadian and U.S. banks are working to program automatic teller machines so customers can gain access to their bank accounts on either side of the border. Manitoba province's tourist agency has negotiated a joint promotion with McDonald's restaurants in Minnesota. In February 1990, New Flyer Industries, a Winnipeg bus manufacturer, opened an assembly plant in Grand Forks, North Dakota (*NYT* 16 April 1990: C1).

Tourism lends itself to cross-border cooperation. Forty percent of all foreign visitors to the United States are Canadian. Substantial numbers of U.S. nationals visit Canada. About 30 percent of Manitoba province's $800 million in tourist income comes from U.S. nationals. Manitoba and Minnesota, as indicated, provide strong examples of cross-border cooperation. Their tourist officials have planned several joint attractions, including an international fishing tournament, a canoe race from Winnipeg to Fargo, North Dakota, and construction of a snowmobile trail that would wind back and forth across the border (*NYT* 16 April 1990: C2).

Cooperation between Manitoba and Minnesota extends beyond tourism and fast food. The increasing scope of their relations illustrates the growth potential between the northern prairie regions of the United States and their Canadian neighbors. Government and private health executives are trying to coordinate the Minneapolis area's impressive health-care services with hospitals in Manitoba, where the Canadian government is building a national disease center. A goal is to coordinate the manufacturing of health-care equipment. One Canadian official noted, "That way we can be more efficient, avoid costly duplication and together sell to the rest of the world" (*NYT* 16 April 1990: C2). This example shows how a free trade area may be a stepping-stone to greater globalization.

While the Free Trade Act is bringing great opportunities for mutual exchange and growth, it has encountered difficulties. In 1991 and 1992 relations between Canada and the United States became strained as a result of simmering trade disputes that began to boil. In June 1991, a special three-judge panel, known as an extraordinary challenge committee, ruled that the United States must give back more than $20 million of duties imposed on Canadian pork. This case was decided under the dispute mechanisms outlined earlier; it is the only appeal so far to have reached the final stage of an extraordinary challenge committee (*NYT* 15 June 1991: 17 and 21).

Other trade battlefields have become automobiles, beer, and lumber. The U.S. Customs Service in 1992 ruled that Honda Civics assembled in Alliston, Ontario, lacked the required 50 percent content of parts made in North America to qualify for duty-free export to the United States. Honda responded that it was not given full credit for the engines, assembled in Ohio, and for its environmental costs. A preliminary ruling from the Customs Service subjects those cars to 2.5 percent import duty. The United States argued that Canada unfairly limited where imported beer could be sold. Canada contended that the tax credits some states in the United States give to beer companies discriminate against Canadian beer imports. The United States increased duties on Canadian lumber exports to the United States in March 1992. The U.S. Commerce Department found that Canadian provinces subsidized lumber exports by charging below-market prices for trees cut on public lands (*NYT* 18 February 1992: A1 and C6; 7 March 1992: 17 and 19; 16 May 1992: 17 and 24).

Buffeting the Free Trade Act is the political situation in Canada. Having won a major victory in November 1988, the Progressive Conservatives have seen the popularity of their government sink very low in the public opinion polls as the Canadian economy ran into problems in the late 1980s and early 1990s. The federal government in Canada is facing its own deficit. The Canadian public has not warmly received a sales tax. Some have blamed almost every plant closing in Canada on the Free Trade Act. In such times the Free Trade Act is an easy target.

Despite all these problems, from the perspective of the twenty-first century the Free Trade Act will most likely be viewed as a historic step in accelerating North American economic integration and creating monumental opportunities for businesses that are up to the challenges of internationalization. One other country became a full partner in this process of North American integration. Mexico, which bestrides North and Central America, and the United States have negotiated a free trade agreement. Canada joined these talks, which produced a North American Free Trade Agreement (NAFTA) among all three countries (see chapter 10).

PART III. CENTRAL AMERICA, SOUTH AMERICA, AND THE CARIBBEAN BASIN

The notion of dependency is a central theme of Part III. Dependency means a harmful reliance on outsiders for one's economic growth and development. All three case studies featured here raise the question of dependency but in different ways. The first studies mining in the Cerro de Pasco region of Peru. It tracks the conditions and historical events that enabled the Cerro Corporation, a U.S.-based multinational, to dominate mining in that area by the early twentieth century. Its main lesson is that dependency is more complicated than just a story of insiders versus outsiders.

The second case study looks at the controversial presence of the Exxon Corporation, another U.S.-based multinational, in the energy industry in Colombia. Its centerpiece is a debate among Colombians themselves in the early 1980s over a key contract with Exxon. No one denied that Colombia would be relying on Intercor, an Exxon subsidiary, to play a crucial role in coal mining, but people argued whether the reliance was harmful and if so, in what ways. Some raised questions that appeared in connection with the United Fruit Company's experiences in Central America. If Exxon did not do it, would another corporation with similar clout undertake the venture? And if no one stepped forward, would Colombia be worse off without the project than benefiting in a flawed fashion with it?

The third case study concentrates on the foundation of the tourist industry in part of the Bahamas in the 1950s and 1960s. The venue of activity changes from mining and mainly supply-oriented foreign investments to an industry—tourism—that uses market-oriented investments but not always in ways that build up the local economy in an equitable and robust fashion. The foreign investment that underpinned the construction of Freeport as a tourist city neglected for a long time the indigenous labor force and relied instead on the services of expatriates or foreigners in important management and technical positions. The emergence of Freeport brought vital foreign exchange to the Bahamas from visitors but fostered a skill and investment dependency on outsiders. The guiding foreign hand in the building of Freeport was Wallace Groves, a U.S. national with long-standing personal ties to the islands. While the Cerro Corporation and especially Exxon exemplify U.S. multinational activity abroad, Wallace Groves and his Bahamian Port Authority fall more into the category of international than multinational business.

Dependency is a concept that has provoked lively debate and penetrating criticism. It originally achieved intellectual force in the 1960s in the work of some scholars of Latin America, most notably that of Andre Gunder Frank, who argued that dependency was a dynamic notion, since it embraced the "development of underdevelopment." There is a distinction, he suggested, between an undeveloped and an underdeveloped region or country. An undeveloped land was one that had not experienced human intervention, especially from foreigners. An underdeveloped land had been the object of harmful manipulation by outside forces. Frank, along with many others, divided the world into various zones. The exploiting countries made up a core, while the exploited areas constituted a periphery. In his own work Frank internalized the notions of core and periphery. The core of Brazil—Rio de Janeiro and Sao Paulo—exploited that country's periphery, which included the northeastern region. Dependency was, for Frank and like-minded scholars, opposed to development: the two could not coexist. Rather dependency caused underdevelopment, an overarching category that stood somewhat vaguely for harms of different kinds.

This is the essence of what some now call the "old dependency" theory: dependency and development are totally exclusive phenomena. One major criticism of the "old dependency" was that it over-simplified what really happened. Its alternatives were too opposite—dependency or development—to capture the twilight zone of relations between outsiders and indigenous residents in which benefits and harms were sometimes interwoven. To correct this over-simplification other scholars proposed variations on the theme of *dependent development*.

By suggesting that dependency and development can coexist in certain situations these analysts try to escape the "either-or" approach of the "old dependency." Among these scholars are Fernando Cardoso and Peter Evans. Cardoso noted how foreign direct investment in an "underdeveloped" country now targets industry, and much less mining and agriculture as it did decades ago. This foreign investment is often advanced in terms of technology and organization and involves a high degree of local participation. Foreign investment is not a zero-sum game in which all gains go to the outsiders at the expense of the host country and its citizens. Significant local participation means that the gains and losses are distributed in more complex ways.

In his 1979 study of Brazil Peter Evans made a stimulating contribution to the notion of dependent development. The key concept he used was the *triple alliance*. The three members of this alliance are the state, international capital, and local capital. Local capital stands for two distinct groups of indigenous businesses: the large-scale and the small-scale. Evans argued that alliance members had evolved a division of labor in regard to the Brazilian economy. This division of labor is based on each member's resources and expertise. The state has financial, legal, and enforcement powers. Multinational corporations have capital, technology, and international clout. Large-scale local business has capital, technology, and some bargaining leverage, while small-scale businesses do not have as much capital but do possess an important strength: detailed knowledge of local markets.

The nature of an enterprise has a lot to do with the location of alliance activities. The state and international capital became involved in areas that are technologically intense and so have high capital and organizational requirements. The creation of *Petrobras* as a state agency, for instance, completed the nationalization of the Brazilian petroleum industry in 1953. Multinational corporations sometimes enter joint ventures or other cooperative agreements with large-scale local businesses in activities that need substantial capital. Small-scale local capital concentrates on those industries where capital needs are not as intense and local market knowledge can prove a decisive competitive advantage. Small-scale local businesses were able to succeed in Brazil's textile industry, whose capital requirements were surmountable and where knowledge of local demand patterns for textiles was a major asset.

Besides Cardoso's analysis of local participation and Evans's notion of the triple alliance, other contributions refined the "old dependency." Another major criticism of the "old dependency" was that it was not sufficiently historical. It did not adequately examine the *process* of becoming dependent. Theotonio dos Santos, himself a Brazilian, presented a useful general formulation of this process and made dependency a more historical concept.

There are three major types of historical dependency, dos Santos suggested. The first form, *colonial dependency*, was the earliest. During this phase foreign trading companies dominated the economic structures of a colony in order to extract food and raw materials for export purposes. The second form, *financial-industrial dependency*, bears some resemblance to Lenin's analysis of financial capital becoming financial imperialism. During this period colonial production was still geared to the export of primary products—food and raw materials. But the type of control changed. Instead of direct domination by foreign trading monopolies, colonies experienced the powerful control of banks. During the second phase foreign banks became important as direct investors and providers of finance for export-related industries.

The third form of dependency is for dos Santos the most recent. It is *technological-industrial dependency*, also known as the "new dependency," which began to emerge after World War II. The core of the "new dependency" is that more multinational corporations based some of their operations in the "underdeveloped" countries themselves. This point is similar to Cardoso's emphasis on local participation in the activities of international capital within a country. Basing operations within host countries makes it more difficult to analyze dependency only as outsiders versus insiders, since the outsiders are becoming insiders in key respects.

The previous discussion presents only a partial sketch of the dependency debate but it does highlight important views that deserve consideration. In some quarters today dependency is not only criticized but also rejected. These reactions come partly from the sweeping nature of the package in which dependency is often presented: linked to the formulation of "world-systems" in which zones of the world set out to exploit other zones. Many of the prominent dependency scholars come from the left on the political spectrum—some are socialists and others Marxists. At a time when Marxism and its kinship theories are in worldwide retreat as operational approaches to human organization, it is all too easy to discard all aspects of ideas from the left even as analytical tools for understanding the most fundamental phenomena of our time. This approach is wrong.

Dependency theorists have drawn attention to a number of important issues. They have provided explanations for understanding the historical origins of two types of dependency that today bedevil more than just countries in the "developing world." These are *debt dependency* and *investment dependency*. From the dependency debate there has emerged a sharper focus on a central question in all relationships between international and indigenous business: when does reliance on outsiders become harmful? The loss of control over one's economic destiny which dependency spotlights is one of the burning issues of our times.

The following case studies present concrete instances of that loss of control. In the Cerro de Pasco region of Peru the local citizenry bears some responsibility for the triumph of foreign capital. In Colombia the government believed it had sufficient controls in place to regulate multinational enterprise, although many contested that view. And in the Bahamas the key agreement that created Freeport was negotiated under administrative and economic colonialism. The residents of the Bahamas had already lost control of their destinies to a British colonial government, which remained in place until the achievement of independence in 1973.

7

Mining at Cerro de Pasco, Peru, 1850–1930s: The Triumph of the Cerro Corporation

Dennis M. P. McCarthy
with Paul M. Kramer

Mining in the Cerro de Pasco region, which lies in the center of modern Peru, has been an important activity for centuries. Begun by Indian groups that came under the domination of the Inca Empire in the fifteenth century, the Cerro mining industry has undergone over the centuries major changes that relate to dependency. The Spanish, who ruled the Pasco region from about the 1570s until Peru obtained its independence in 1821, organized the mining industry in Peru as a source of revenue for their empire.

During the Spanish period, many of the problems in the Pasco mining industry that were to intensify after independence appeared. The industry was cyclical, beset with drainage problems, and under domestic leadership that would turn more and more to external sources for financial help. Until the early twentieth century, the Pasco mining industry was monometallic. It concentrated exclusively on one metal: silver. Monometallism (one metal) and monoculturalism (one crop) are kinds of dependency. People producing one product are economically vulnerable. Significant price declines for their product can devastate them financially. Other hostile forces can hurt them, since they are not diversified and have nothing on which to rely in times of crisis. The Pasco miners faced several adverse forces. The major one was water in the wrong place; namely, in their mine shafts. It was the drainage problem and attempts to solve it that had a huge impact on the fate of the Pasco mining industry.

As the shafts went deeper, flooding became more difficult to control. Over the years a number of adits were constructed to expedite drainage. An adit is a nearly horizontal passage leading into a mine. The deeper the shafts, the more complex were the problems involved in building those drainage adits. The more intricate the problems, the greater were the technological requirements for their solutions. The larger the technological demands, the greater became the need for capital. This chain of necessity—mining deeper required more capital—is central to the process by which the Cerro de Pasco mining industry became more reliant on outsiders for capital.

Pasco's capital or investment dependency is rooted late in the Spanish period, when three local businessmen sought British capital and technical assistance. In 1812 José Arismendi and Pedro Abadia, two of Lima's wealthiest businessmen, and Francisco Ulville, a Swiss immigrant, formed a partnership to raise capital to purchase steam engines for draining the Pasco mines. Their efforts produced the Steam Machine Company. Ulville worked on the spot to get a contract between the Pasco Mining Guild and the company and in Great Britain to sell shares of its stock to British investors. British specialists played significant roles in the greater mechanization of the Pasco mines from 1814 on. The involvement of British capital and technical assistance initiated a process that culminated in the triumph of the Cerro Corporation, a U.S.-based multinational, in the early twentieth century. The case study picks up the story in detail in the aftermath of the boom of the 1850s. This period of prosperity at Pasco resulted from discoveries of rich veins of silver ore, price declines for salt and mercury, and government action. Salt and mercury were two key elements in the refining process. The government raised the price of silver at the local bank that purchased the metal.

LOCAL CONTROL SLIPS AWAY, 1850–1900

The boom of the 1850s was truly a boom for the few. The skewed distribution of benefits had characterized earlier booms. As time went by, the deepening of the shafts required more expensive water control projects. The local mining elite, well positioned politically and financially, was able to capture an increasingly disproportionate share of the returns. It was able to have taxes levied on all miners, even those who did not directly benefit, to support the drainage improvements that helped the few more than the many. While membership in the inner circle increased over time, concentrated power became more entrenched as ownership of different phases of the mining industry interlocked in the same people. A major trend during the 1870s and into the 1880s was for mine proprietorship to concentrate among the large refinery operators. This concentration resulted from an intensification of that chain of necessity—mining deeper required more capital.

Once again, the nature of the extractive struggle with water determined the timing of the onset of another crisis. In 1860 miners reached the depth of extraction made possible by the steam pumps installed from 1848 to 1851: 30 meters below the Quiulococha adit. In 1860 silver output dropped to 194,435 marcs (1 marc = 8 ounces) and effectively ended the boom conditions of the 1850s. Anticipating 1860, the Pasco Miners Association in 1857 sought 60,000 pesos from the Peruvian Congress for the construction of another drainage project—the Rumillana adit. The ravine of Rumillana, located northeast of Cerro de Pasco, constituted the natural geographical drain for the area. Juan Languasco and Augustin Tello, powerful Pasco miners, led the 1857 endeavor, which failed. They, along with other members of the Miners Association, tried to support construction with their own capital. But building the Rumillana adit, which involved a distance of some 8,000 meters (4.96 miles), was too formidable a task for only local private capital. By the late 1850s, there had been at least three unsuccessful attempts to construct the Rumillana adit.

The Pasco miners again turned to the government. In 1861 the Peruvian government did agree to provide assistance but not as a grant or even a loan. Instead the government would help arrange a loan, of up to 1 million soles (the sole replacing the peso in 1863), and would guarantee an interest rate of 6 percent. Development rights, according to the 1861 accord, would go to the lowest bidder at public auction. The loan was to be repaid by a 2.5 percent per marc assessment on all silver produced at Cerro de Pasco. To fund this project the government and the mining association, in another example of public-private cooperation, sent a special loan commission to Europe. At this point problems began.

Despite its efforts, the commission could not put together financing under the 1861 law. Consequently, in 1865 the Miners Association negotiated a contract with Weyman and Harrison Company of England. The company was to provide three large 70 horsepower pumps at a cost of 250,000 soles. Expectations were that these three pumps would drain a large number of mines from their positions in centrally located shafts in the districts of Mesepata, Yauricocha, and Huancapucro.

Installation started in 1868. W. R. Rutter, an English engineer for a company of technicians hired by the contractor Henry Weymouth, began excavation of three shafts. He and his work force attempted to dig these shafts to a depth of 135 feet below the 300-foot level of the Quiulococha adit. The first pump in place at the Mesepata shaft began operating in 1872. It drained only the shaft itself, leaving the mines in areas surrounding the shaft flooded because of the permeability of the rock formations.

This failure angered members of the Miners Association, who had been paying tax since 1865 to pay for the pumps. As if the limited capacity of one pump was not disheartening enough, Weyman and Harrison Company never even brought the other two pumps to Cerro de Pasco. Their parts were left scattered along the road leading from the port of Chancay. Scattered parts, no benefits: the miners were left with nothing after making a payment of 229,000 soles to the company.

Weyman and Harrison did leave one legacy with significant public benefits. Its ultimate disposition was to have portentous consequences for the entire Cerro de Pasco mining industry. Under the company's aegis the Mineral Railway of

Cerro de Pasco was constructed. This railway was only seven miles long, from Cerro de Pasco to Sacrafamilia, but it did measurably reduce the costs of ore transport for no fewer than 36 refineries. For instance, the hacienda Esperanza experienced a decrease in transport costs per caxon (6,000 pounds) from 7 to 2.5 soles, while refineries along the river of Sacrafamilia paid about 9.50 soles. This amount was still about 2.50 soles below the average cost of 12 soles per caxon.

The railroad did not rescue the company from a bungled performance, however. Weyman and Harrison failed to honor their contract to drain the mines, and the firm never recovered from that fiasco: it was unable to correct its finances. Consequently, the Peruvian government confiscated the railway and held a public auction. It is here that another fateful involvement occurred. In 1874 the Public Works and Development Company acquired the railway. This was a company of a U.S. engineer and contractor named Henry Meiggs, who was to play a critical role in the future of the Cerro de Pasco mining industry.

Meanwhile, matters worsened at Cerro de Pasco. Failure to drain the mines adequately led to a decline in silver output by 1871 to 177,942 marcs. In 1876 production plummeted to only 149,878 marcs. Water was relentless in its capacity, sooner or later, to thwart extraction, organization, and technology. After a total investment of nearly 3 million soles in drainage projects during the 1824–1876 period by the government and the Miners Association, the water won. But this downside seemed and was more ominous. The big pumps were asked to perform in a drainage plan that was not realistic.

Many people were worried. In 1874 the Peruvian government commissioned a special study of the problems of the Cerro de Pasco mining industry. Alejandro Babinski, a Polish engineer, undertook an extensive survey of previous drainage projects in order to determine the best means of rejuvenating the Pasco mines. His analysis is an instructive example of an internalist approach that neglected a number of key factors in the wider environment. Directed to recommend the best way to revive Cerro silver mining, he concentrated exclusively on the mines themselves and their intertwined histories of drainage and extraction. He concluded that construction of the Rumillana adit 80 meters below the Quiulococha adit was essential to mine revitalization. Cerro's sliver output had declined, he argued, not because of a lack of mineral riches or only on account of an inadequate drainage system. Excavation procedures used for nearly three centuries, whereby the run of the ore veins determined the direction of digging, had resulted, he suggested, in the collapse of hundreds of rich mine shafts. He also recommended that government support the formation of more *companias* like the Sacrafamilia and Esperanza, which refined the large amount of low quality ore assaying at from 4 to 7 marcs per caxon available at Cerro de Pasco.

In a final suggestion that prefigured Cerro's metallic diversification, Babinski urged the government to facilitate the construction of a railway from Cerro de

Pasco to the rail line at La Oroya, a distance of about 71 miles. This line would reduce transport costs and permit the export of the abundant industrial minerals and metals of the province, such as coal, iron, lead, and copper, in addition to enhancing the movement of silver. All these projects required the formation of a large development company with sufficient capital to acquire state-of-the-art mine technology.

Babinski overlooked the world beyond the mines. Pasco's problems were related not only to drainage difficulties and excavation techniques. The price of silver itself on the New York and London markets was plunging: from 59.2 pennies per ounce in 1873, to 51.2 pennies by 1879, to a low of 28.9 pennies in 1894. Basic supply-demand factors in the metals markets, along with government decisions, contributed to the more than 50 percent reduction in price. The supply of silver had increased significantly in global markets, especially after the discovery of the Comstock Lode in 1859 near Virginia City, Nevada, in the United States. The supply of gold had also risen, in the aftermath of its discovery in California and Australia.

The increasing size of the gold supply had a great impact on the extrinsic value of silver as reflected in its price. With more gold available, a one metal gold standard (gold monometallism) became more feasible. England had already adopted such a standard in 1816. In 1873 Germany began to demonetize silver. It sold 114 million ounces between 1873 and 1879, which exerted downward pressure on silver prices. At the same time, the Scandinavian countries formed a monetary union that unified their currencies on a gold standard. In the United States the Congress decreased the amount of silver for coinage in 1873. This action was not a technical demonetization of silver as such, but it was a significant retreat from bimetallism, in which both gold and silver, though of unequal intrinsic value, are treated as authentic precious metals and accorded proportionate roles in the currency system. The 1873 action of the U.S. Congress authorized coinage of silver money below standard weight, which departed from both authenticity and proportionality. Then in 1876 Russia suspended the coinage of silver, except for trade with Asia. The Latin Monetary Union (France, Belgium, Switzerland, and Italy) and Spain also suspended the coinage of silver for public use. As all these actions made silver less prized, its price continued to fall.

In Peru itself the economic and financial situation was darkening. The rate of inflation was high. The boom in guano, which had brought nearly $600 million on the retail market since 1840, collapsed in 1875. Guano is natural fertilizer made from the excrement of sea birds. The abrupt end of the boom reversed the capital infusion associated with its heyday. Many Lima banks and commercial houses were forced to recall outstanding debts and loans. The Peruvian government was operating on a budget deficit. It also faced an internal debt of about 17.5 million soles, and a foreign debt of 202,132,587 soles negotiated since 1825. The government's demand for money to stay in business meant that there was even less available than there might have been for private borrowing. In very local terms, miners at Cerro de Pasco found it exceedingly difficult to arrange financing.

Their industry had deteriorated to grave levels by the mid-1870s. In 1875 Apolinario Franco and Hilarrio Parra, Pasco mining deputies, submitted a special report to the Ministry of Public Finance, which detailed the extent of Cerro de Pasco's problems. The mining industry was running at a loss: in 1875 the expenses for refining some 43,897 caxones of ore, which yielded 174,550 marcs of silver, exceeded revenue earned by about 205,625 soles. Only about 153 mines out of some 734 were then actively in production. The others lay abandoned because of flooding or the cost of having low-quality ore refined. Thirty-eight refineries in the province of Pasco had stopped operations; 80 remained functioning. The conditions portrayed in that 1875 report continued to worsen. By 1876 the population of the city of Cerro de Pasco declined to about 6,400 people. Many small-scale miners had abandoned their claims or sold them to the refineries still operating.

This situation made Cerro de Pasco vulnerable to the events that would result in the loss of whatever local control remained over its resources. An interesting duo had an enormous impact on Pasco's future. José Prado, Peru's first civilian president, and Henry Meiggs, the U.S. engineer-contractor whose company had recently acquired the Cerro de Pasco–Sacrafamilia railway, came up with a plan to develop the mineral wealth of the province of Pasco. This unusual partnership originated in necessity and desire. President Prado desperately needed money to service or pay interest on the country's debt. Meiggs was searching for financing for his various railway projects at a time when the available capital pool in Peru was shrinking. Together they decided, probably inspired by the Babinski report, to diversify Cerro de Pasco's export production. Their goal was to develop Pasco's industrial metals, along with the continued encouragement of silver production—all metals and minerals destined largely for export. The projected revenues from these export sales would fund Prado's debt servicing and Meiggs's railroads.

Meiggs certainly thought big. He proposed that the Callao–Lima–La Oroya railway, already 352 kilometers long, be extended another 71 miles to Cerro de Pasco. The Rumillana adit, the primary recommendation of the Babinski report, received attention. Meiggs advanced a plan to construct that adit through his Public Works and Development Company, with capital guaranteed by the state at 7 percent interest. He also asked for important local items. He wanted to receive all mineral claims at Cerro de Pasco not worked, as well as all "public works" machinery. This category included three steam pumps at Mesepata, Yauricocha, and Huancapucro and two others held by the government. This was the major beginning of a process of foreign acquisition of indigenous properties and property rights that led to virtually complete local dispossession. It is important to grasp the essentials of greater foreign penetration and the extent to which it received opposition and begrudging, and sometimes willing, local cooperation.

At Cerro de Pasco itself Meiggs obtained the support of about 100 hard-pressed mine proprietors and refinery owners. These people had halted operations. Among their number were some of the local luminaries of the industry, including Edward Steel, Henry Stone, Augustin Tello, Lagravere and Sons, Manuel Chavez, and M. A. La Torre. Still, many members of the Miners Association opposed the Meiggs plan for constructing the Rumillana adit. They preferred that the government and miners guild together build the adit and the railway as public works projects. Economic necessity rendered such calls for public-private cooperation impractical. The collapse of the guano boom had then almost completely dried up domestic capital sources. It seemed to Prado, Steel, Stone, and like-minded colleagues that only a capitalist and contractor with international financial connections, like Meiggs, could provide the necessary capital at this crucial juncture in the history of the Cerro de Pasco mining industry. Their view won, with enormous implications for undermining local control of local resources.

In 1877 J. R. de Izcue, the Director of Public Works, negotiated a contract with Meiggs. This document, based on the 1861 drainage contract development law, gave him the rights to construct the railway and adit. Capital for constructing the rail link from La Oroya to Cerro de Pasco, at a projected cost of 1,800,000 soles, and the Rumillana adit, at an estimated 700,000 soles, was to come from various sources. These included the sale of 200,000 tons of guano, a state monopoly, with Meiggs as concessionaire selling it on the U.S. market; the net profits from exports of metal carried on the Callao–Lima–La Oroya– Pasco railway; the duties on the export of silver, coin, copper, and lead from Cerro de Pasco; and the Peruvian government's share of the profits from working Cerro de Pasco (25 percent).

Meiggs was to receive all abandoned mine claims in the Pasco district and those steam pumps. Those miners who remained were given the following alternatives under the 1877 contract: continue to work but sell to Meiggs 30 percent of the ore they mined, or turn over ownership of their claims to Meiggs and receive 20 percent of the ore extracted. Meiggs acquired claims from 50 miners and an unspecified number of abandoned claims, the water rights of the Quiulococha and Rumillana adits, and the steam pumps at Yauricocha, Mesepata, Huancapucro, and Conan. Legal dispossession of several kinds was well under way: of the minerals in the land itself, of those already extracted (partial dispossession of the usufruct), and of water.

The infrastructure projects did not begin smoothly. Immediate financing for operations of the Public Works and Development Company came from special notes issued by the company itself. These were known as "billete de Meiggs" and totaled 1,030,000 soles in 1877. They were not universally well received: about 27 major Lima commercial establishments refused to accept them. This rejection curtailed the company's activities, but only temporarily. After considerable litigation and debate in the press, President Prado, to support the company, authorized the issuance of government securities, to the extent of 5,333,333 soles and bearing 6 percent interest. To finance projects designed in part to service the public debt required in this case the creation of more debt.

Some progress was made on the adit and rail link during 1878. But Henry Meiggs died that year, and his rights became the subject of litigation by his heirs, which slowed progress. The Peruvian government eventually acknowledged that John Meiggs, his brother, and William Cilley held the development rights at Cerro de Pasco. Silver production continued to decline, reaching an output of 145,236 marcs in 1879. The price per marc remained on the downside, falling from 10 soles in 1878 to about 8 soles in 1879. Many Pasco miners were wondering how much worse the situation could become—much worse, as the War of the Pacific broke out in late 1879 and lasted into 1883.

This conflict, which pitted Chile against Peru, seriously damaged the Cerro de Pasco region and its mining industry. Twice during the war invading Chilean armies from the south ravaged Pasco. They confiscated large amounts of silver from the miners and tried to destroy the productive capacity of the industry. Andres Caceras, a Peruvian general, led a large force in the Central Sierra that was resisting a Chilean-imposed peace. In 1883 his supporters demanded money from 83 residents of Pasco province; these "requests" varied in amount from 16,000 to 20,000 soles.

Battered from all sides, miners and their industry still managed to maintain a wartime production that averaged about 161,000 marcs per year. Most went to the Chilean and Peruvian armies. To return to production levels associated with the silver industry's heyday would have been difficult in any event after the war, but several factors made full-scale recovery impossible. The price of silver then seemed on a perpetual downside; it fell to 28.9 pennies per marc in 1894 (22 pennies = 1 sole in 1894). Silver output continued to decline in the 1890s; fewer than 70 of the remaining 300 mills at Pasco were operating. In 1897 the government of Peru administered the financial death blow to some of the old silver mining enterprises at Pasco: it stopped buying and coining silver and adopted the gold standard. Silver mining continued for export, but on a reduced scale.

By 1883 many miners had been reduced to a low level of operation or had sold or abandoned their claims. The trend toward greater concentration continued during all these troubles. By 1886 most major mining and refinery proprietors had increased the number of mines under their control, which contrasted with a decline in the amount held by smaller miners. Yet even these larger miners had financial difficulties that persisted through the rest of the nineteenth century. By the first decades of the twentieth century, they found themselves completely displaced by foreign capital: the giant Cerro de Pasco Mining Company backed by U.S. money.

The process of indigenous dispossession had begun with seemingly unentangling overtures to foreign equity investors in the early nineteenth century and then involved total foreign ownership of some local assets from the late 1870s. It accelerated during the 1890s as the Cerro de Pasco silver mining industry completely disintegrated. By 1899 the wind had blown down 2,832 of the 3,222 houses listed in the 1895 census, which put the total population of the district at 5,000. As the nineteenth century ended, except for several dozen houses around Carrion Square, the city of Cerro de Pasco had become a virtual wasteland as miners, shopkeepers, and prostitutes all left. Fewer than a dozen of the old *haciendas minerales* continued refining operations, and Cerro's silver output dropped to only 12,500 silver marcs in 1901.

Out of such depths emerged a diversified Pasco mining industry producing for export. But during the variegated resurgence local control slipped away. Production of industrial metals had been one of the objectives of Henry Meiggs in the 1870s, but death denied him whatever progress he might have made in that direction. Others took concrete steps toward diversification. Augustin Tello constructed an *oficina* for smelting copper ores in 1878, and Eulogigia Fernandini built another *oficina* and began exporting smelted copper, lead, and silver ores over one decade later. By the late 1890s more than 20 *oficina* employing about 200 workers operated in the province. In 1900 the export of copper from Cerro de Pasco to England amounted to 5,138 tons, worth 4,500,000 soles, as electrification in Europe generated an increased demand for copper and other industrial metals. These early efforts hinted at the economic potential of diversified production.

An important report prepared by outsiders underscored Pasco's great possibilities. Participating in a special investigatory commission organized and financed by Michael Grace in the 1890s, some U.S. engineers came to a central conclusion that was to further excite external interests. Beneath the rubble of exhausted silver veins, they concurred, lay a fabulous lode of minerals and metals, including copper, lead, coal, iron, gold, zinc, vanadium, bismuth, and more silver. Cerro de Pasco apparently still contained immense mineral wealth, even after nearly three centuries of enriching kings, viceroys, and the citizens of an independent Peru.

But the problems that bedeviled miners for centuries awaited the new economic conquistadores from the north. The awesome threesome of flooding, transport, and capital remained, ready to discourage the hardiest of entrepreneurs. Nonetheless, efforts picked up to diminish all three constraints. The organization of these endeavors facilitated the greater intrusion of foreign capital. As to flooding, the Rumillana adit had to be completed. During the period from 1883 to 1895 three separate groups sought from the Peruvian government the concession to construct this adit. One was a New York banking syndicate, represented by Michael Grace, which had acquired the rights to this enterprise from the Meiggs heirs in 1884. A second was the British Peruvian Corporation, Ltd. A third was the *Sociedad Nacional de Minería de Pasco*, composed of the remaining members of the Pasco Miners Association. The government eventually chose collectively, not separately, and sanctioned a mix of foreign and domestic financing. It awarded rights to the project to the *Empresa Socavonera del Cerro de Pasco* (the Cerro de Pasco Tunnel Company), with financial involvement of all three groups. Construction of the adit resumed in 1901 under the direction of a British engineer. In that year there also began work in earnest on a rail link between Cerro de Pasco and La Oroya, which would connect Cerro with the Lima–Callao port lines on the coast. Undertaking this project and completing it by 1904 was a newly formed North American enterprise, the Cerro de Pasco Mining Company and its subsidiary, the Cerro de Pasco Railway Company.

THE TRIUMPH OF U.S. CAPITAL AND LOST INDIGENOUS OPPORTUNITY: THE CERRO DE PASCO MINING COMPANY

The organization of the Cerro de Pasco Mining Company was a watershed in the history of the region: it marked the beginning of large-scale industrial mining at Cerro. This company, attracted by those favorable engineering assessments of the mineral wealth of the area, received considerable assistance from the Peruvian government. It did not have to pay production taxes for twenty five years. Favored by the government and bolstered by U.S. capital, the company moved quickly to establish domination over the Cerro de Pasco mining industry. By 1904 it controlled about 75 to 80 percent of all mining claims in the entire province. Four years later, it supposedly possessed a total of about 1,250 claims, with partial interest in another 122. By 1912 it had absorbed the Cerro de Pasco Tunnel Company.

With such an overwhelming power base the company transformed the nature of the Cerro mining industry. Over the next several decades it introduced state-of-the-art metallurgical technology, which had profound consequences. The Pasco mining industry, which had for so long been largely monometallic, very labor-intensive, and reliant on hand-tool procedures, became something else. There emerged a diversified mining industry that was mechanized and capital-intensive. Evidence of this transformation was abundant: a half-dozen hydroelectric dams, four large smelters, tramways, internal-combustion engines, machine loading gondola cars, and compression air hammers for use in mine shafts more than 1,000 feet beneath the surface. The push toward greater capital intensity required an increase in the labor force, at least for several decades. Labor contractors recruited Indian farmers, fugitives, and impoverished ex-miners from surrounding areas to provide the work force necessary for this massive transformation. The company's total labor force numbered about 4,880 by 1908 and reached nearly 10,000 people by 1920.

The Cerro de Pasco Mining Company can stand as an archetype of foreign involvement that produced excessive one-way benefits. It swiftly achieved financial success for itself and its stockholders. Later known as the Cerro Corporation on the New York Stock Exchange, it had a registered book value in Peru, which likely understated its worth, amounting to $70,667,358 in 1920. It had an annual export capacity of more than 100 million pounds of ore. Between 1916 and 1936 the corporation paid out nearly 71 million dollars in dividends on some 1,123,000 shares of stock held in the United States. The greatest profit came from the sale of industrial ores, but the corporation continued to extract silver as a byproduct of its mining operations. Even as a secondary product silver output totaled 42,297,989 marcs between 1901 and 1944. As an annual rate of production the corporation's twentieth-century record almost doubled that of the previous century, when silver had been the focus. Only when mining ceased to be monometallic was the full economical potential of the area realized. Only when production diversified did the Cerro mining industry escape from the boom and bust cycles so common to regions that are monometallic or monocultural. The Cerro Corporation did achieve the sustained growth of industrial ores for export, which masked the ups and downs of any particular metal.

Yet this record was based on a too familiar combination of factors: state-of-the-art technology, foreign capital, cheap labor, and monopoly control. There is nothing inherently wrong with modern technology or foreign capital, but when cheap labor and monopoly control were added to this mix, the results were disastrous from several important perspectives. The kind of dispossession that occurred meant that local control over local resources was lost. This was a surrender of control not only over the assets themselves, but also over their product or usufruct. Too great a share of the profits was repatriated, or sent abroad, rather than locally reinvested.

This outcome was not, however, preordained or inevitable. Foreign participation in mining at Cerro de Pasco did increase throughout the nineteenth century, but a balance of sorts between foreign and domestic efforts existed during the first half century of the national period (from 1821 into the 1870s). The government then seemed committed to support both indigenous and foreign efforts to drain and operate the mines. President Prado, under financial stress, departed greatly from this approach in the 1870s when he granted extensive "development" rights to Henry Meiggs. Meiggs's death slowed the shift to foreign domination, and the government returned to a more balanced policy toward the Cerro mines. The Cerro de Pasco Tunnel Company, which received the rights to construct the Rumillana adit, blended both internal and external financing. When the Cerro de Pasco Mining Company swallowed the Tunnel Company whole, there ended the last best hope and opportunity for preserving some semblance of balance.

It need not have turned out that way. One major key to understanding the process of foreign penetration and economic conquest of the Cerro de Pasco mining industry is the notion of vacuum. Throughout the nineteenth century and into the twentieth century there were usually new sources of external capital and foreign entrepreneurs ready to take advantage of the economic vacuum created by the failures, in varying degrees, of Pasco miners. The most telling setback to the prospects for maintaining a balance between domestic and foreign interests was the inability of the Pasco miners to arrive at a solution for financing and constructing the Rumillana adit during the 1860s. This project in itself would not necessarily have prevented the decline in silver production that was to follow, in view of the strength of such factors as the declining price and international monetary role of the metal. But it was the inability or unwillingness of the miners to cooperate, in the fashion the times demanded, as they had done on several important occasions in the past, that was most ominous. Despite the best efforts of Augustin Tello and Juan Languasco, the level of cooperation that funding and excavating the adit required did not materialize. The government was not notably generous during these critical years, and the diminution of its financial role surely contributed to upsetting whatever balance of power existed between external and internal interests.

Had a more dynamic mining economy been achieved in the nineteenth century, perhaps a balance of an evolving sort might have continued at Cerro de Pasco into the twentieth century. Greater dynamism required, as subsequent experience was to demonstrate, diversification. The inability, or unwillingness, of significant numbers of Pasco miners to begin working in a major way the deposits of copper, lead, iron, and coal in the nineteenth century came from several factors. The nature of opportunity in the past greatly influenced its definition in the present. It was only natural, given the experience of the colonial era, for the miners of Cerro de Pasco to perceive silver production as the primary source of potential wealth. And silver bullion, which had served as the basis for the currency during the Spanish colonial era, retained this function for a long time in the newly independent states of Latin America. Market considerations also reinforced monometallism. The new countries in Latin America had then not industrialized enough to create a sufficiently powerful demand for industrial metals, whereas there were long-standing silver markets in Latin America and elsewhere. In those the high intrinsic value of silver, at least until prices unraveled during the 1870s, 1880s, and 1890s, usually rendered most considerations of diversification entirely theoretical.

Besides perceptions, markets, and prices, transport costs greatly configured the definition of practical economic opportunities. Before the La Oroya–Pasco railway was completed in 1904, transportation was usually so costly between Pasco and the coast that any project that would have required the export of a substantial tonnage of industrial ores was, on this count alone, deemed grossly impractical. Perhaps most compelling of all, silver did prove profitable for many miners at various times during the nineteenth century and earlier. Hence, it is entirely understandable, for a number of reasons, that many miners persevered in the search for more and richer lodes of silver and/or continued to try to refine silver from lower grade ores rather than turning to a broad-based attack on industrial ores. Even in the midst of numerous failures it was the success stories that were more motivating. Struggling miners were inspired to keep at it, in the hope that they could accumulate sufficient capital to invest in land, continue silver mining, and live the Peruvian Hispanic seignorial way of life.

Counterpointing those personal dreams was the ominous reality of the nineteenth century for not only the Cerro de Pasco region but also Peru itself. This was the crucial transitional period. The opportunity to develop a strong, independent Peruvian national economy slipped away. Sown during this epoch were the seeds of another version of dependent economy, one that was not embodied in the structures of government colonialism. The twentieth century manifestation of dependency had a broader export base—sugar, cotton, oil, silver, and industrial ores—and was sustained by massive European and U.S. capital investments.

8

Mining in Colombia:
Energy Contracts and Exxon,
1951–1983

Dependency can blend harm and benefit such that one must take both or neither. The area of El Cerrejón in the Colombian region of La Guajira has been the location for a coal mining venture that interweaves the interests of international capital and the Colombian people in ways that illustrate the above proposition. In 1976, Intercor, a subsidiary of the U.S. multinational Exxon, entered into a contract with the government of Colombia to extract coal. This contract, the North Cerrejón agreement, was the subject of heated debate among Colombians themselves. The contract itself and the surrounding debate highlight this case study.

To appreciate this argument one needs background about Colombia's energy history, the types of contract models, the state energy bureaucracy, and other agreements with other corporations that antedated the North Cerrejón contract with Intercor. This case study takes the phrase "government-business relations" and shows what it means in specific circumstances. The complexity of these energy arrangements compounds the difficulty of assessing each party's gains and losses: Intercor (Exxon), the Colombian government, and the Colombian people. The debate over the North Cerrejón contract makes the theoretical sparring over the merits and demerits of dependency theory come alive. Despite strong contrary viewpoints, the Colombian government chose to go ahead with the agreement because it believed the gains for Colombia far outweighed the losses. The pointed arguments that all sides in the debate made will challenge readers to make up their own minds on the question.

Colombia, located on the northern tip of South America with access to both the Pacific and Atlantic oceans, is endowed with immense and varied natural and human resources. Its geographical spectrum ranges from deserts to snowcapped mountains, from rainy tropical forests to vast plains. Its population of over 27 million people reflects a diverse ethnic mix, which contains Spanish, African, and indigenous elements. Some Colombians still debate the extent to which the glorious Spanish custom that considers material work undignified undercuts the willingness of their fellow citizens to do certain kinds of work. However Colombians feel about this issue, there is no shortage of human energy in the country. Colombia has a democratic form of government that has survived numerous civil wars since the 1900s, a military coup, overt political repression at times, and intense activity by a number of guerrilla movements.

The region of La Guajira has never been integrated into Colombia other than in a formalistic way. Located in the northeast on the Atlantic Ocean and next to Venezuela, it has mostly been known for its contraband trade with Venezuela and its marijuana production (Kline 1981: 74). Its relatively small population is basically indigenous and its desert topography makes it ill suited for sustained agricultural production. For a long time only two roads connected the region with the interior of the country. La Guajira's state of alienation from the rest of the country is such that national laws are sometimes very difficult to enforce locally.

ENERGY HISTORY AND CONTRACT MODELS

On the national level, energy developments in Colombia have been traditionally undertaken by multinational corporations. In 1920 Gulf and Exxon entered into long-term *concession* contracts with the Colombian government for the extraction of petroleum, which lasted until 1951. In that year Ecopetrol (the Colombian Petroleum Enterprise) was founded to continue production in the areas returned by Gulf and Exxon to the Colombian government. In 1970 *joint venture* contracts started replacing concession contracts. In 1974 President López Michelson issued a decree that made concession contracts illegal. In 1975 Colombia became an oil importer for the first time since the 1920s. Coal production in the 1970s was dispersed among a few large producers and numerous small ones (Kline 1981: 73).

There are four possible contract models in this case study. A *concession* contract gives no equity (ownership) to a host country. An *association* agreement grants 50% of equity to a host country. A *joint venture* can give more than 50% of equity to a host country. A *service* contract grants 100% equity to a host country: either to a state company, a private company, or a joint state-private company (Kline 1983: 6).

The El Cerrejón area itself, located in the south central state of La Guajira, has an important energy history. Coal was discovered there in 1872. These deposits exist on 130,000 acres, on which 316 people lived in 1982. The *proven* resources are 2 billion metric tons of coal, with an additional *probable* two billion tons. These are the largest known deposits of coal in South America.

They were long neglected for a number of reasons. The seven major civil wars fought during the late nineteenth century and the twentieth century absorbed the energies of most politicians; developing El Cerrejón's coal deposits was not a high priority. There was no economic incentive from within Colombia itself to extract that coal. Before the 1930s Colombia's railroad and other industries used the coal found in other parts of the country, as well as other forms of energy. As Colombia became an oil exporter in the late 1920s, railroads and other industries were led away from coal. There was no economic incentive from without to mine El Cerrejón's coal. This was an era of cheap oil; therefore, the global demand for coal was limited.

GOVERNMENT AGENCIES AND THEIR ACTIVITIES

Some of the institutional framework that would be instrumental in various endeavors concerning El Cerrejón's coal in the late 1960s and beyond was already in place by the early 1950s. In 1951 Ecopetrol had been founded, as noted, to deal initially with continuing petroleum production in areas returned to the government by Gulf and Exxon. In that same year the IFI (Industrial Promotion Institute), set up by the Ministry of Economic Development as a decentralized agency, began to study the Cerrejón area (Kline 1981: 75). For energy purposes government divided the El Cerrejón area into three zones. There are two major stories here: the first involves the central zone; the second, the northern and southern zones combined.

In 1969 the government allocated the central zone to IFI, which soon took the first step for production. In that year it negotiated a contract to buy the subsoil rights of the area from an entity designated as "the indigenous community of La Guajira." The name of this group is somewhat deceiving, since its members were not indigenous in the pre-Spanish sense. The group had supposedly owned the subsoil rights since Spanish colonial times. But subsoil rights in both colonial and independent Colombia usually belonged, in the ultimate sense, to the state, which made the status of the La Guajira community confusing. In 1969 the IFI also created *Cerrejón Carboneras*, Ltd., a commercial enterprise with the express purpose of developing the central zone (Kline 1981: 76). The legal ramifications of insulating the IFI aside, *Cerrejón Carboneras*, Ltd., is for all practical purposes the IFI on the spot in the central zone.

In 1970 *Cerrejón Carboneras* began its activities. It entered into an exploration contract with Mining and Engineering Technical Services, Ltd., of South Africa. Subsequent investigation proved coal reserves of at least 100 million tons in those areas of the central zone explored by the South African company. In December 1970, a public bidding took place for the development of the central area, but no contract emerged. Then in 1971 a private bidding was offered to six international firms. This procedure did produce an agreement. Peobody Coal, a subsidiary of Kennecott Copper, was awarded a contract (Kline 1981: 76).

The provisions of this document are important. It was a stage agreement without sufficient detail. The first stage required that Peobody undertake initial exploration, investing at least US $300,000, but it had *no* time limit. The second stage was to be mutually consensual. If both parties—*Cerrejón Carboneras* and Peobody—agreed to continue, they would enter a formal contract, which would constitute the second stage. The costs of implementing this stage would be equally divided between the two parties. The third stage was to consist of the construction and operation of the mining infrastructure in the area. At this time a final ownership arrangement was to be worked out. Each company was to have equal equity participation, but here again details are murky. That equal share for each company was to be somewhere in the 40 to 47 percent range, with the remainder to be allocated somehow to other parties that were not specified (Kline 1981: 76-77).

The time imprecision in stage one led to the unraveling of the agreement. By the mid-1970s Peobody had still not completed the first stage, which was within its rights under the agreement. But the leaders of *Cerrejón Carboneras* wanted a better deal for Colombia, in light of the realities of the post-1973 energy world. The price of oil was rocketing and coal was becoming more attractive (Kline 1981: 80).

They tried to change the agreement. They demanded that the state hold the majority of the stock. They wanted an agreement that seemed in some ways an association contract made into an arrangement that was unmistakably a joint venture, with the majority held by the state, representing the people, rather than by individual Colombians. Peobody refused. The agreement was canceled.

The outcome was different, though no less troublesome, in the northern and southern zones. In 1975 both the IFI and Ecopetrol asked the Ministry of Mines for the right to explore in these areas. Ecopetrol was awarded these territories. The IFI had submitted its request several days before Ecopetrol, but sequence apparently was not decisive in the deliberations of the Ministry of Mines. In October 1975, Ecopetrol sent letters asking for bids for the northern and southern zones to seventeen international firms. Ecopetrol suggested an approximate production target of 5 million tons per year. It enclosed a contract of the association type. This was an attempt to employ for coal a contract model that had worked in the past in Colombia for petroleum. February 1976, was the final date for entries. Six were received. Since two were proposals for service contracts and did not follow the association model, they were disregarded. At the last moment, a group of Colombian capitalists had made an offer, but it was not studied because it lacked the appropriate formalities. Of the four remaining proposals, Exxon's offered the highest royalties (Kline 1981: 78-80).

In November 1976, another important bureaucratic entity emerged. Carbocol (the Colombian National Coal Company) was founded as a "second-level" commercial and industrial enterprise of the state. In such an organization "first-level" state agencies own all the capital. For Carbocol the distribution of ownership was as follows: Ecopetrol, 49 percent; IFI (*Cerrejón Carboneras*), 40 percent; and others (Ministry of Mines), 11 percent. Carbocol received the areas of Cerrejón previously assigned to both the IFI and Ecopetrol (Kline 1981: 81). Then in December 1976 a major event occurred. Carbocol signed a contract with Intercor for the development of the northern zone. Intercor, which stands for the International Colombia Resources Corporation, is a subsidiary of Exxon, the U.S. multinational.

This contract divided into three periods. The first—exploration—was to be done in three years and undertaken completely at the risk of Intercor. At the end of this period Intercor could declare commerciality, if it found the project economically feasible. The second—installation—was to be accomplished in four years. It covered the construction of the mine facilities, a railroad from mine to port, and a port at Bahía Portete. During this stage investments were to be shared equally between Carbocol and Intercor. The third—extraction—was to begin when the first coal was loaded at the port and was to last for twenty three years. During this phase both investments and coal were to be shared equally. During both installation and production periods Intercor was to be the operator of the mine and all related facilities. It could choose all contractors and hire all employees (Kline 1981: 82).

Other aspects of the contract are important. Consider key financial details. Intercor was to pay royalties of 15 percent of its production to the Colombian government. This would come to 15 percent on 50 percent of the coal, since Intercor and Carbocol would be dividing the coal output equally. The coal would, therefore, be apportioned 57.5 percent to the government (Carbocol's 50 percent + 7.5 percent as royalty), 42.5 percent to Intercor. Intercor was to pay an income tax on its profits and a tax on those profits remitted to the exterior or repatriated. In addition, an excess profits tax was to start when Intercor's profits exceeded 35 percent of something described as its "accumulated investments." According to Intercor, its profits would be going, under this tax code, 83 percent to the government and only 17 percent to itself (Kline 1981: 82).

There was *no* mention of the amount of production in the agreement. Each partner was to be free to sell all of its coal, but each was to offer 50 percent of any contract that it might negotiate to the other. The entire operation of installation and extraction was to be governed, in theory, by an Executive Committee, which was to consist of one person chosen by Carbocol and one by Intercor. Unanimity was to be required for all decisions. Different provisions of the contract created an intriguing governance situation. As operator Intercor would choose all contractors and hire all employees. As seemingly equal member of the Executive Committee, Intercor was to be subjected to checks and balances from Carbocol. What happened next is fascinating (Kline 1981: 83).

From 1 January 1977, to 1 July 1980, Intercor carried out exploration. It declared commercial feasibility at a minimum extraction level of 15 million tons per year, which was three times the 5 million tons suggested at the bidding. It indicated the machinery to be used and the characteristics of the mining towns. It affirmed that the port would be constructed at Bahía Portete, about 150 kilometers (93 miles) from the mines. Carbocol had sixty days to reply, either accepting Intercor's conditions or asking for more information. In September 1980 Carbocol accepted (Kline 1981: 83).

This acceptance was very controversial. There were serious problems of both information and finance. All of the necessary information was not yet available. The environmental impact study, required for the agreement to be consummated, had not been submitted. The absence of this document, as well as other missing data, bothered Parsons Brinckerhoff, a New York–based firm of international consultants. This firm was assisting the Colombian government; it had been hired by the United Nations Development Program and was being supervised by the World Bank, the likely lender to the government for this project. Parsons Brinckerhoff stated that the information was not complete and Carbocol should ask for more. Finance had also become troubling. The cost of the project had inexplicably risen for its first part—before coal revenues covered costs—from US $1.5 billion to US $2.5 billion (Kline 1981: 84).

Meanwhile, back in the central zone, Carbocol had taken action. By early 1976 Peobody Coal, which refused to renegotiate its contract with *Cerrejón Carboneras* had left the country. In 1977 Carbocol began work in the central zone. It tried to use service contracts for development, which would ensure, on paper, virtually 100 percent equity participation by Colombians themselves and/or their representatives. Bidding was opened in 1979. By 1981 a contract was awarded to a Spanish-Colombian consortium.

This document linked production with time, unlike the North Cerrejón contract. Production was to begin in 1982 with 300,000 tons, rise to 700,000 tons in 1983, and from 1984 to the end of the contract in 1989 was to total 1.5 million tons per year. The consortium was to undertake all investment and import all necessary machinery at cost to itself. Carbocol was able to buy coal at the mouth of the mine but would not take over the machinery when the contract expired. Part of the coal from the central zone was destined for domestic consumption (Kline 1981: 85-86).

Neither the northern nor the central zone contracts dealt with the questions of appropriate technology or social costs. There was no clause in either that considered in detail the transfer of technology. That it would take place at all was doubtful, since Carbocol's role was insufficiently determinative. In the northern case, while on the Executive Council, Carbocol was not the operator, but at best a partial supervisor. In the central example, Carbocol would not necessarily have obtained the technical know-how to run the machinery, even if it had been able to get control of it later. The northern contract was defective in its lack of production goals or limits. Since there was no agreed upon amount for extraction in the northern contract, the question soon became how much coal, if any, would be left after twenty three years?

CONTROVERSIES OVER CONTRACTS

Both contracts became the subjects of increasingly heated controversy in Colombia. The northern document in particular triggered a widespread discussion of the basics of foreign participation in Colombian development. While both contracts were flawed, the northern agreement invited special attention because it was an association agreement. It did not give locals majority equity participation in the project. Granted, the central mix was not on the surface 100 percent Colombian, as it was a combination of Colombian and Spanish financiers who provided the capital. But it could be argued that Colombians themselves predominated or that the Spanish financiers had deep roots in Colombia or were just monetary adjuncts to the agreement. No such defense could be made of the North Cerrejón contract because it legally accorded, though in an unclear manner, equality to both Carbocol and Intercor.

The ensuing debate over the North Cerrejón contract was comprehensive. The decision to use an association contract was both defended and criticized by Colombians themselves. Some Colombians argued that the only remedy for the "chaotic" state of industry, which supposedly resulted in part from the "laziness" and "disorganization" of Colombians themselves, was more multinational involvement with appropriate safeguards. These MNCs, the argument continued, would provide organization and contribute greatly to the industrialization of the country.

While part of the problem was allegedly "laziness" and "disorganization," another supposedly came from a lack of ability among too many Colombians. Some who called for greater multinational involvement under certain conditions conceded that the "lack of ability" or capacity was itself partly the result of years of domination by mncs in the industrial sector without adequate technological transfer. But they contended that the only realistic hope for accelerating industrialization in the short term was intensified MNC participation, this time with rigorously specified conditions concerning technology transfer. It was necessary, in short, to have multinational involvement for effective industrialization, and safeguards could be devised that would ensure some transfer of technology to the country and its citizens (Angel and Navia 1983: 6).

Critics, too, had their general preferences for a more nationalistic approach to resource development, one that made greater use of local capital in conjunction with service contracts. It was in this respect—choice of contract—that the debate became more focused. Recall that the contract required a substantial up-front investment by Intercor, a sum that rose from US $1.5 billion to US $2.5 billion during exploration as estimated by that company. The contract defenders had argued from the start that the principle of association was necessary to attract a multinational partner. Where substantial front money was required, no mnc would settle for less than 50 percent of the equity and production.

Having a company completely financing exploration conferred another benefit, proponents contended. The government would not have to spend any of its funds during this risky period but would still be positioned to reap revenues when extraction went on-line. These revenues would in turn allegedly contribute to political stability, which meant in this case the maintenance in power of the decision makers, described by their critics as "oligarchical," who had brought about the agreement.

The fact that one multinational was to control all three major operations—the mine, the railroad, and the port—was deemed to be necessary by contract proponents. They buttressed this part of their defense by suggesting that the ability of the Colombian government to organize at least one of these enterprises—the railroad—was nonexistent, in view of the alleged disarray of the national railway system. Carbocol could not be assigned the mining railway operations, since this division of labor would supposedly create conflicts as all three operations were interconnected.

Critics answered that the contract was grievously flawed. Since many of these people saw Colombia as a "victim" of multinational involvement in unison with the "ruling oligarchy," they argued that this contract further favored this relationship. Even though critical of the government in many respects, they contended that it should have control, which the association contract did not confer (Angel and Navia 1983: 7).

This particular association contract had other problems, critics suggested. The risk factor in the case of El Cerrejón coal was not as great as some believed, certainly not as high as that associated with oil and natural gas exploration in Colombia. Therefore, the terms of the contract were too favorable to Intercor, and possibly the government itself might have undertaken a greater financial role in the first phase. Contrary to proponents' repeated statements about the need to have stricter safeguards guaranteeing technological transfer, these provisions in the North Cerrejón contract were not rigorously specified.

Critics further argued that other multinationals were willing to participate with minority equity shares in a joint venture approach to El Cerrejón coal. An association contract with one major partner was an unwise narrowing of the pool of potential international involvement. In cases where international participation is deemed essential, Colombia should devise a diversified arrangement that avoids an over-reliance on one international partner. Joint venture contracts with multiple foreign members may, therefore, be appropriate in certain cases.

Critics also vigorously questioned the wisdom of having so long a production period in the contract (twenty three years). Differences between multinational and state goals were likely to emerge in a harmful fashion over the long term. The state could possibly face situations in which the multinational partner would gain bargaining leverage from the fact that the government was locked in for so long.

As debate intensified, other criticisms sharpened. Exploration should have been done by a company other than the one that was awarded the contract for installation and extraction. It was alleged that Intercor, as the recipient of the total contract, could present the information from exploration in a way that favored its own interests. Exxon could overcharge by increasing prices on imported machinery for which the state had to pay 50 percent of the cost. If this were done, the cost to Colombians would be higher than it should have been. Exxon by transferring prices could also hurt Colombia's investment. Were Exxon to charge more than the "real value" for the use of the railway, Carbocol would supposedly suffer extensive losses. Some calculated that by the year 2008, assuming production of 15 million tons per year, Exxon could, by overcharging US $50 a ton for transport, "steal" US $750 million every year (Kline 1983: 16-17).

It was further claimed that Exxon was paying low royalties. Since the minimum production quota rose from 5 million to 15 million tons a year, so should the scale of royalties be raised, critics contended. They asked for a revision of the contract here, but it was never carried out. Some estimate that Colombia may have lost about US $8.3 billion by not obtaining an adjustment of royalty payments (Kline 1983: 20). To strengthen their case in this regard, critics cite the fact that other multinationals interested in El Cerrejón coal had supposedly proposed higher royalties after the contract with Intercor had been signed. These more generous figures may have been exercises in public relations, if the non-participating companies thought the contract was set. But if one company or more believed that there was a possibility of contract revision, then the higher numbers may have been part of a strategy to bring that about.

Exxon had allegedly received excessively favorable tax and tariff treatment. The relevant tax and tariff laws were approved by the Colombian Congress before the contract was signed. Critics charged that because of the low rates to which Exxon would be subjected, the country would lose another US $42.3 billion dollars. Some asserted that when the tax and tariff laws were being debated in the Congress, Exxon's lobbying efforts were powerful and efficient. Others complained that many government officials had been bribed. President Turbay was sometimes included in these allegations. As one opposition saying went, "Some Colombian leaders, probably including the Minister of Mines, wear Exxon T-shirts" (Kline 1983: 19).

Contract defenders did not let these attacks go unanswered. On the question of price manipulation, they said that it would be difficult for Intercor to transfer prices by overcharging railroad rates, since there is nothing mysterious about these rates. The contract was signed at a time when Exxon had offered the highest royalties. To stand by a signed contract was a matter of national integrity, even if others at a later date had proposed higher royalty payments. As to the issue of tax and tariff undercharges, the laws generating these rate structures were incorporated into Colombia's legal system prior to the contract's approval.

Defenders stressed the significant economic gains for Colombia that would come during the lifetime of the contract. For a country that was legally monocultural (coffee exports) and practically bicultural (coffee and drug exports) it would be advantageous to have another major source of income, one that was not part of the "underground economy." Coal exports would help reduce the large deficits the country was running on its international balance of payments. The government would have money to reduce its operating deficits. The multiplier and accelerator effects, two techniques economists employ to measure the overall impact of spending a certain amount of money, would significantly boost economic activity in the environs of the mines and throughout the country.

Increased employment because of the project is one outstanding example of those ripple effects. About 8,000 people were to be employed in the initial construction of the mine, railroad, and port. The work force was to stabilize later at about 4,000 people. It was agreed that 96 percent of those employed had to be Colombians. Contract enthusiasts estimated that about 100,000 to 200,000 additional jobs would be created because of the multiplier effect. Local industry would also benefit, as a very high percentage of the construction subcontracts was being allocated to Colombians and a significant amount of the materials used was coming from within the country. Local subcontracting and materials purchasing did take place (Kline 1983: 22).

Critics found the 96 to 4 employment ratio between locals and expatriates misleading. While 96 percent of the total labor force would be Colombian, the other 4 percent of foreigners would occupy the top managerial and technical staff. This distribution would have grave consequences for Colombia when the contract ended, critics alleged, because Colombians themselves would still not be able to run the project (Kline 1983: 24). Well into the installation period Intercor still had located its main office out of the state of La Guajira, in that of Barranquilla. This lack of proximity deprived the mines and environs of some of the immediate direct and indirect economic benefits. Intercor and Carbocol did take steps to train thousands of La Guajirans to take jobs in the operation. And the government moved to stimulate general industrial development in La Guajira state so that the local economy could more effectively provide for the needs of the operation.

The effects of all the operations on La Guajira itself received special attention from the participants in the debate. Supporters of the contract argued that implementation would bring the possibility of cracking down on the illegal marijuana industry. Greater access to its environment would supposedly disrupt the normal trading routes used by the Mafia and jeopardize the very large-scale operations of that organization. As a replacement for the economic stimulus supplied by the drug trade, the project might possibly bring about an increase in tourism and commerce, stimulated by the road that was to be built alongside the railway.

La Guajira might be the point of departure for economic vitalization in two more respects. The project's railway could be the beginning of a network extending to the interior of the country, which would open up the possibility of shipping coal from the interior to Bahía Portete on the Atlantic Ocean. The revenues realized from the project might go in part to the establishment of industries in the areas of gasification and liquefication of coal in El Cerrejón and beyond. Development of these related enterprises would extend the useful life of some of El Cerrejón's coal.

Critics were as unrelenting here as they were elsewhere in the debate. The benefits cited for El Cerrejón were suspect. Some maintained that disrupting the cultivation and trading of marijuana would irreparably damage the only true industry of La Guajira. Extending the project's railway into the interior would again raise the problem of overcharging by Intercor for use of the 150 kilometers of track that it oversaw. Overcharging would have even more serious implications in this case, since it would affect products coming from the interior of the country. As to enterprises designed to prolong the useful life of the coal, critics wondered again about the coal itself. They asked not only how much would be left at the expiration of the contract but also if any remained, how accessible would it be.

All this discussion of the North Cerrejón coal contract did prompt reconsideration. The government decided to go ahead with the contract, nevertheless, mainly since Exxon was willing to invest so much money in the country. The hope was that any problems could be solved along the way.

9

Tourism in the Bahamas: Foreign Capital and the Creation of Freeport

Dennis M. P. McCarthy
with Peter W. Deveaux-Isaacs

Tourism has been touted as an economic development strategy in many quarters. But relying heavily on foreign capital to create tourist complexes can entrench dependent relations of various kinds. The host country can become too reliant on outside sources for financing and skills. The Bahamas, which gained legal independence from Great Britain in 1973, experienced these types of dependency in connection with the development of Freeport on Grand Bahama Island.

In 1955 the British colonial administration headquartered in Nassau entered into an agreement with Wallace Groves, a U.S. businessman with a tarnished reputation, that laid the basis for the emergence of Freeport, the "second city" of the Bahamas. Known as the Hawksbill Creek Agreement, this document gave Groves land at bargain prices and other concessions thought necessary to establish a tourist complex. How the Hawksbill Creek Agreement originated, what its provisions were, and how it affected the people of the Bahamas are all concerns of this case study. Relations between expatriate (foreign) and local labor are spotlighted to illustrate skill dependency. The development of Freeport relegated local labor to the most menial and least powerful jobs while assigning the more skilled and better paying positions to foreigners.

This case study of accelerated development through foreign investment and tourism has international significance. A number of countries in Africa, Asia, and Latin America are today considering tourism as a beginning or greater feature in their development plans. This case study does not rule out tourism as a possible approach; however, it does strongly suggest that the details of tourism, especially the impact on the local labor force, be as fully thought out as possible in advance of binding contractual decisions.

BACKGROUND

After World War II, several events occurred that set the stage for the Hawksbill Creek Agreement. Treasure from a Spanish galleon, valued at over $1 million, was found about a mile off the coast of Nassau, which is on New Providence Island, about 130 miles south of Grand Bahama Island. This discovery, along with careful planning, advertising, and the opening of two offices in Toronto and New York, generated a significant tourist trade. Travelers, mainly from the United States and Canada, entered the islands in great numbers, usually in the environs of Nassau. This traffic underscored the potential of the Bahamian archipelago for tourism.

Besides the tourist boom, another important happening was the initiation of a more planned approach to development. The decision for more planning followed several studies on the British Caribbean, the most important of which was the *Moyne Report*. Though Atlantic islands, the Bahamas were included within the sweep of these Caribbean documents. The planning that British bureaucrats had in mind featured industrial incentive programs in their Caribbean basin territories, wherever feasible. These were designed to stimulate investment in local industry by both local and foreign business people. Business was to play a crucial role in the colonial development planning that was envisioned for Britain's part of the Caribbean basin. In the Bahamas it turned out that foreign business people, in fact one businessman, exerted great influence on local development. The Hawksbill Creek Agreement of 1955 was one such industrial incentive program, and Wallace Groves was the point man for deepening foreign involvement in the Bahamas.

WALLACE GROVES AND THE "BAY STREET BOYS"

Groves had a fascinating though sullied business background, but he was a man of vision. A U.S. citizen, he had been active on Wall Street, perhaps excessively so, as he was convicted of securities mail fraud in 1941. He was a frequent visitor to the islands and liked the environment so much that he had made a home in Little Whale Cay (key). In 1946 he bought a pulpwood lumber operation on Grand Bahama and concentrated on the "development" prospects of this island. At first he appears to have thought only about constructing a resort for himself and his wife. But he soon grasped the significance of Grand Bahama's strategic location: about 70 miles east of Florida, ideally situated on key western hemisphere shipping lanes, and reasonably close to markets in North America, the Caribbean, and Latin America. He conceived the idea of a custom-free manufacturing and trading area for Grand Bahama, which might bring riches to himself, Grand Bahama, and the islands as a whole.

He explored his notion with the government of the Bahamas, which was then greatly influenced by the "Bay Street Boys." This was a group of powerful British businessmen, the location of whose businesses in Nassau gave them their popular name. Several of the "Bay Street Boys" usually sat on the Executive Council, through which the governor ruled. In the Bahamas this council, unlike similar agencies in other British territories, did exert considerable force on the direction of policy. In fact, it was the governor in consultation with his Executive Council that signed the Hawksbill Creek Agreement in 1955 with Wallace Groves. Sir Roland T. Symonette and Sir Stafford Sands, two prominent "Bay Street Boys," were most instrumental in bringing about this agreement. Whether any of these people knew about Groves's criminal background remains an unanswered question. What is clear is the nature of the agreement.

THE HAWKSBILL CREEK AGREEMENT OF 1955

Wallace Groves, representing the Grand Bahama Port Authority (PA), proposed to establish a port and an industrial complex in the vicinity of Hawksbill Creek on Grand Bahama Island. The government of the Bahamas contracted to sell 50,000 acres of land to the PA at the nominal price of 1 British pound sterling per acre. The PA further agreed to purchase an additional 80 acres of land in the Hawksbill area from private owners, and arrangements were made to secure 1,420 acres more. Still other transactions occurred. In 1958 the PA contracted to buy another 40,000 acres from the British Crown, again at the price of 1 pound per acre. This was a conditional purchase agreement: the PA had to spend 1 million pounds on developing the existing port area within three years. By 1960, the PA had invested about 2 million pounds and was therefore able to take control of 40,000 more acres at bargain prices. This acquisition brought the PA's total holdings to almost 139,000 acres. It is this land that officially became known as Freeport.

Land was only part of the agreement. The government furnished other generous incentives. The PA was to be exempt from customs duties on all building materials, supplies, and other products necessary for the dredging and construction of the port area. The PA would not have to pay duties on manufacturing or administrative supplies. These clauses were important, as customs duties were (and are) the principal source of national revenue. The government's largesse extended to other taxes. For thirty years, no personal property taxes or levies on capital gains were to be imposed or extracted within the port area or upon any personal property within it. For that same time period, the government agreed not to collect taxes on the earnings of the PA, or a licensee operating in the port area and outside the colony. For its part the PA agreed to provide certain educational and medical services, furnish rent-free living and office accommodations for government personnel, and abide by the laws of the Commonwealth of the Bahamas.

The vagueness of those clauses concerning educational and medical services proved the harbinger of worse things to come for the local labor force. These people by and large had not been adequately prepared to perform well a number of the tasks associated with the creation and development of Freeport, a project that represented at the time high-technology industrialization. A major cause of widespread inadequate preparation was the British colonial educational system. It was very selective: there was a constant "weeding out of the crop." As a result two groups emerged from this process. The first was a small elite, which managed to make it through all the winnowings. The second was the great majority, largely uneducated in a formal sense beyond the grammar school level and unskilled in technical fields. The trades that the system did encourage, such as masonry, carpentry, and plumbing, were a holdover from the "apprenticeship system" that was instituted after the abolition of slavery in 1834. Building Freeport required other types of skilled workers, in addition to masons, carpenters, and plumbers. Satisfying the demands for many kinds of skilled workers brought about an inequitable situation for the indigenous labor force.

The PA argued that if it were to succeed, it had to find a source of "qualified laborers." And it wanted to know whether the impact of the "developing process" would be borne by government or by foreign or local investment. At the time these issues were intensifying in the early 1960s, some facts, or perceptions of them, were working against a solution that would have upgraded the local labor force. The government then apparently had little money in its treasury for spending on enhanced technical education or anything else. The Bahamas had a population of fewer than 150,000 and there was the perception in decision-making quarters that "full employment" was commonplace. It is more likely that widespread underemployment, in which many people perform tasks that are not really full-time jobs, was the rule. In any event, the Hawksbill Creek Agreement did not specifically commit the PA to the educational upgrading necessary to train local workers at the required levels. The indigenous labor force was seen as unsuitable or otherwise occupied. And the PA was in a big hurry.

THE IMMIGRATION ACT OF 1963

The result of these conditions was the government passage of the first Immigration Act concerning the PA. Passed on 20 December 1963, this act supplied a major part of the answer to the PA's inquiry as to who or what would bear the impact of the "developing process." The local labor force was to bear a disproportionate share of the costs coming from that process and benefit only marginally. This act empowered the PA to employ any qualified or skilled foreigner it felt would help in developing Freeport. The government's Immigration Department would not interfere in the PA's decision to hire a person, unless that individual had a criminal record. This proviso was ironic, since Wallace Groves himself possessed one. The 1963 Immigration Act was not on paper the virtual carte blanche for the PA that it became in practice. Section 3 appears to sketch a mechanism whereby the PA would notify the government of the workers required and the administration would then try to recruit them, perhaps locally. But if the government did not meet the target, the PA or its licensee would have the right to import the number of laborers that the administration was unable to produce. Nobody had to worry about making that mechanism work. Foreign labor was usually preferred right away for those skilled posts, just as foreign investment was to finance the birth of Freeport.

THE LABOR REVOLUTION AND THE TOURIST BOOM

The Hawksbill Creek Agreement (1955), reinforced by the Immigration Act (1963), set off a labor revolution in Freeport. Expatriate workers, skilled and qualified in industrial capacities, came from many countries to work for the PA; the majority were from England and the United States. These foreigners supervised the "less skilled" local labor in the Freeport area, an arrangement not designed to ensure harmony. The government had tried, with Section 3 of the 1963 Act, to obtain some security for the average Bahamian worker, but that laborer was the less formally skilled, and bound to become entrenched in secondary and tertiary roles as the "development process" unfolded. Still, for several years following the implementation of the 1963 Act, most Bahamian workers seemed satisfied, or chose not to vent their displeasure, with their own situation, which repeated the pattern of the 1950s.

And it was difficult to protest too loudly, if at all, during the immediate aftermath of the 1963 Act because Freeport began to boom. Tourism had increased to 1 million people by 1964, which represented a 20 percent increase from 1963 and almost a 100 percent rise from 1960. The government was very pleased and allowed the PA to promote, in addition to the factories and industrial undertakings in Freeport, the establishment of other enterprises outside of the port area that might benefit the Bahamas as a whole economically. The PA took advantage of this decision and opened business offices and other companies throughout the Bahamas, especially in Grand Bahama and Nassau. These activities also contributed to the influx of foreign workers, as people involved in construction and hotel management, accountants, lawyers, doctors, and others were brought into Freeport, Nassau, and elsewhere. By the mid-1960s expatriate labor could be seen almost everywhere. Most foreign investors at that time began to predict future prosperity for the islands and began to invest greater sums of money.

The prosperity was magnetizing. People from Caribbean islands like Jamaica and Barbados became aware of what was happening in the Bahamas. Some people from these islands, particularly Haiti, entered the country illegally, others legally, in an attempt to capture some of this prosperity for themselves. Other Bahamians wished to participate for the first time. In the midst of this boom many people on the out islands of the Bahamas, those other than New Providence, were still pursuing their seafaring livelihood, which often depended on the sponge. This industry, which had been profitable for at least forty-five years (1920–1965), collapsed when the sponges were afflicted with some unknown disease. Some of these fishermen became aware of the "other economic boom" generated mostly by expatriates, the large investments, and the increasing number of tourists, which had gone up by more than 1.5 million in 1966. They, too, wanted some of the prosperity for themselves.

There were now four types of workers in the Bahamian labor force. First, there was a large number of expatriate workers brought in by government but primarily by the Port Authority. These included bankers, doctors, lawyers, engineers, geologists, architects, managers, supervisors, and technicians. Second, there was a moderate number of skilled and qualified Bahamian workers, who had acquired some knowledge and skill at institutions and universities mainly in England and the United States. There were Bahamians in all of those above mentioned expatriate job categories, but not nearly as many as there were foreigners. Third, there was a large number of manual Bahamian workers, augmented by the influx of Out Island Bahamians. These included carpenters, masons, fishermen, and custodians. Though not unskilled in the true sense, these laborers lacked the skills that result from years of technical education and are essential to the industrialization process. Fourth, there was a moderate but increasing number of manual laborers from such places as Jamaica, Barbados, and especially Haiti.

It seemed as if the prosperity would never end. Up until 1966, matters moved along smoothly. More tourists came into the Bahamas, investors had high expectations of obtaining large profits, and more foreign workers entered the labor force. But there was great latent dissatisfaction among many Bahamians with the results of this process. National income was increasing, but the average Bahamian laborer found that his or her share of the returns from this expansion was much, much less than that of the expatriate worker. Though this gross differential was galling enough, the situation was made thornier by the fact that many Bahamian workers had been relegated to a position of even greater inferiority in their own country.

THE CRYSTALLIZATION OF DISSATISFACTION

In 1966 dissatisfaction began to crystallize. Bahamians questioned more openly the right of the Port Authority to bring workers into the colony when they maintained that they could do the work themselves, given the proper training and opportunity. This rising call for greater Bahamianization of the labor force extended to all positions, high executive posts as well as seemingly more ordinary jobs. Also in 1966 the colonial government of the Bahamas, which did not officially receive its legal independence from Great Britain until 1973, began to respond seriously to the more publicly articulated requests for greater Bahamianization. It began an educational drive. Higher education had not been completely stagnant in the Bahamas during the 1950s and 1960s, as many parliamentary members were able to finance some family members through university education. But it was a trickle, not a flow, of graduates. In 1966 the government acted to create that flow. With the treasury showing a surplus, the Board of Education started issuing scholarships for the first time. Most importantly for the future of the Bahamas, its most authentic citizens, also in 1966, took specific steps in the political process to bring about major change. In that year the Progressive Liberal Party (PLP), a predominantly black organization, announced that it would mount a serious electoral challenge to the United Bahamian Party (UBP), the political vehicle of the influential "Bay Street Boys."

THE ELECTION OF 1967, BLACK POWER, AND EXAMINATION OF THE EXPATRIATE ROLE IN DEVELOPMENT

The general elections of 1967 brought to power for the first time in the history of the Bahamas a government that was largely black. In the campaign the PLP had accused the "Bay Street Boys" of having stereotypes about blacks. It argued that the government had not educated many blacks in the past because it was believed that they could not be educated. The PLP also suggested that the government's advertised educational drive, begun in 1966, was too little, too late and, in any event, copied its own platform. As both opposition and new government the PLP promised many things to many people, but concentrated on two issues. Its first priority was education; it also pledged to improve the labor conditions prevailing in the colony at that time.

As to its educational promise, in 1967 more people went off to technical schools and universities than ever before. Concerning labor conditions, the government, headed by Prime Minister Lynden O. Pindling of the PLP, passed a key amendment in 1967 to the Immigration Act of 1963. Section 9 of the amendment stipulated, in its essentials, that businesses and companies should make a major effort to employ Bahamian-born persons, if they are available and willing to work, and also to train them to fill "high positions of employment" in the colony.

An important report then appeared in the following year, which intensified debate over the imbalance in the labor force. In 1968, Clapp and Mayne, Inc., U.S. management consultants, surveyed the number of people employed in the first quarter of 1968 in establishments with five or more employees in Freeport. The results troubled many. In no occupational group did Bahamian-born people or those who had acquired Bahamian status together make up at least 50 percent of the labor force. This was true, though, only for Freeport. The islands as a whole did not reflect such domination by various groups of outsiders—expatriates, Haitians, and residents. Freeport itself had become excessively non-Bahamian, and the government regarded this situation with great apprehension.

The PA's position was, however, at best gradualist. Using the Clapp-Mayne survey and assuming a context of near-full employment that seemed to prevail, the PA argued that there were not enough Bahamians or people of Bahamian status, either in numbers or in skills and proficiencies, to maintain the economy at its present level, let alone permit its expansion. The PA and other licensees offered to help the government to educate Bahamians by offering scholarships to technical institutions and universities. The PA endorsed the principle that qualified, competent Bahamians and persons of Bahamian status should be preferred over non-Bahamians for any and every employment. But, and this was a major endorsement of the status quo, to satisfy labor requirements it would still be necessary to continue to attract and permit non-Bahamians to enter and take up work.

THE IMMIGRATION ACT OF 1968 AND BAHAMIANIZATION

The government favored the higher education policy of the PA and other licensees. It was not satisfied with the unrestricted continuation in practice of expatriate immigration to fill choice slots in the labor force. It, therefore, enacted another major Immigration Act in 1968, which affected all businesses but had a special impact on the PA. This act, which covered both skilled and nonskilled workers, considerably tightened the conditions pertaining to the employment of expatriate labor in the Bahamas. Expatriate contracts were limited to a period of three years, with a maximum renewal of three more years, with the consent of government. The act also contained explicit provisions about the government's right to investigate expatriate workers and exclude whomever it wished from the Bahamas. This power of exclusion included those recruited but not yet arrived as well as those already present and working.

In these connections the language of the act is couched in terms of "undesirable" persons. But "undesirable" was never defined, and this vagueness proved most detrimental to foreign workers, both prospective and actual. Many permits to enter and work were denied and some workers were asked to leave the colony under the "undesirability" proviso. The PA continually complained about the restrictions placed on immigration. The government, in some cases of exclusion, appears to have been motivated by rumors that certain "shady" underworld characters were controlling the famous gambling casino in Freeport.

It took some time for the acceleration of higher education for Bahamians and the reduction of local working opportunities for expatriates to take full effect. The PA had in 1970, two years after the passage of the restrictive Immigration Act, essentially restated its gradualist position concerning Bahamianization, but it sharpened its analysis of the impact of government actions. The delay or refusal of work contracts "without good reasons" would hinder the progress of the Bahamas and "tend to discredit the government." These warnings notwithstanding, the government persisted. The recently created Labor Department, working along with the immigration office, refused most work permit applications, and when granted, these were usually not renewed. As more Bahamians returned from their advanced schooling abroad, the Bahamianization of high working positions accelerated. There was still a role for expatriate labor in the Bahamas, especially for school teachers and others brought in by the government itself. On the whole, though, the foreign labor force was sharply contracting.

But Pindling's Bahamianization—secure the Bahamas for Bahamians—did not involve reducing every outside component of the labor force. The role of Haitians stands as an intriguing counterpoint to the overall trend toward diminution. When Haitians began to enter the Bahamas in greater numbers in the 1960s, the government tried to keep as many of them out as possible. Total exclusion proved impossible: there are 700 islands in the Bahamian archipelago, much coastline is not patrolled, and Haiti is not far away. And it soon became obvious that their labor was needed. Many Bahamian workers longed for a job in which they could at least act or appear to be "high class," which included dressing in a suit, necktie, and so on. Many refused to do jobs deemed to be "lower class," such as collecting garbage, cleaning yards, and the like. So as Bahamian workers sought seemingly more prestigious positions, the less desirable but no less critical posts were filled by Haitians.

Nor was Bahamianization cost free. Disputes concerning immigration began to have a significant cumulative effect by the mid-1970s. Until that time, tourism and many other businesses had been flourishing, but the growing acrimony eventually poisoned the investment climate. Many investors concluded that there was excessive risk involved in keeping their money in the Bahamas and began withdrawing it. Prospective investors shied away because of perceived conditions of instability. Banks reported a decline in the number and value of deposits and savings accounts. Business slowed down throughout the financial squeeze and some companies closed down. Tourism dropped for the first time since 1960. The Bahamas slipped into recession. The government then faced the tasks of restoring a favorable climate while preserving the essential features of Bahamianization. To some extent it succeeded in doing both, though foreign investors were understandably more selective and cautious. They knew that the unrestrained post–Hawksbill Creek days would never return.

This agreement did set in motion a series of largely unanticipated events that changed the nature of Bahamian society and as such provides an opportunity to reflect on the merits and demerits of tourism as a development strategy. It is clear that the colonial government of the Bahamas, whatever its rhetoric, did not have the best interests of the country at heart in its relationships with Wallace Groves and the Port Authority. One may reasonably argue about what were the "best interests" of the Bahamas in the 1950s, but there is no doubt whose interests the controlling United Bahamian Party (UBP), dominated by the "Bay Street Boys," had in mind. It is reported that this group—Sir Roland Symonette, Sir Stafford Sands, Harold Christie, Norman Soleman, and others—received over $2 million in "consultation fees" from Groves and the PA. In return they practically gave Freeport away to foreign financiers who subsequently made millions from its resale. So much for massive investment deals decided mainly on the narrow business interests of those immediately involved in the negotiations, with little or no reference to the broader environmental impact and its implications in the near, medium, and long term.

CAUTIONS AND QUESTIONS

Tourism has a potentially disruptive effect on the social and cultural fabric of any country. Proposals to create resort towns, which are usually off limits to the locals either legally or financially, should be thoroughly thought through before any decision to proceed is made. Moreover, before introducing any kind of development program a variety of studies should be undertaken, including those dealing with demographics and labor. People need jobs, but speedy programs designed to alleviate what appears to be unemployment or underemployment may have serious social and cultural repercussions. In the case of the Bahamas, the Hawksbill Creek Agreement created a foreign enclave in Freeport and resulted in the alienation of Bahamians from their booming second city.

There are a number of questions arising from this case study that deserve further research and analysis. For one, the exact relationship between the disputes over restricted immigration, associated with the implementation of the 1968 Act, and the downswing of the Bahamian economy in the mid-1970s requires more study. Was acrimony the only major factor weakening investor confidence? Was investor confidence the only relevant variable here? Might a downside have naturally occurred after such a powerful and long-lived upside?

A second set of issues relates to the Port Authority. Could the PA have accomplished its goals, albeit over more time, without relying so heavily on expatriate labor? What happened to the PA's worker training program? If some expatriate labor was necessary, as was conceded by the actions of the government itself in bringing in school teachers and other specialists, what was a proper ratio between indigenous and expatriate labor in various job categories? That is, what ratio would have most facilitated the achievement of two essential goals that involve trade-offs—spurring economic growth and protecting the social and cultural fabric.

The central conclusion that the Freeport evidence vividly illustrates is that any approach to development must conform to a country's own unique historical circumstances. Planners, business people, and other potential investors should not borrow models from other countries and mindlessly try to superimpose them on a particular country, region, or locality. They should strive to ascertain what those unique historical circumstances are and when borrowing from others be very selective and adapt with maximum sensitivity and preparation those imported aspects to local conditions. It would have been interesting to see what would have happened had the indigenous Bahamian labor force been better prepared for the introduction of high-technology industrialization.

10

Vignette: International Business and Economic Integration: The U.S.-Mexico Free Trade Act

Important attempts at economic integration are unfolding, sometimes with difficulty throughout the western hemisphere. The U.S.-Canada Free Trade Act began on 1 January 1989. A southern cone common market (*mercosur*) may embrace Brazil, Argentina, Uruguay, and Paraguay sometime in the 1990s. On 26 March 1991 the presidents of these four countries signed the Treaty of Asunción, which pledges the formation of a tariff-free common market by January 1995 (*FT* 26 March 1991: 18). In December 1991, members decided to create an arbitration tribunal whose decisions will be binding (*FT* 19 December 1991: 6). Chile, a natural geographical candidate, has spurned the southern cone common market and opted for a free trade agreement with the United States (*FT* 26 March 1991: 18). The Caribbean Economic Community (Caricom) remains committed to a customs union, but its thirteen members are having problems implementing a common external tariff wall. Significant policy differences exist between the "more developed" members (Jamaica, Trinidad and Tobago, Barbados, and Guyana) and the "less advanced" (some smaller islands in the eastern Caribbean and Belize on the Central American mainland) (*FT* 25 April 1991: 3). In 1990, U.S. President George Bush proposed "Enterprise for the Americas," a prospective free trade zone stretching from Alaska to Tierra del Fuego. This zone would receive U.S. investment and government debt relief (*FT* 26 March 1991: 18). The five countries of the Andean Pact have accelerated their economic integration. On 19 May 1991 the presidents of Bolivia, Colombia, Ecuador, Peru, and Venezuela set a 1995 deadline for forming a regional common market (*NYT* 20 May 1991: C9).

The Andean Pact originated in the dissatisfaction of some members of the old Latin American Free Trade Association (LAFTA) with the policies of that organization. Five nations originally signed the Cartagena Agreement on 26 May

1969, which created the Andean Pact. These were Bolivia, Chile, Colombia, Ecuador, and Peru. Venezuela joined in 1973; Chile withdrew in 1976. A conviction had grown among the countries that formed the Andean Pact that LAFTA was benefitting disproportionately its big three: Argentina, Brazil, and Mexico. The aggrieved members of LAFTA felt that the "big three" were getting more out of that organization than they were (LaValley 1983: 1).

The Andean Pact, named after the mountain chain that runs 4,500 miles from northern Colombia south to Cape Horn, began as a customs union. Its members pledged to harmonize their economic and social policies, foreign trade regulations, and standards for treating foreign investments. The Treaty of Cartagena, reflecting the surging economic nationalism of its time, forbade foreign investment in the steel industry and endorsed nationalization as a legitimate policy tool. In the early 1970s some member states did nationalize the operations of some multinational companies within their borders. In 1970 Peru nationalized the local businesses of the International Petroleum Corporation (IPC) and the International Telephone and Telegraph Corporation (ITT). Bolivia nationalized Gulf Oil. And in 1971 Chile nationalized its copper mines, owned 49 percent by Kennecott and Anaconda, two U.S. multinationals (*Newsweek* 11 October 1971: 77).

As time went by, hostility toward international businesses diminished. By the mid-1980s countries in Central and South America (and indeed elsewhere) were actively seeking foreign investment, which was no longer viewed as a zero-sum game. More people were concluding that both international business and the host country gained from many foreign investments, though not necessarily in equal shares in every instance. In 1984 the United States and Ecuador negotiated an agreement to get around the Andean Pact's then strict guidelines for treating foreign capital. In 1985 the United States and Colombia entered into a similar pact. Talks continued between the United States and other Andean Pact members to prepare the way for a mutually beneficial multinational presence in their countries.

The spirit of greater cooperation that characterizes many hemispheric economic relationships faced a difficult test in trade talks that produced a North American Free Trade Agreement (NAFTA) in 1992. President George Bush received from the U.S. Congress the authority to negotiate a comprehensive free trade agreement with Mexico. This is the so-called fast track legislation that permits Congress to vote any eventual agreement up or down but not become involved in negotiating its details. Canada, already a free trade partner of the United States, participated in the discussions along with Mexico and the United States. These talks yielded not only a U.S.-Mexico Free Trade Agreement but also a free trade agreement among Canada, Mexico, and the United States; that is, a North American Free Trade Agreement.

Mexico has much to bring and gain from a free trade pact with the United

States and Canada. Mexico has a growing population, which exceeds 85 million people. It has important natural resources, including significant supplies of oil. It already has an established and growing industrial base. Mexican industrialization has gone beyond the numerous assembly plants, known as *maquilladoras*, in northern Mexico, which began to emerge in the early 1980s. From imported parts these plants put together largely finished products, which are then exported. In 1989 the *maquilladoras* accounted for only 30 percent of Mexico's $12.5 billion in manufacturing exports. Now such companies as Ford, General Motors, Nissan, Volkswagen, and Chrysler are "putting down deeper roots" and carrying out most of the manufacturing process in Mexico. These companies are succeeding in this phase of an industrialization that uses foreign investment constructively because they are tapping into a hitherto neglected segment of the Mexican labor force. There are thousands of Mexicans with little manufacturing experience but who are graduates of technical and vocational schools. Foreign capital together with this skilled local labor force have helped to double Mexico's manufacturing exports since 1985 (*NYT* 25 September 1990: C1; C2). Its people, natural resources, and established industrial tradition give Mexico a substantial base upon which to continue building. The extent of Mexico's potential may be a secret to some, but a number of U.S. corporations and some Japanese firms have already given Mexico a significant role in their overseas investment strategies.

Mexico has problems that other nations in the hemisphere share: a burdensome international debt and an excessively large public sector. It has taken action on both fronts. These initiatives come from the government of President Carlos Salinas de Gortari, who assumed the presidency on 1 December 1988. To reduce Mexico's $93 billion foreign debt, his administration negotiated a historic debt accord. This agreement forces about 500 banks, which hold a significant portion of that international debt, to choose one of several options. A creditor bank can either reduce the principal of its loans by 35 percent, or accept a fixed interest rate of 6.25 percent on the unpaid principal, or work out new loans. Most banks appear to have chosen the first or second option—debt reduction or servicing readjustment. The debt accord restored investor confidence in the Mexican economy. The president estimated that about $3 billion in capital that had fled the country returned to Mexico by the end of 1989. From May through October 1989 Mexico received commitments for foreign investment projects worth about $2 billion and foreign investment has continued to increase (*NYT* 2 November 1989: 23).

Like Argentina and Brazil, Mexico seeks to reduce the size of its public sector. President Salinas de Gortari is committed to fostering a market economy through deregulation and privatization. On 2 May 1990, he sent to the Mexican Congress a constitutional amendment that would reprivatize the country's banking system, which had been in state hands since 1982, and allow private interests to set up new financial institutions. Since taking office he has liberalized the foreign investment code, significantly lowered tariffs, and put state-owned companies like Mexicana Airlines and the telephone company TelMex up for auction (*NYT* 3 May 1990: C1). Mexico's privatization program has proven to be one of the world's most successful. In fewer than three years the government sold 160 companies for about $13 billion. In late 1991 the government began the severest test of privatization to date—the sale of three state-owned steel companies (*FT* 6 November 1991: 24).

In agreeing to consider negotiations for a free trade agreement with the United States, President Salinas de Gortari made another move in line with his philosophy. This decision represents an enormous political gamble for the president, since it signals the most important break with the policy of economic nationalism that has prevailed in Mexico since the Revolution of 1910 (*NYT* 29 March 1990: 1). His decision to take seriously a possible free trade pact with the United States set off a spirited debate in Mexico.

A Mexico-U.S. agreement would have to take into account sensitive issues between those two nations. The U.S. government expects a trade agreement to intensify cooperation with Mexico in the energy sector. Mexico exports about half of its 2.5 million barrels of oil daily. The United States buys about 60 percent of those exports, Japan 15 percent, and Europe most of the rest. In the Persian Gulf crisis Mexico agreed to lift overall exports by 100,000 barrels to help ease pressure on global oil supplies (*NYT* 14 September 1990: C1). But the United States will have to respect Mexico's sensitivity on the energy question. It is not likely that U.S. business people will ever participate directly in oil and gas exploration, for fifty years the exclusive preserve of the state-owned *Petroleos Mexicanos* or Pemex (*FT* 11 June 1992: 5). President Salinas de Gortari can break with the Mexican tradition of economic nationalism in crucial ways, but he can not eradicate its wellsprings, which are concerned with guarding the basic resources of the country. One suggested solution in the energy area is a financial mechanism, like a trust fund established in a Mexican bank with which Mexican operators would carry out drilling activities. In the energy area, then, there would be cross-border circulation of capital but not entrepreneurial ability (*NYT* 14 September 1990: C1; C6).

Concerns over the unrestricted circulation of people complicate U.S.-Mexican relations in other ways. Mexico had wanted to push for the freer movement of both workers and goods, but the United States warned that this could doom the talks. The United States won this point and immigration was not negotiated. Organized labor in the United States opposes any agreement because it fears that more Mexicans will be able to reside legally in the United States and more U.S. jobs will be lost to Mexicans working in their own country.

Other groups have joined organized labor in a coalition to oppose a free trade pact. Environmentalists, for example, are concerned about contaminated water irrigating crops exported to the United States. Some people did not object to negotiations, but wanted discussions expanded to include a social charter addressing issues of labor rights, health, and environmental standards (*FT* 30 January 1991: 4). Most U.S. industry groups favor a pact. If it makes Mexico more prosperous, it will lessen pressure on workers to come north and thus address a central labor concern.

The first years of the Canada-U.S. free trade agreement hold lessons for a North American Free Trade Agreement. Increasing trade friction between the United States and Canada demonstrates the need for clearer rules of origin than exist in the U.S.-Canada agreement: the Honda dispute underlines this lesson. The NAFTA requires a more detailed dispute settlement process than exists in the U.S.-Canada agreement (*FT* 13 March 1992: 13). This process should cover trade disagreements, but also other issues that became central concerns in NAFTA negotiations. These include Mexico's environmental and labor laws (*FT* 15 June 1992: 4).

The opportunities for international businesses lie in increased exports to Mexico as well as in direct or indirect participation in privatized Mexican industries. The potential for U.S. business, which would have an inside advantage, is huge. The stakes for Mexican businesses are as important: increased exports to the United States and greater access to capital and knowledge.

In discussing the NAFTA one must always keep the following facts in mind. Mexico is the third largest U.S. trading partner after Canada and Japan. In 1989 two-way trade between Mexico and the United States exceeded $51 billion; in 1990, it approached $60 billion (*NYT* 14 September 1990: C6; *FT* 12 June 1991: 2). The United States is Mexico's primary export market. A North American Free Trade Agreement would constitute one of the greatest opportunities for international business ever.

PART IV. AFRICA

International business has had a mixed history of involvement on the African continent. For a long time this relationship brought more harm than benefit to Africa. The Atlantic and Indian Ocean slave trades are major examples of international business inflicting monumental damage upon Africa. The Atlantic slave trade, which began in the fifteenth century and continued almost to the twentieth century, forcibly removed at least 10 to 12 million people from their homes and transported them to the western hemisphere. The Indian Ocean slave trade, in which Arab slavers played prominent roles, took millions of people from East and Central Africa and put them to work on islands in that ocean. The slave trades, which enmeshed Africa in webs of international exploitation, are among the worst episodes of business conduct in history.

As the nations that had supported the slave trades sought to stop them in the nineteenth century, Europe got even more involved in the affairs of the African continent. To replace the "illegitimate commerce" in slaves Europeans sought "legitimate commerce." The search for such "legitimate" trade items as palm oil, coffee, cocoa, and cotton carried European nationals and eventually their governments ever more deeply into the interior of the continent.

Chartered companies played important roles in this penetration and illustrate a blend of business and politics that was to have enormous consequences for Africa. Among the most important were the Royal Niger Company, German East Africa Company, German South-West African Company, British East Africa Company, and the British South Africa Company. These companies simultaneously advanced economic penetration, laid the basis for European colonization, and created conditions in which their respective governments would become directly involved in the administration of Africa.

The activities of two companies demonstrate this process. The Royal Niger Company (RNC), led by Sir George Goldie, was instrumental in some areas of what was to become Nigeria in establishing the antecedent to formal administrative colonialism. Incorporated as the Royal Niger Company in 1886, this organization made treaties with chiefs along the Niger and Benue rivers, obtained from them trading and territorial concessions, and levied taxes to meet its administrative expenses (Wickins 1981: 301). It was, in key respects, a "shadow government," with responsibilities for introducing a British version of law and order into its operating region. This task required considerable pacification.

The RNC was, by all accounts, a financial success in terms of trade generation; it was less able—and this is a crucial point—to pacify the area on its own. The kinds of economic penetration associated with legitimate trade, unlike the slave trade that throve on disorder and insecurity, needed a more stable climate. This meant eliminating warfare that sometimes flared up between

African societies and the slave raiding that continued. The RNC was a quasi-government in its area, but the preservation of "law and order" required a real government with sufficient military forces. For this reason, and the fact that the company had aroused opposition because of its informal monopoly on trade, the British government itself in 1900 took over effective administration of its operating area. The company kept only its trading assets and warehouses (Wickins 1981: 301).

The German East Africa Company (GEAC), like the Royal Niger Company, proved to be the advance agency of formal administrative colonialism in its area. Carl Peters and his associates traveled through parts of what is now Tanzania, especially in the north, during the 1880s and produced a series of documents that were presented to the public as "treaties." Various African chiefs had allegedly, by their Xs or other marks on these pieces of paper, placed themselves under the GEAC's "protection" or otherwise granted it concessions. What these documents meant to their respective African signatories remains ambiguous.

What was clear was how Germany viewed the "treaties." The German Chancellor Bismarck, already having established a foothold in Africa by his declaration of a protectorate over Angra Pequeña in southwest Africa in 1884, chose to recognize the false treaty rights of Carl Peters in East Africa in 1885. The German East Africa Company (*Deutsch Öst-Afrika Gesellschaft*) then sought to extend its own control, but in 1888 and 1889 it encountered the traditional stiff resistance of the peoples of the Swahili coast along the Indian Ocean. Just as the Royal Niger Company had been unable to pacify its area, so also would the GEAC discover that its resources were insufficient to defeat its opposition. Both deficiencies triggered formal governmental intervention. With the GEAC in deep trouble, the German Imperial Government "was obliged" to intervene militarily. In 1891 it assumed responsibility for the administration of German East Africa, secured control of the coast, and proceeded to the arduous task of inland pacification, most of which was completed by 1898. Business activities, as exemplified by the chartered companies, are an important part of the story that led European powers to divide up much of the continent among themselves in the 1880s and 1890s.

This partition did not start European colonialism in Africa. The Portuguese, Dutch, French, and British had already established bases for their colonies well before the 1880s. Dutch involvement in South Africa dates from 1652, and the French penetration of Senegal had been going on for centuries. What the "partition of Africa" brought was the formal period of widespread administrative colonialism in Africa, which ended for most of Africa by the late 1960s. European powers set up or expanded bureaucracies to run their respective spheres of influence on the continent. These colonial administrations, which represented their home countries in Africa, developed minds of their own and achieved an autonomy of operation in important respects.

Colonial bureaucracies had various relations with international businesses, which went through at least four phases. These are the eras of "robber colonialism," mature colonialism of the interwar years (1919–1939), reformist colonialism after 1945, and independence. "Robber colonialism" is graphically embodied in the Congo Free or Independent State, which was almost a company itself and did not have the backing of a metropolitan state. Leopold II of Belgium ran the Congo Free State as his own colony and handed over part of it to concession companies. France imitated Leopold II and gave over much of French Equatorial Africa to the same kind of company. During "mature colonialism" companies gained more power and the state provided a wider range of facilities and services for firms. States, in ways that differed considerably on the spot, invested in infrastructure, controlled labor through taxation and other forms of coercion, manipulated "peasant" production of certain commodities, and fixed or otherwise tinkered with prices (Clarence-Smith 1983: 5-6).

During "reformist colonialism" after 1945 what had been a partial alliance between the state and big business began to unravel. In some cases, as in the Belgian Congo and Portuguese Angola, a more autonomous state appeared to be more understanding of the demands of white settlers, while exploring at the same time the strategy of focusing both economic and political activities on the masses of Africans. The altered relations between states and companies during the "reformist" period may also have originated as much in the evolving structures of big business as in the changing nature of the colonial state. The fourth phase of "flag independence" marked, in one significant way, a sharp break in the interplay between states and large corporations. The "weakness and instability" of many post-colonial states brought about changes in strategy on the part of large companies. Governments in such conditions encouraged the emergence in some cases of a new kind of "rip-off" capitalism, "which acts in the role of asset-stripper and leaves nothing behind" (Clarence-Smith 1983: 7). Matters have come almost full circle, as the "rip-off" capitalism of the independence era resembles in key respects "robber colonialism": whether the robbers or the rippers-off were more rapacious can be argued.

This four-stage periodization, while suggestive, must be used with caution and refinement. During the phase of "mature colonialism," as in all other phases, the role of the state must be analyzed on a case-by-case basis. It is vital to know as much as possible about how a particular territorial bureaucracy invested in infrastructure, tried to control labor through taxation and other forms of coercion, manipulated farmer production of certain commodities, and tampered with prices. Knowledge is crucial because state action in these areas and others affected all sizes of businesses and had great consequences for the configuration of economic activity at the time and later. The legally independent African state still, in crucial respects, embodies the colonial bureaucracy. It is misleading to overemphasize aspects of perceived "weakness, instability, and corruption" in the operation of post-colonial states. The state, whatever its actual flaws, remains a dominant, in many cases the predominant, influence on economic and business activity within its borders. The twin needs to distinguish more rigorously "the state" and "business" apply as well to the continuing era of independence (McCarthy 1988: 143-49).

The three case studies in Part IV all fill out different aspects of this introduction. The South African study deals with an intricate case of ongoing administrative colonialism over 21 million African people. In this case the current colonizers are the Afrikaners, descendants of the Dutch who as noted began their presence in South Africa in 1652. The Afrikaners, while not ethnically indigenous to Africa, have really become Africans in their loyalty to the land and tenacity in preserving their kinship structures. One topic of this case study is the ongoing divestment/reinvestment controversy concerning South Africa. Divestment or disinvestment means withdrawing business in some way. This debate has become more complicated in recent times as the African National Congress and the ruling National Party engage in dialogue about the country's future and President de Klerk has legally abolished all aspects of apartheid or race separation. Our contextual approach here consists of providing essential background about the past and present of South Africa to make business people better informed about the wider implications of their decisions concerning that country.

The Namibian case study focuses on a country in whose victimization business played prominent roles. This victimization went through several phases. The penetration of traders from South Africa north into southwest Africa (now Namibia) in search of cattle pushed the peoples of that area into relations of exploitation. The Germans, who declared a protectorate over Angra Pequeña in southwest Africa in 1884, expanded their control over the entire territory. In this process they expropriated hundreds of thousands of acres of land and thousands of livestock. German companies were active in these "acquisitions." These depredations grievously hurt many indigenous peoples of Namibia, especially the Herero and Nama-speakers. During World War I Germany was defeated militarily in southwest Africa by forces representing the British Empire. South Africa acquired control of southwest Africa as a mandate from the League of Nations after World War I and refined its mechanisms of oppression there from the 1920s on. After World War II, international business became more deeply involved in Namibia. The activities of the Tsumeb Corporation in the country are spotlighted in the case study. Readers should compare and contrast the Tsumeb Corporation with the Cerro Corporation, which came to dominate mining in the Cerro de Pasco area of Peru in the early twentieth century (Chapter 7). The "flag independence" of Namibia on 21 March 1990 means only that the country has shed its shackles of legal subservience, not that it has wrested control over its own economic destiny from the foreign corporations that for so long maltreated it.

The theme of how best to control one's economic destiny in the post-independence period informs the final case study in part IV. This chapter focuses on the Republic of Tanzania in East Africa but speaks to issues that affect post-independence Africa. What ideology or intellectual framework best serves the purposes of rapid economic development with threshold fairness? Is it capitalism (a larger private sector) or socialism (a larger public sector) or some mix of the two? Or is it some blend of pragmatism (doing what works) with utilitarianism (striving for the greatest good for the greatest number)? What roles can or should international business play?

The most popular way to phrase these issues today is to talk about creating the best public-private sector mix for a country. The trend in Africa, as it is in Eastern Europe and much of South America and Asia and the former Soviet Union, is for the private sector to play an increasingly more important role in economic development. Not every government in independent Africa has committed itself to the private sector or even a market economy with equal enthusiasm. But the economic future in Africa is on the side of a greater role for private agents and agencies. This holds much promise for international businesses that seek types of involvement on the continent that benefit all parties.

11

South Africa: A Complicated Situation for International Business

South Africa today is a land of tragedy and promise unfolding together. Recent events underscore this entanglement. In early 1990 the South African government released Nelson Mandela from prison. Mandela is the president of the African National Congress (ANC), an organization dedicated to the abolition of apartheid, or race separation, and the foundation of a "new South Africa" that recognizes the rights of all its citizens. Later in 1990 the South African government, led by state President F. W. de Klerk, began talks with the ANC aimed at clearing away obstacles to actual negotiations. In 1991 President de Klerk abolished the rest of apartheid, including its core, the Population Registration Act. Negotiations on the constitutional future of South Africa are underway; most political parties in South Africa are paritipating in these talks. On 17 March 1992 white voters in a referendum endorsed by a two-thirds majority the state president's continuing negotiations on the future of South Africa (*FT* 19 March 1992: 1).

As these discussions take place, violence in some African townships has escalated. These clashes are party interethnic, since they often pit Zulus against Xhosas. But the struggles are also political in several senses. The Zulus are members of Inkatha, the Zulu political movement led by Chief Buthelezi and centered in old Natal province, now called by some KwaZulu or KwaNatal. The Xhosas are supposedly associated with the ANC, Inkatha's major rival in organizing Africans against the South African government. The brutal confrontations had other origins. Extreme right-wing groups of white South Africans, upset with President de Klerk's determination to fashion a fairer South Africa, fueled the so-called black violence. They either participated directly or worked through agents. There was a disturbing connection between this right-wing white involvement and the activities of some members of South Africa's own security forces. The state president himself, along with Nelson

Mandela, has acknowledged the existence of some kind of "conspiracy" to derail the fragile dialogue between the government and other parties.

The sharp contrast between the promise of constitutional negotiations and the tragedy of recurring deep-seated violence intensifies the risks and uncertainties that becloud the South African business environment today. Increasingly buffeted by international sanctions, the economy of South Africa, which had been lackluster for years, entered an official slowdown in 1989. The Reserve Bank, the country's central bank, produced statistics that show that real gross domestic fixed investment declined at an annual rate of 1.5 percent in the five quarters to mid-1990. The private sector was largely responsible for this decline: fixed private investment decreased over the period at an annualized rate of 3 percent, double the overall rate (*FT* 13 September 1990: 3). The slowdown began before the township violence of 1990 escalated and continued through 1992.

Political disruption compounds the disincentives to business investment that a slowing economy and high interest rates already present. The economy of South Africa, previously hurt by the decisions of many international businesses to close down, cut back, or transform their activities there, now faces a problem of domestic investor confidence. President de Klerk's reform program, given strong support in that 17 March 1992 referendum, has led to the relaxation of international sanctions against South Africa. Yet its economy remains fragile and continues troubled. In 1992 South Africa was in the grip of its worst drought since the 1930s; this drought has affected a large part of Africa from South Africa, through Zimbabwe, Tanzania, Kenya, Somalia, Sudan, and Ethiopia (*FT* 14 February 1992: 24). Agriculture, the livelihood of so many South Africans, is under severe stress at a time when the country is already beset by serious problems.

Businesses face in South Africa a troubled environment but one that holds immense potential. The land is rich in gold, silver, and a host of other metals and minerals. The land also contains great possibilities for agriculture when and where there is enough water. South Africa is today struggling with the consequences of apartheid, a word that comes from the language of Afrikaans, which is the tongue of the Afrikaners. Members of this group currently run the central government and administration of South Africa. Apartheid means the separation of people based on a concept of race defined by skin pigmentation. There had been racial segregation, sometimes coming from voluntary association, in southern Africa for centuries. But after the Afrikaner-based Nationalist party won the 1948 elections, its leaders began to impose apartheid on South Africa. Afrikaners, descendants of the Dutch who settled in South Africa from 1652, argued that apartheid meant separate development, which was supposedly different from racial segregation.

THE DIVESTMENT CONTROVERSY
AND INTERNATIONAL BUSINESS

During the 1980s a controversy intensified over the proper roles of international business in a South Africa that was becoming more polarized. In the 1990s the divestment controversy entered a new phase: the legal abolition of apartheid and continuing constitutional negotiations produced promise and hope that had not existed before. International businesses that had reduced or sold off their South African operations as they disinvested or divested may be wondering whether to reinvest. International businesses that chose to stay may be considering how to refine their strategy of working from within.

It is worthwhile to review the essentials of the divestment controversy because they apply to the reinvestment debate. South Africa presents an enormously difficult problem for business ethics or what is proper conduct. This case study first summarizes the basics of the divestment controversy then sketches essential features of the history of South Africa. To make an informed decision about investing in South Africa today one needs to know how South Africa became what it is: a land of many divisions, the worst of which has been apartheid. Businesses need to integrate this historical sketch into their investment decision making about South Africa.

In the 1980s and earlier people debated whether international business had any role in South Africa and if so, what it was; what stances should holders of equity in businesses involved in South Africa take toward their investments; and what policies should individual people, government entities, and other enterprises doing business with firms operating in South Africa adopt. The divestment or disinvestment debate had several dimensions: international business in South Africa, equity holders in those companies, and those who conducted business with the involved enterprises.

Insofar as international business operating in South Africa itself was concerned, defining divestment became controversial. Some companies, such as General Motors, General Electric, and Merck, sold their South African subsidiaries to local investor groups. But these legally independent local firms continued to sell the products of their former parent enterprises. Should complete divestment have included product withdrawal as well as equity withdrawal? This question complicated the divestment debate. Equity withdrawal may have placed the former parents in technical compliance with various statutes enacted by some states and other local jurisdictions. But maintenance of their product links, critics argued, violated the spirit or intent of divestment legislation.

The divestment controversy raised fundamental questions concerning relations between business, on the one hand, and morality, ethics, and religion on the other. It did not present those issues in a clear fashion. While most agreed that apartheid was wrong, there was energetic argument over how best to right a wrong so that it does not perpetrate more harm. Some people stated that more than financial and economic considerations should guide investing and other business behavior. Everyone, they suggested, should adopt and systematically use their own *social concern investment criteria.* These would guide investment toward those areas with the best economic return compatible with social sensitivity. People so inclined supported various measures of business disengagement from South Africa and formal sanctions imposed by governments or economic communities. Other people, as concerned with the welfare of all the people of South Africa, contended that for international business interests to depart completely from the scene would cause even greater harm than the the the maintenance of their sometimes socially ambiguous presence.

Some disputed and still do question the appropriateness of social concern investment criteria in themselves. Their case rests on the following propositions. Economic growth is central to social change. Businesses can best contribute to social change by fueling economic growth. Businesses can maximize their contribution by striving for their own greatest growth and returns. Investors can best assist this process of social change through economic growth by selecting those companies that operate with a growth- and profit-oriented philosophy. To limit the universe of choice of one's investments by ruling out a company because it is not as socially conscious as one would like is itself a self-defeating approach. Those who reject the necessity of social concern investment criteria are not proceeding in a vacuum because for them businesses can have their most beneficial impact on a society by specializing in what they do best: their own work, without excessive politicization.

All these approaches figured in the divestment debate. This controversy furnishes an excellent opportunity for people to think through their own philosophies of business behavior in any environment, especially those that pose acute social dilemmas. With what particular stance just mentioned or combinations do you identify? Can you work out your own approach based on values or premises derived from your previous experience? In order to help people form or refine their notions of appropriate business conduct, particularly in the South African situation, a thumbnail sketch of some main features of the history of South Africa follows.

To understand apartheid it is necessary to remember the central premise of South African history: it is the story of many different peoples from many different places coming together, affecting one another in many different ways, of which not all the consequences are yet known (Wilson and Thompson 1969: v). The indigenous peoples of South Africa included first the Khoikhoi and Bush people and then the many communities of Bantu. Different groups of Europeans, first the Dutch and then the British, established important settlements in South Africa. Over time the descendants of the Dutch became known as Afrikaners. Indians from the subcontinent across the Indian Ocean came to

South Africa and became prominent traders but also functioned in a wide spectrum of occupations.

Soon after the Dutch came to South Africa in 1652 they came into conflict with the Khoikhoi, who had long pastured their livestock in the environs of the Cape during part of the year. The Dutch claimed that land and wanted the Khoikhoi's livestock for food. The Khoikhoi regarded their livestock as wealth, income, money, status, and social cement, least of all as food. The conflicts between Dutch and Khoikhoi over land and stock led to the Khoikhoi's defeat and subservience. They set the stage for the struggles over land and stock that would dominate so much of South Africa's history for the next two centuries.

Struggles for land and stock continued into and throughout the eighteenth century between and among South Africa's peoples, but it was not until the nineteenth century that the situation along the plateau and coast of southeastern Africa, where most people lived, would undergo significant transformation. Between 1800 and 1870 change took place in three overlapping phases, which resulted from the impact of three distinct processes (Thompson 1969a: 334).

DECISIVE TRANSFORMATIONS: 1800–1870

The first phase featured the revolutionizing from within of some types of African social organization that had existed for several centuries. The process that powered the first phase was the fact that some chiefdoms developed into powerful kingdoms by absorbing other chiefdoms. The classic example of the first phase and process was the emergence of the Zulu kingdom. The Zulu kingdom originated among Bantu who were Nguni speakers. Dingiswayo laid the foundation upon which Shaka built the Zulu kingdom. The rise of the Zulu kingdom had repercussions from Cape Colony in South Africa to Lake Tanganyika to the north in east Africa. It disrupted the lives of thousands. One of the peoples who suffered most during this violent eruption was the Sotho, another Bantu group which lives in what is now known as Lesotho. The severe turbulence that produced a general collapse of Sotho political organization provided an opportunity for a person with superior attributes to emerge. Moshweshwe, a Sotho, came to the fore as a result of his outstanding political and military talents. Less military minded and power preoccupied than Shaka, Moshweshwe used his skills as an arbitrator to weld a confederation of his people.

The first phase and process featuring those larger African kingdoms were still going on when the second phase began. This period features Afrikaner thrusts into the interior of South Africa and highlights the Great Trek (c. 1836–1854), a sudden, dramatic, and substantial acceleration in *trekboer* movement into the interior that dated from the start of the eighteenth century. A *trekboer* is an

Afrikaner farmer or countryperson on the move. By mid-1837, about 5,000 Voortrekkers, or pioneers, had crossed the Orange River on their way into the interior of southeastern Africa. By 1845 the number had risen to 14,000. Many Voortrekkers sought a new life, free from perceived British oppression in Cape Colony, which Great Britain then controlled (Thompson 1969b: 406).

The second process was Afrikaners carving out settlements for themselves in the interior. These locations became the Orange Free State and the Transvaal. The creation of these settlements, and the thrusting into the interior that made them possible, had significant costs. As the Voortrekkers pushed into the interior, they confronted and defeated the two most powerful African kingdoms in their way. Major fighting occurred in the late 1830s. The Boers beat the Ndebele during 1837 and 1838, and then the Zulus from 1838 through 1840.

The second process did not have time to work itself out before the third phase began. This consisted of British intervention. British involvement was not linear; it was a mixture of advance and withdrawal. The British annexed, or declared possession of, Natal in 1843. They annexed all territory between the Orange and Vaal rivers in 1848, only to renounce that responsibility in 1854. They had already disengaged from the Transvaal in 1852. But then at the request of King Moshweshwe, they assumed responsibility for Basutoland (Lesotho) in 1868.

The third process, which reprises elements of what preceded it, delineated the emergence of three different kinds of polities. The first was the British Colony of Natal. The second consisted of the Afrikaner Republics of the Orange Free State and the South African Republic (Transvaal). The third featured a number of weakened African chiefdoms and kingdoms on the outskirts of Natal and the Afrikaner republics. One of these was Basutoland, which came under British protection in 1868. The results of all these processes reinforced the opposing themes of conflict and commingling that characterize the history of South Africa. Increasing antagonism strained relations between Boers and British, black and white, and among Africans themselves. At the same time, the mixing of different cultures and traditions accelerated as the peoples of South Africa came into contact with one another (Thompson 1969a: 334-35).

From 1870 to 1910 there were two more distinct processes at work that built upon tendencies that had already emerged. The first was the subjection of African chiefdoms to white control. The second was the establishment of British supremacy over the Afrikaner republics. Of the many examples of African subjection to British rule four can represent a variety of paths to the same end: intensified repression.

DECISIVE SUBJUGATIONS (1870–1910):
AFRICAN CHIEFDOMS TO WHITE CONTROL

Consider first the fate of the West Griqua, a community of people who came from so-called racially mixed marriages. The Griqua were not a major South African population group nor did they occupy a vast tract of land. In 1870 they numbered fewer than 1000 people, most of whom were poor and nearly all of whom lived west of the Vaal River (Thompson 1971a: 253). But their fate gives them special significance in the steamrolling of white power inland. One commodity determined their destiny: diamonds. The discovery of diamonds under their territory gave the Griqua an importance in the colonial land grinder they would never have possessed. Great Britain annexed Griqualand West as a Crown Colony in 1871, and then in 1880 incorporated it into Cape Colony. This latter action harmonized with the British imperial approach of devolving direct responsibility for some colonial possessions onto other colonies.

All the while, the Griqua continued to decline. The British did allot them farms, other locations, and even some villages within Griqualand West. But the Griqua were "persuaded" to sell their land to white people for cash or liquor, which included a cheap, rotgut brandy known as "Cape Smoke." By 1900 the Griqua had ceased to exist as an organized community. Those who survived worked for white people (Thompson 1971a: 257).

Griqualand West did not benefit the Griqua at all, but its incorporation into the British Empire helped the British in three ways. Its strategic location, to the northeast of Cape Colony, checked the expansion of the Afrikaner republics to the southwest. Its position kept the roads to the north open for British missionaries and traders. The road to the north was not a paved expressway, but a series of trails and dirt roads that went into Bechuanaland (Botswana) and further north. Keeping roads to the north open preserved a lingering vision in the minds of some that would have the British Empire occupy African territory from Cape to Cairo, from the southern tip of the continent to the Mediterranean Sea in the north. Besides these two geopolitical objectives, the absorption of Griqualand West was geo-economic. The empire asserted control over the diamond fields and then made them the responsibility of its self-governing colony, the Cape Colony.

Natal, the other British colony in South Africa, was the scene of another vignette of repression. The four principal "western-style" creations in South Africa—Cape Colony and Natal by the British, and the Transvaal and the Orange Free State by the Afrikaners—may have had rough if fluctuating boundaries in the minds of those who ran them, but African groups, which were either obstacles or servants in foreign state formation, sometimes found themselves living uneasily within one of these entities. Some Nguni-speaking Bantu reside in Natal and are designated as the Natal Nguni to distinguish them from the southern Nguni.

This episode concerns the Natal Nguni. In the 1870s Natal was a colonial wedge between two still independent African states—those of the Zulu and the Mpondo. A fragile peace existed there until 1872 when the government of Natal ordered the chiefs to register all firearms held by their people. One famous chief, Langalibalele, refused, and the government decided to make an example of him in order to reassure the white settlers. A force composed of 200 British troops, 300 white volunteers, and 6,000 Africans set out for Langalibalele's place. He fled, but his pursuers seized his people's stock, confiscated their land, and distributed his people among white farmers. The chief himself was eventually captured, tried in a kangaroo court, and exiled to a farm in Cape Colony. Africans in Natal remained quiet, on the whole, until 1906, when there was another act of defiance and another violent white reaction. The seeds of African discontent are deeply planted in Natal (Thompson 1971a: 260-61).

The Zulu, whose preliminary defeat the Boers had administered in the late 1830s, remained by far the most powerful African state south of the Limpopo River in the 1870s. But "a diplomatic and military noose gradually tightened around the Zulu kingdom," as the British subjugated it in four stages (Thompson 1971a: 263). They first conquered it militarily and broke up its army. They then split Zulu country into thirteen separate units. White magistrates then supplanted the chiefs as the most powerful men in their districts. Finally the British partitioned the land itself. When this process was complete, only one third of the former kingdom was left in Zulu hands. One British official expressed the hope that the warriors of Cetshwayo, a proud successor to Shaka, would turn into laborers working for wages. This transformation had already begun by the end of the nineteenth century (Thompson 1971a: 266).

British officials defended the Zulu war as a campaign "to liberate the Zulu people from a tyrannical ruler, and South Africa from a menace to Christianity and Civilization." The reality was different. British forces destroyed the Zulu kingdom because British officials "on the spot managed to foment a crisis," partly by provoking Cetshwayo, and "then to persuade the British government" in London "that the kingdom stood in the way of British interests" (Thompson 1971a: 266-67).

While the British dismantled the Zulu, they almost smothered the Sotho in a protectorate that was at first mismanaged. Moshweshwe, readers will recall, had asked Great Britain to establish a protectorate over his people. He feared the further depredations of the Zulus and others on his people and their land and was concerned in particular that the Orange Free State, one of the two Afrikaner units, might completely carve up Sotho territory. Great Britain complied with his request in 1869 and then followed its practice of giving responsibility for some of its colonial possessions to its other colonies. Cape Colony assumed control over Basutoland in 1871 and then proceeded to behave poorly. The Cape legislature passed a series of ill-considered acts that poisoned ties with the Sotho. The legislature ordered all Africans to hand in their weapons. It raised a major levy on the Sotho, the hut tax. It opened the Basutoland district of one very uncooperative chief to white settlement.

Most of the Sotho resisted these impositions. Over 20,000 formed the military resistance, and Lerotholi, their leader, successfully employed guerrilla tactics against the forces of Cape Colony. The British in England gave little direct aid to Cape Colony in this war. Defeated by the Sotho, the Cape Colony government asked Great Britain itself to reassume direct responsibility for Basutoland, which it did in 1884.

Great Britain also "protected" the Tswana and Swazi. The result was that these three territories—Basutoland, Bechuanaland, and Swaziland—were never included in the Union of South Africa, which was created during the 1902–1910 period. Direct control by London meant that when Great Britain decolonized many of its African possessions in the decade or so after 1957, the territories became "flag independent" as Lesotho, Botswana, and Swaziland.

The West Griqua, Natal Nguni, Zulu, and Sotho all provide studies in the subjection in different ways of various kinds of African communities to British rule. All took place with violence of one type or another—physical, mental, or combinations of the two. British subjugation of the Afrikaner states also exhibited comprehensive forms of violence, nowhere more than in the Anglo-Boer War (1899–1902). The Great Trek and this war are perhaps the two major events that have shaped the historical memory of Afrikanerdom in South Africa today. The Anglo-Boer War pitted the Boers against the British Empire. It involved paramilitary and extramilitary tactics on both sides and made entire populations participants in the struggle. The excellent Australian film *Breaker Morant* focuses on three different Australian men who fought with the British Imperial forces in South Africa contesting the Boers. It captures the brutality and pervasive moral ambiguity of actions taken by both sides in a conflict that prefigured Algeria and Vietnam.

DECISIVE SUBJUGATIONS (1870–1910): THE AFRIKANERS TO THE BRITISH

The origins of the Anglo-Boer War reflect a mixture of politics, diplomacy, strategy, economics, and business that invalidates any single-factor explanation. A condensed analysis of origins looks first at the British side, then the Boer side, and how the two collided.

The vast majority of late nineteenth-century British officialdom believed that Great Britain should hold at least the Cape peninsula because of its strategic and commercial importance on a major sea route between Europe and Asia. The opening in 1869 of the Suez Canal, which shortened Euro-Asian water links by connecting the Red and Mediterranean seas, did not weaken that conviction.

There was no guarantee, many pointed out, that Britain could or would dominate the canal in a time of war or other serious disturbance (Thompson 1971b: 290). Holding the Cape peninsula can be called the Table Bay imperative, after Cape Town's famous natural harbor. The Nilotic imperative drove the British to control as much of the Nile River and its adjacent territories as possible. The Table Bay imperative compelled the British to move further inland to gain as much land as possible to protect the Cape peninsula. It is another version of the hinterland doctrine, which decrees that the coast can only be controlled by securing the interior.

The Table Bay imperative gained strength from other sources. One was ideological. Some British, especially in South Africa, saw a twofold obligation that they thought history had imposed on their government. The first part was to safeguard the interests of the British communities in the Cape Colony, Natal, and later the Transvaal. The second was to protect the African peoples from oppression by Afrikaners and British South Africans. That these missions were not completely compatible did not lessen their appeal. Another source was economic. The discovery of precious metals by Europeans and the subsequent growth of the diamond-mining industry in Griqualand West and the gold-mining industry in the Transvaal strengthened economic arguments for greater territorial supremacy (Thompson 1971b: 291).

There was an ominous strategic twist for the British. Toward the end of the nineteenth century the Transvaal was emerging as a powerfully armed Afrikaner state. The Transvaal began diplomatic overtures to Imperial Germany. Anglo-German relations became more tense after 1890, as Kaiser Wilhelm II directed a substantial program to upgrade the Germany navy. A stronger German navy would challenge British supremacy on the high seas, which had been one of the major keys to the successful imperial expansion of that country. In the southern African theater the British feared relations between the Transvaal and Germany for several reasons. An alliance between an expansionist Transvaal and a supportive Germany might produce a hostile barrier to the north. This wall would consist of German South West Africa, the Transvaal itself, and German East Africa, with the intervening territory up for forcible acquisition by the alliance. A graver possibility was the specter of the Transvaal's becoming the strongest state in South Africa and, with German assistance, forcing the British out of South Africa altogether.

British policy toward the Afrikaner republics was not consistent in practice. The 1870s and 1890s were more aggressive than the 1880s. Whoever held two posts in the British government—the Secretary of State for Colonies at the cabinet level and the British High Commissioner for South Africa—could influence the rhythm of intervention. There were two colonial secretaries and two high commissioners who had strong imperialist convictions and pursued policies that led to greater involvement and military conflict with the Boers. These were in the 1870s Lord Carnarvon as Colonial Secretary and Sir Bartle

Frere as High Commissioner and in the 1890s Joseph Chamberlain (C.S.) and Sir Alfred (Lord) Milner (H.C.) (Thompson 1971b: 290).

The Boers drew enormous strength from an Afrikaner nationalism that began to emerge after 1870. Nationalism refers to the creation and fostering of not only a common community to which people belong, but also a shared sense of participation among those individuals. Before the 1870s the Boers lacked a national consciousness. Since the Great Trek of 1836 through 1854, they had been thinly spread over a vast subcontinent. They were divided among four different states and three churches. They lacked common institutions and loyalties (Thompson 1971b: 301).

The Boers, however, possessed well before 1870 some of the necessary ingredients for a nationalist movement. They had a common historical background. Most of the Afrikaners were descended from the thousand free burghers who were enumerated in the Cape Colony in 1691. Virtually all of them could trace their ancestry back to the 17,000 who were counted in 1795. Many Afrikaners were aware that they had kinfolk in different parts of South Africa. Besides ancestors and present blood kin, Afrikaners shared some common attitudes. They regarded Coloured (or mixed "race" people) and Africans as inferiors; yet they were acutely conscious that some white people of British origin looked down upon them (Thompson 1971b: 301).

Events during the 1870s began to crystallize expression of that nationalism. At the same time, Afrikaner insecurity and pride increased, a combination that provoked the articulation of Afrikaner nationalism. The British increased the group's insecurity. During the 1870s Carnarvon and Frere aggressively intervened in the Orange Free State, the Transvaal, and Cape Colony, but the Afrikaners, at least those in the Transvaal, gained a great victory over a British force at Majuba in 1881. As these events were transpiring, some Afrikaner intellectuals were giving reasons to all Afrikaners for respecting Afrikaner culture. The central concept that these intellectuals promoted has great importance for understanding Afrikaners past and present. The Afrikaners, they argued, "were a distinct people or nation, occupying a distinct fatherland, South Africa, speaking a God-given language, Afrikaans, and endowed by God with the destiny to rule South Africa and civilize its heathen peoples" (Thompson 1971b: 301-2). These intellectuals were also showing how individuals could channel their own frustrations into group grievances against a common enemy.

With this self-image, self-belief, sense of mission, and an ingrained need to have a common enemy, the Afrikaners were becoming formidable. Give that force a common enemy—the British—and the potential for explosion would be enormous. The collision course that these two powers followed is illustrated by the careers of two men: from the British side, Cecil Rhodes; from the Afrikaner, Paul Kruger.

Cecil Rhodes became prime minister of the Cape Colony in 1890. The son of an English clergyman, he had migrated in 1870 to Natal for health reasons at age seventeen. He moved to the diamond fields and organized the consolidation of claims held by individual people and syndicates. By 1891 his diamond company, DeBeers Consolidated Mines, had virtually complete control over the production and marketing of diamonds worldwide. He also founded Consolidated Gold Fields, which became one of the strongest gold-mining corporations on the Witwatersrand, the richest gold fields in the world located near Johannesburg in the Transvaal. Cecil Rhodes thought big. He wanted to promote the expansion of the British Empire in Africa. He wished to see the map of Africa from Cape to Cairo colored in the red of the British Empire. He had exceptional means to further his fantasies: he was very rich and very persuasive (Thompson 1971b: 305-6).

Paul Kruger became president of the Transvaal in 1883. He had taken part in the Great Trek as a child. The country of which he was now president had achieved some measure of independence from Great Britain as a result of the battle of Majuba in 1881, but this freedom was fragile. More non-Afrikaners were entering the Transvaal, mainly in connection with the growing gold-mining industry. These immigrants were called in Afrikaans *uitlanders*, or foreigners.

The growing immigrant presence created difficulties for the Transvaal Afrikaners. Many *uitlanders* were British; Anglo-Boer relations were strained. The British *uitlanders* constituted a potential fifth column, and the leadership of the Transvaal was acutely aware of this possibility. Throughout the rest of the 1880s and well into the 1890s the *uitlanders* protested their treatment by the Transvaal government. They accused the Transvaal of depriving them of political rights because they could not vote in local elections.

In Kruger and colleagues the British met the immovable object. Public relations pressure would not persuade the Transvaal government to alter its policies toward the *uitlanders*. This intransigence, as the British viewed it, or steadfastness, as Afrikaner partisans saw it, was provoking a growing impatience. Cecil Rhodes was becoming increasingly frustrated in his desire to extend the domain of Cape Colony northward. The panorama of Cape to Cairo, always excessively visionary in its complete geographical realization, was becoming a mockery even in southern Africa. There was virtually no prospect that the growing *uitlander* presence might influence Transvaal politics through the ballot box.

Cecil Rhodes was in a hurry. The British had satisfied geopolitical and geo-economic needs simultaneously when they incorporated Griqualand West and its diamond fields. The Transvaal Afrikaners were now frustrating them on both fronts. The gold fields, more dominion, more protection for the Cape, all these seemed unreachable through diplomacy and politics. Rhodes decided to take action unilaterally. His goal was to spark and support a coup d'état against the Afrikaner leadership of the Transvaal. He reasoned that since the aggrieved *uitlanders* constituted a potential army of insurrection, all they needed was a force to trigger their uprising. However, a fifth column on paper is not necessarily a fifth column in the field. Rhodes and his associates realized the truth of this dictum too late.

Rhodes needed a front man in this operation. He contacted Dr. Leander Starr Jameson, who put together a group of about 500 men. They were not even an average fighting force for straightforward maneuvers, and their task in this case was more intricate: to enter the Transvaal secretly and inspire and lead the *uitlanders* to victory against a well-armed and deeply entrenched government that was popular with its Afrikaner constituents.

The Jameson Raid was poorly planned from the start. An *uitlander* uprising upon the entry of Jameson's raiders was assumed, not coordinated in any way. Such defective organization doomed the raid. Events played themselves out with a certain tragic consistency. Jameson and his raiders invaded the Transvaal from Bechuanaland in late December 1895. The road to Johannesburg proved their path to nowhere. There was no "indigenous uprising" against "tyranny" by the *uitlanders*. Afrikaner forces easily defeated the ragtag Jameson operation. The failure of the Jameson Raid had disastrous consequences for Anglo-Boer relations. Afrikaners were furious: the raid strengthened Afrikaner solidarity and the Transvaal continued to arm itself. Through 1896, 1897, and 1898 relations between Great Britain and the Transvaal deteriorated. One is not sure that when the Anglo-Boer War broke out in 1899 it was, borrowing from Clausewitz, the continuation of diplomacy by other means. A diplomatic solution may never have been possible, given what the British really wanted—Afrikaner subservience, land, and gold.

THE AFTERMATH OF THE ANGLO-BOER WAR

The war itself was a struggle between Boer commandos and much larger numbers of regular British soldiers. The British won the military phase of the conflict. The Peace of Vereeniging (1902) formally ratified the end of physical hostilities, but it did not solve Anglo-Boer problems. After the war the British government engaged in a complicated series of negotiations that aimed to reconcile British and Boer in a new union of the four major units of white settlement in South Africa. The process of putting together the Union of South Africa took about eight years and apparently had succeeded when the Union Act of 1910 legalized the unification of the Cape Colony, Natal, the Transvaal, and the Orange Free State.

The Union Act was costly. Great Britain may have on paper achieved a veneer of reconciliation between the two major "white" groups in South Africa. Its primary goal in the unification process was to promote that reconciliation. But movement toward that first goal had entailed sacrificing Great Britain's secondary goal—racial equality. When Great Britain formally withdrew from South Africa after the Union Act, it left its government in control of an Anglo-Afrikaner coalition. What remained after centuries of tension and conflict, many years of war, and eight years of negotiations was a caste-like society, dominated by its white minority. The price of white unity and reconciliation, Leonard Thompson has written, was the institutionalization of white supremacy (Thompson 1971c: 364).

THE EMERGENCE OF APARTHEID

Refinement of that institutionalization, which pervaded every aspect of society, achieved special coherence around the midpoint of the twentieth century. The Nationalist party, the fortress of Afrikaner political power, campaigned in the pivotal 1948 elections, which it won, on its twin goals of guardianship and apartheid. Guardianship was an elastic notion that encompassed everything needed to preserve *baaskap*, or white racial domination. Apartheid was advertised as separate development, which supposedly meant more than racial segregation. One major justification for this approach, an argument not unique to Afrikaner intellectuals, was that each population group needed its own space to develop to the fullest its own distinctive genius in its own time and in its own way. Apartheid was almost exclusively separatist, with its developmental aspects a rousing self-mockery.

Separation in South Africa was based on a concept of race defined in terms of skin pigmentation. The legislative core of apartheid was the Population Registration Act of 1950, which was amended several times. It defined a Coloured Person (one of mixed descent) as a "person who is not a white person or a native." A "native person," the act continued, "is one who is in fact or is generally accepted as a member of any aboriginal race or tribe of Africa," that is, a "black person." A "white person" was one "who in appearance obviously is or who is accepted generally as a white person, but does not include a person who, although in appearance obviously a white person, is generally accepted as a Coloured person." A 1956 amendment attempted to tighten the definition of a "native" or "black" or "Bantu" or "African." "A person," the amendment directed, "who in appearance obviously is a member of an aboriginal race or tribe of Africa shall for the purposes of this Act be presumed to be a native unless it is proved that he is not in fact and is not generally accepted as such a member" (de Villiers 1971: 402-3).

A 1962 amendment addressed the still vexing question of who really is "white." "A white person," the amendment insisted, "means a person who (a) in appearance obviously is a white person and who is not generally accepted as a Coloured person or (b) is generally accepted as a white person and is not in appearance obviously not a white person, but does not include any person who for the purposes of his classification under this Act, freely and voluntarily admits that he is by descent a native or a Coloured person unless it is proved that the admission is not based on fact" (de Villiers 1971: 403). Numerous racial classification boards were mandated to determine to which group a person belonged. They could reclassify people as they saw fit.

Racial designation determined the legal and, in many respects, the economic conditions under which people lived in South Africa. In the early 1950s the government enacted other legislation that specified some of those conditions. The Group Areas Act of 1950 aimed to separate the "races" physically as much as possible. It decreed complete residential segregation. It directed that non-whites refrain from using the sports facilities of whites and that non-whites not attend public functions with whites. This act made possible the forcible relocation of whole communities, wherever they constituted a "black spot" in a white area (de Villiers 1971: 410).

Another piece of legislation was the Abolition of Passes and Co-ordination of Documents Act of 1950. This pronouncement coordinated existing pass laws and tried to make them easier to implement and administer. All African men and women had to carry a "reference book," or identity card, which contained details about the holder, where he or she worked and for whom. This act abolished "passes" as these were then defined but instituted the requirement that Africans had to have "reference books" or "identity cards" on their persons. Its original purpose was to stop the flow of blacks to urban areas and restrict the African population already in the cities, which were considered as "white areas." The legislation failed to accomplish these objectives. It did, however, aggravate and extend the system of migratory labor in which a wage-earning father would live in one place and his family elsewhere, because he was not allowed to bring his family into an urban area (de Villiers 1971: 409-10).

NEO-APARTHEID

During the 1980s the government of South Africa tried one or another version of neo-apartheid, or new form of apartheid. It abolished or reduced restrictions that some called "petty apartheid." Some disputed whether any aspect of apartheid was "petty." The government, for instance, cancelled some of its prohibitions on "racial mixing" in sports contests, among players as well as spectators. To modernize apartheid the government tackled more integral elements of the system. In 1985 legislation abolished the prohibition of interracial marriages and in 1986, for yet another time, the pass laws. This revision eliminated the legislation, directed only at Africans, that required them to carry "reference books." In its place was a law that dictated that everybody, including those classified as "white," carry "identity cards."

The government also began grappling in the 1980s with the difficult question of substantive power sharing among different racial groups. It established another legislative house for some of those of "mixed race," not "black." This was not substantive power sharing because real power remained entrenched in a determined elite within Afrikanerdom itself. This approach attempted to graft onto the basic trunk of apartheid a layer of consultation. The government defended its action as a cautious first step in a delicate transition from apartheid to a non-apartheid future. Its critics attacked its tentative and limited nature and wondered what kind of non-apartheid future the government had in mind.

The government has answered part of that question with the complete legal dismantling of apartheid. The abolition in 1991 of the Population Registration Act struck at the core of the system. But a physical infrastructure of apartheid remains. There is the long-standing Bantustan or homelands program. The government has set aside pieces of land designated as home states for the country's black ethnic groups. Bophuthatswana, the location of Sun City, and Kwazulu are homelands. If this program were completed, there would be twelve of these mini-states.

Separate homelands were seen as a prerequisite for separate development. They would supposedly give each African group a chance to develop to the utmost. Some dismissed the homelands program as a ludicrous exercise in the creation of entities that will never become states. The government responded that it was a first step in generating the conditions necessary for developing the distinctive ethnic geniuses of black South Africans.

Several homelands in South Africa achieved their "flag independence" but only from the viewpoint of the South African government. No other country diplomatically recognized them. Some homelands are not unified blocks of land: they are land archipelagoes, islands of land assembled as a unity by government order. The homelands have inadequate resources. Those trying to govern a land archipelago face troublesome questions of economic unity and integration. The homelands program is a classic hybridization of racial discrimination and dependency. Should the homelands remain, which is difficult to envision in a post-apartheid country, they would continue to be dependent on the government of South Africa.

THE FUTURE OF SOUTH AFRICA

There is considerable speculation about the future of South Africa. Much depends on the ability of mainstream Afrikaner and African leadership. President de Klerk and his supporters appeal to moderate Afrikaner opinion. To their right they find the Conservative party, which broke away from the Nationalist party. On the far right of Afrikaner opinion is the Afrikaner Resistance Movement (ARM), which threatens armed struggle to preserve a "white" homeland in South Africa. Many groups claim to represent Africans, but two have emerged as primary contenders for African support. The African National Congress (ANC), founded in 1910, is one. It apparently favors a unitary state, with real power at the center exercised on the basis of "one person-one vote." The electorate would also be unitary: "blacks," "coloureds," "whites," and others would all be together in one pool of voters. The outcome of this arrangement would seemingly consist of majority or in this case "black" rule, construed in numerical terms. But whether the minority groups of "coloureds," "whites," and others would receive a share in the exercise of power proportionate to their voting strength or a certain number of constitutionally guaranteed seats in the main legislative body is not known.

The Zulus, who have their own homeland in Kwazulu, their own political organization in the Inkatha Freedom Party, and their own internationally known leader in Chief Mangosuthu Gatsha Buthelezi, are another force to be reckoned with in their own terms. These are now ambiguous. Some have suggested that the Zulus are seeking a middle ground between white minority rule and the prospect of "radical rule" by a black majority. Chief Buthelezi does seem to be trying to keep one foot in the "white world" and one in the "black." He accepted the position of Chief Minister of Kwazulu, which made him part of the widely criticized homelands program, but then as minister, he refused to accept the South African government's interpretation of what "independence" for his homeland meant. Survival in two worlds has been the overriding objective of others caught in a cultural and sometimes military crossfire. Whether he and his 6 million ethnic brothers and sisters can straddle this vortex remains to be seen.

BUSINESS CONDUCT IN A TROUBLED LAND

In such a situation how should business proceed? With caution. Businesses must know as much as possible about the South African context. Decisions made or implemented in a historical or cultural vacuum would not serve their interests. No one can predict the outcome of current negotiations, but it may be time to consider South Africa more as land of promise than tragedy.

12

Namibia: Multiple Victimizations, from the Nineteenth Century to the Present

Dennis M. P. McCarthy
with Timothy Joseph O'Rourke

On 21 March 1990, Namibia became an independent nation after seventy-five often turbulent and painful years under South African control. The achievement of Namibia's legal or "flag" independence brought to fruition negotiations that had gone on for years between the South African government and groups representing Namibians, especially SWAPO (the South West Africa People's Organization). These negotiations, sometimes conducted under international auspices and with the diplomatic good offices or help of foreign diplomats, resulted in the free and fair elections that gave SWAPO majority representation in the Namibian legislature and made Sam Nujoma, the SWAPO leader, the president of the new country (*NYT* 21 March 1990: 1).

The achievement of "flag" independence could not in and of itself break the patterns of dependency and victimization that over a century and a half of outsider manipulation had fastened on the country. This case study examines that outsider manipulation and the dependency and victimization that accompanied it. Namibia's travail unfolded in several phases. Certain trading relationships, which exported livestock and imported guns, involved Namibia in international economic arrangements during the nineteenth century. These business connections created conditions that both undermined indigenous societies and invited foreign political intervention.

In 1884 Germany declared a protectorate over part of Namibia and began a second phase of outsider manipulation. In subsequent years Germany expanded its control over the entire territory. Germany, which had emerged as a unified nation-state only in the 1860s, became involved in southwest Africa (and east and west Africa) as part of the wider "scramble for Africa" that led to that continent's partition among the European powers in the 1880s and 1890s. Germany was eager to help its settlers establish themselves in Namibia. The

German organization of Namibia, which featured the brutal subjugation of its ethnic groups and their coerced participation in the mining and settler economies, came to an abrupt and unfinished conclusion in 1915. Then Allied forces defeated the Germans in southwest Africa during World War I.

The German phase of victimization turned out to be only preparatory in light of what South Africa did to the country during its seventy-five years of manipulation. South Africa, which had acquired German Southwest Africa as a Class C mandate under the League of Nations, carried through with a policy of creating "native reserves" or constrained living spaces for the indigenous peoples of Namibia. A legal framework of increasing complexity was designed to control the basics of people's everyday lives: where they worked, for whom, what they did, for how long they did it, how much they got paid, how far they could travel, whether they could take their families with them, and so on. The South African government used a principle of race based on skin pigmentation to organize Namibia much as it operated at home.

During the period of South African rule, multinational corporations became deeply immersed in an extraction of Namibia's resources that was exploitative or abusive. These corporations came from many countries and broaden the scope of an indictment of the foreign business presence in Namibia as destructive. The Tsumeb Corporation, named after the location in Namibia of its principal mining operation, exemplified the modus operandi of international business in Namibia: insensitive, taking out much more than it was returning, paternalistic, and very shortsighted. Tsumeb was a narrowly focused, supply-oriented investor in Namibia. The South African period, with a special feature on the Tsumeb Corporation, focuses this case study.

The Cerro Corporation in Peru (Chapter 7), Intercor in Colombia (Chapter 8), and the Tsumeb Corporation all touch upon the related themes of dependency, victimization, and exploitation but not in the same way and degree. Tsumeb seems the most inconsiderate corporate guest. The Cerro Corporation consolidated itself on the backs of less powerful Peruvian miners, but the historical record indicates that indigenous mining interests must share some of the blame for the eventual triumph of foreign capital. This was clearly not the case in Namibia, where international business seized local resources. Intercor's behavior in Colombia produced an entangled mix of harm and benefit for the country, which does not lend itself to easy generalization. These three supply-oriented companies exhibit different modes of behavior in very different local contexts.

BACKGROUND: THE LATER GERMAN PERIOD

In 1911 and 1912 the Germans divided the territory into spheres of influence for different enterprises and decided to create spheres of influence for Africans, though of a different kind. The realization finally took hold that the African population needed some kind of protection in order to regenerate itself after the bloody repression of the Herero and Nama rebellions from 1904 into 1907. The present situation, which featured Herero and Nama survivors living dispersed on white farms, did not bode well for the continuation of either Hereros or Namas as distinctive ethnic groups. The central premise behind African reserves was to provide a minimal support structure for an ethnic community. The reserves would permit the maintenance of a semi-autonomous social structure but entrench economic dependency, essential to the economy of labor mobilization. Restrictions would ensure that the reserves would never become productive enough to support their populations without income from wage labor.

SOUTH AFRICA TAKES OVER AND
REFINES ETHNIC EXPLOITATION

The Germans did not have time to establish those dependent African reserves on the scale envisioned. Germany lost South West Africa in 1915 to forces from the Union of South Africa, representing the British Empire. The only reserve created, in a small area near Rehoboth, was set aside for the "Basters," a community of mixed Afrikaner-African descent. The concept remained for the South Africans to expand. After Germany's defeat in World War I, the Union of South Africa acquired South West Africa from the new League of Nations as a Class C mandate: least able to stand alone in the international community. Whether those who designed that ranking knew it or not, expanding contact with white traders and settlers over a century had dislocated and then destroyed the local African economies of Namibia. The indigenous basis for autonomous development was gone. The South African presence in the years to come would reinforce the bonds of the economy of labor mobilization and the debilitating dependency associated with it.

The South African government used South West Africa as a place to relocate its own poor white population. Poor whites mocked the European success ethic that was one pillar of the implicit ideology upon which the controllers rested their claim to rule. The hope was that in their new lands the poor whites might become prosperous and examples of the success ethic. The South African government began in 1920 to take a series of measures that would open up Namibia for a substantial intrusion of white settlers from South Africa. It cancelled all land concessions held by German syndicates. All German Crown lands, which included land confiscated from the Herero and Nama after their rebellions, passed over to South Africa. It gained ownership of the entire country, with three exceptions: the Ovambo territory north of the Police Zone, the "Baster" reserve, and the land owned by German settlers.

The South African government dissolved the German firm *Diamenten Regie* and gave the diamond-mining rights to Consolidated Diamond Mines. This was a newly created subsidiary of DeBeers, the South African based corporation that dominates diamonds worldwide. The government allowed the Otavi Company to continue its base-metal operations at the Tsumeb outcrop.

But the South African government could do little with German settlers under the terms of its mandate. It did deport all German military and administrative personnel and expel a number of "undesirable" settlers who had resisted occupation in 1915. These actions reduced the size of the German population by half and added 3 million hectares to the land available for alienation to South African settlers (1 hectare = 2.471 acres). A substantial German settler presence still remained: about 7,000 people holding 11 million hectares of land. These holdings constituted about 80 percent of the total land in private ownership before the South African occupation. The land was by and large prime. Most of it was located in former Herero territory, the richest grazing land in the entire country.

This irreducible German presence had significant implications for potential South African settlers and their government. Since those Germans could not be expelled, the newcomers would have to settle on less productive lands. To compensate for the fact that much of the land available for alienation was less than choice, larger acreages seemed necessary. Increasing farm size brought larger operating expenses. Greater expenses placed another burden on those South African settlers, the vast majority of whom were poor whites without land, sometimes called byowners. The prospect of greater settlement costs implied increased government financial assistance.

Despite expenses, the government pushed ahead. It established a Land Board to survey farms and alienate the new holdings. By the end of 1921 the board had alienated 414 farms, which covered an area of 3,721,026 hectares: the average alienation amounted to 22,209.312 acres. By the end of 1921 the South African population exceeded the German. Former residents of the Union of South Africa accounted for 57 percent of the 18,558 whites in the country. By the end of 1922 white farms occupied about half of the central plateau.

The poor financial condition of the settlers compelled the government to pay a substantial share of their expenses. The large size of the average alienation was deemed necessary for successful farming in the less fertile areas of the south central plateau, where many of the new settlers located. They could not meet the start-up costs, let alone the expenses of continued maintenance and expansion. In 1921 the average assets of the Afrikaner settlers amounted to about 867 pounds. In 1922, as still poorer people entered the territory, that figure declined to 682 pounds. The landless Afrikaners needed much help simply to start. Their government responded with generous loans often never recovered, with remissions on rent arrears, and with considerable upgrading of the settler-oriented infrastructure. The government built dams, bored holes for water, and tried to maintain strategic transport arteries.

THE INTENSIFICATION OF LABOR MOBILIZATION

The settlers got much; the Africans, nothing, except more repression. The Herero had petitioned the government for land and were refused. The administration would not let local African economies recover because regeneration would create work for Africans at home and reduce the necessity to seek employment with the settlers and miners. The labor shortage, already significant before the Afrikaner influx, became acute as their settlement increased. There were not enough Herero and Nama males to meet the demand for labor from the farms and mines. The only other major indigenous source was the Ovambo population in the north. The Ovambos had not participated in the 1904–1907 rebellions.

However, laboring as a ranch hand was among the least desirable alternatives available to the Ovambo. After the Germans had designated Ovamboland as the exclusive labor pool for foreign mining operators in 1911 and 1912, a number of Ovambo, particularly those who had no cattle, took up jobs as mine workers. Their pay was not substantial, but it was still above what the settlers, especially the byowners, could afford. From an Ovambo perspective, cattle keeping, cattle raiding, other farm work for themselves, and then if driven by necessity laboring in the mines all yielded greater returns than would farm work for already financially strapped settlers. Once again, from the government's perspective, the laws of economics would have to yield to the laws of force—the foundation of the economy of labor mobilization.

The administration moved to eliminate or repress by law Ovambo alternatives to wage labor. A central strategy was to increase the number of Ovambo without cattle by suppressing cattle raiding. The government knew that if it could extend effective administrative control over northern Namibia, it would be able to shut down all cattle-raiding operations. Ovambo herds were recovering from the rinderpest epizootic of 1897, but not fast enough. As a consequence, cattle raided from others, including members of their own ethnic group, were sometimes necessary to maintain political power and, in increasing numbers of cases, to ward off starvation. With cattle raiding for the most part closed down, more Ovambo would be driven to seek wage labor in order to survive. There were only so many mining jobs available, so increasing numbers would have to settle for work on European farms, a primary objective of the administration in its nurturing of white settlement.

The suppression of cattle raiding continued the German modus operandi of brutal force in Namibia. The fate of Mandume, a chief of the Kwanyama Ovambo, illustrates this repression. Driven out of Angola by Portuguese attacks, he settled in northern Namibia and began raiding the cattle of other Ovambo groups. From 1915 on the South Africans repeatedly warned Mandume to stop these activities, but he ignored their orders. By making the area unsafe he interfered with the efforts of recruiters to induce Ovambo men to move south as wage laborers. The South Africans dealt with Mandume in a fashion that befit the German legacy. In 1922 a military force went to Ovamboland, killed Mandume and over 100 other Kwanyamas, and placed the survivors under the direct authority of a government bureaucrat, called a native commissioner. This commissioner acted as a recruiting officer to channel the now completely impoverished Ovambo to jobs on the central plateau. The economy of labor mobilization was slipping into higher gear.

To suppress cattle raiding the South Africans preferred to rely on fines. The raiders had to pay those fines in cash, which sent the following riptide through Ovambo society. To get cash chiefs raised taxes, which came to them in cattle, which enlarged the group of Ovambo without cattle, who had to seek wage labor. The chiefs then had to sell the cattle to traders or the South African government in order to obtain cash for the fines. Success as a cattle raider was, in the end, self-defeating because each acquisition only triggered more fines. Those who did not pay their fines experienced the laws of the economy of labor mobilization.

The fate of Ipumbu, a chief of the Kuambi Ovambo, shows the fate of those who refused to pay their fines. He was fined repeatedly from 1922 to 1932. When he did not pay in 1932, the South Africans bombed the chief's homestead and surrounding community from airplanes. The Kuambi lost all of their cattle and became instant paupers, instead of slipping into this status less quickly as a result of the continued payment of fines. The government deposed Ipumbu and drove him into exile. The circumstances surrounding the removal of Mandume and Ipumbu were somewhat different. The former ignored warnings; the latter, fines. Their fates were very different. One was murdered; the other lived, though in restricted conditions. But the survivors among their people went down the same road. After exiling Ipumbu, the government appointed a resident commissioner for the Kuambi. This bureaucrat facilitated the flow of labor onto white farms. The economy of labor mobilization, as a result of this and other episodes, was slipping into even higher gear. In 1921 virtually no Ovambo worked on white farms. By 1936 over 17,000 farm laborers were Ovambo.

The Herero and Nama also faced increasing government repression. The central South African objective with them, as it was with the Ovambo, was to eliminate alternatives to wage labor. In 1920 the government extended the Land Act of 1913 from South Africa to Namibia. Since at that time effective administrative control had not penetrated Ovamboland, extending the Land Act adversely affected the Herero and Nama first.

The Land Act harmed indigenous autonomous economic activity in several ways. It prohibited Africans from purchasing land. It abolished sharecropping arrangements. Here Africans did all the work in connection with producing a crop on a white owner's land and then turned over a share, often half, of that crop to him in return for the right to use his land for crops, livestock, and their dwellings. The Land Act forbade landowners to rent any portion of their land to Africans.

Extending the Land Act to Namibia ratified an already entrenched dependency. The Herero and Nama owned no land as a result of earlier German and South African actions, but now they could not legally change that situation. Nor could the Ovambo expand their limited grazing areas. Abolishing sharecropping and straight renting took away forms of farming that were dependent in some respects but autonomous in others. The extension of the Land Act foreclosed the possibilities for independent or semi-autonomous African stock farming to emerge in any significant way.

The legal web contained other constraints. The administration was concerned that some Africans, as alternatives to wage labor, might forage for food in the unoccupied areas of the territory or graze a few head of small stock. Its solution was the Vagrancy Act of 1920, which resembled a German statute. Any "suspicious" African was liable to arrest. In the early 1920s white settlers had occupied only about half of the central plateau. They had taken the best grazing area, but there was still a substantial amount of bush land on which Africans might forage or graze stock. Roving Africans in that region were special targets of the Vagrancy Act.

Once mobilized, African farm workers were, in a sense, immobilized. In 1920 the government decreed the Masters and Servants Ordinance, which dealt with both employees and employers. Africans were prohibited from quitting their farm jobs. The white owners were empowered to exact specific job performances from their African laborers. Africans were to work on one-year contracts, either written or oral. In the case of a dispute, the existence of a contract was taken for granted. Breach of contract through job desertion was a criminal offense, with the perpetrator liable to fines and/or imprisonment. African "servants" were liable to fines and/or imprisonment for various offenses, which included refusing to obey, intoxication, neglect of duty, and simple impertinence. The ordinance aimed to prevent "masters" from applying corporal punishment to their "servants," but in most respects the legislation resembled the German Imperial Ordinance of 1896 for South West Africa.

NATIVE RESERVES

This legal infrastructure of land, vagrancy, and masters and servants statutes was not sufficient to deal with the labor problem. More Africans had to be mobilized. The Herero and Nama populations needed space to recover from German reprisals and to regenerate their own economies. The South Africans accepted the first point but not the second because revival would provide alternatives to wage labor for whites. The solution, which paralleled German thinking before World War I, was to establish native reserves in 1921 and 1922.

These reserves offered several administrative advantages. The government could more effectively control the African population once it was confined to fixed locations. The Vagrancy Act, for instance, could be administered more easily. By limiting the size of the reserves, the government could ensure that the population increase that did occur would pressure already sparse resources and force more men to seek outside work. The government could contain the effects of one decision it had made that significantly departed from German practice. The South Africans had lifted the German ban on African stock acquisition, which might seem at first glance a major key to indigenous economic regeneration, but stock need suitable land and enough of it to thrive. On neither count did the reserves prove acceptable for livestock, let alone their care-givers.

The African reserves were demarcated in the least desirable areas of Namibia. In 1922 the government designated as reserves some 10,487,377 hectares, or about 20 percent of the Police Zone excluding the Namib Desert. Of this total the Herero received about 6 million hectares. These people, who numbered about 32,000 in 1922, were confined to an area that was 40 percent of the land mass held by the 14,000 white settlers in Namibia. Half the Herero reserve was located on the border of the Kalahari Desert. This land was useless, the "thirstland" into which von Trotha had driven the Herero in 1904. It was almost entirely arid; water had to come from boreholes sunk over 250 feet. The government sank only one borehole in the half of the Herero reserve bordering the Kalahari in the early 1920s. In 1921 and 1922 it sunk a total of thirteen on all African reserve lands, only six of which yielded water. By contrast, during that same period, the government sank 198 boreholes for white farmers; how many yielded water is not known to the authors.

The Nama reserves to the south were no better. The Nama received 1 million hectares. They numbered about 15,000 in 1922, or more than the total settler population; yet the government allocated them an area that was only 6 percent the size of white occupied land. Their 1 million hectares would have made up about 100 white farms under the Land Board's alienation policy in the early 1920s.

The reserves facilitated administrative efforts, which included the levying of more taxes. In 1921 the government enacted a hut tax, which created a further need to work for wages: 12 shillings per year for every dwelling an African possessed. In that year the government enacted several types of taxes that aimed to control alternatives to wage labor. The first was a tax on African livestock: every month an African had to pay 1 shilling for every head of cattle and six pence for every sheep or goat he possessed. The tax discouraged stock accumulation. An African possessing twenty head of cattle might, for example, have his entire monthly wage go for stock taxes.

A dog levy worked against hunting. Deprived of their guns, some Africans had turned to using dogs to track and run down game in order to supplement their own food production. The South Africans feared that successful hunting would undercut the labor supply. Under pressure from white farmers, the government introduced an escalating scale of taxation on African dogs. Every year an African had to pay 1 pound on the first dog he owned; for a second, 2 pounds and 10 shillings; for a third, 4 pounds and 10 shillings, and so on. This scale limited the size of an African's hunting force to one or two dogs and, in so doing, destroyed its effectiveness.

The dog tax precipitated a crisis among the Bondelswart, the southernmost Nama group. These people, disarmed by the Germans before the general Nama rebellion, had made effective use of dogs to obtain game. They refused to pay the dog tax and to give up their leader Abraham Morris, a veteran of the 1904 Nama rebellion who had returned from exile in South Africa. On 29 May 1922, South Africa attacked. Its planes bombed and strafed the Bondelswart; its mounted riflemen broke into the reserve. Over 100 Africans were killed, including Morris, and several hundred, many of them women and children, were wounded. All Bondel stock were confiscated and all dogs were shot. The South Africans had definitely eliminated the predominant Bondelswart alternatives to wage labor: the economy of labor mobilization once again operated as the economy of brutalization.

The web of control over Namibia was not yet complete. The Native Proclamation of 1922 implemented a pass law. An African could not leave his place of employment without a pass issued by his employer. No African without a pass could be employed, and any African found outside a reserve without a pass was liable to arrest as a vagrant. Non-whites could not enter the Police Zone without a pass. Africans had to obtain passes from their employers or magistrates, who could refuse their requests for any reason. The pass law interlocked with the statutes on vagrancy and masters and servants to hamper severely African freedom of movement. With mobility largely eliminated, there was no need to pay a higher wage to attract African labor. Low wages became the rule for Africans working for foreign businesses of all kinds.

These enterprises were not growing at the same rate. The business of settler farming was expanding in dramatic fashion. The Land Board continued to sell off huge tracts of land to incoming whites from South Africa. By 1935 white settlers had received 25,467,628 hectares, or 62,930,508 acres of land, about 56 percent of the arable land of the Police Zone. The government continued to provide massive grants to the settlers. By contrast, the mining industry did not grow at all from 1921 to 1929, and then it declined from 1929 to 1935 as a result of the Great Depression. The stagnation and distress of the mining industry benefited white farmers. They enjoyed from the early 1920s through the mid-1930s an adequate supply of labor paid low wages because demand for labor in the mines was flat through most of the 1920s and then diminished during the Great Depression.

ACCELERATING BUSINESS COMPETITION
FOR SCARCE AFRICAN LABOR

After 1935 the situation changed and precipitated another labor shortage. White settlement continued to expand, but mining began to recover slowly from the effects of the depression. While the industry would not reach production levels averaged during most of the 1920s until 1948, its comeback began to reclaim African workers who had gone to labor on farms. A second factor increasing the demand for African labor was a change in settler farming. Some farmers on the south central plateau began to substitute Karakul sheep for the smooth-haired variety that had predominated in the region. Karakul sheep yield lambskin fur. Farmers decided to raise this breed aggressively. This move meant increased herd sizes, which required more land and African laborers.

All these factors—the continued expansion of white settlement, recovery of the mining industry, and emergence of Karakul sheep-farming—triggered more than just another labor shortage. After 1935 some old and some new government fears intensified. There was the perennial concern that wage competition between miners and farmers would break out, despite the legal infrastructure constructed in the early 1920s, and that many farmers would be losers. The new specter originated in how the environment would affect different groups of farmers. Drought was a major problem at all times in Namibia, but the 1920s and 1930s were decades of special devastation. Over the sixteen years from 1920 to 1936 ten years were classified as drought years. Drought did not affect very much the ways the mining industry operated in Namibia, but it had a varying impact on farmers. Drought harmed Karakuls, a hardy breed of sheep, less than other small stock. The government feared that mine operators and to a lesser extent Karakul ranchers would be able to offer higher wages than the cattle and smooth-haired sheep farmers. These settlers might be unable to get any labor at all and have to go out of business. A group of impoverished whites, having lost their land to the larger-landowning Karakul farmers, might emerge. This specter drew strength from strong memories of what the situation had been in South Africa itself before 1920, when many of the landed in Namibia had been the landless in South Africa.

These fears drove the government to impose more infrastructure after 1935 on the Ovambo peoples north of the Police Zone. Laws enacted in the early 1920s were controlling the Herero and Nama peoples effectively. But the Ovambo posed a special threat to white rule. The Ovambo population was greater than that of the Herero, Nama, and whites combined. Though they were now within the sphere of effective South African administration, the Ovambo had never been humiliated as had the peoples of the central plateau. Ovambo had for some time been working for wages in mines. The South African government had kept the division of Namibia whereby mining operators had to recruit north of the Police Zone. In practice, mining recruiters had concentrated on Ovamboland, although a few Okavango also entered into "contracts." The government was now worried that Ovambo, attracted to higher wages offered by mining operators and Karakul ranchers, might pour into the central plateau and undermine the prevailing structure of low wages. These higher wages would never materialize, but the government again followed one of its central administrative canons: when worried, repress.

LABOR MOBILIZATION FURTHER REFINED

The administration spelled out in greater detail certain control principles that were already on the books. In 1935 it enacted the Extra-Territorial and Northern Natives Control Proclamation. Its twin aims were to prevent that Ovambo influx and suppress wage competition. A "northern native" could not enter the Police Zone without a pass issued by an employer. Ovamboland became a "proclaimed area": whites could not enter without government approval. The Ovambo were blocked in two ways. They could not respond to the prospect, real or illusionary, of higher wages to the south. They could not contact potential employers directly. Recruiting agencies licensed by the government received requests from various employers for labor and then unilaterally assigned workers to jobs. The economy of labor mobilization was also an economy of rapidly disappearing choices.

Government-directed labor recruiting in Namibia received its fullest expression in the creation of the South West African Native Labour Association (SWANLA) in 1945. SWANLA was empowered to control completely labor recruitment north of the Police Zone and to set minimum wages for all Namibia. Every African north of the Zone who wished to work for wages outside his homeland had to report to an office of SWANLA, where its agents continued the earlier practice of unilaterally assigning jobs. Employers forwarded a request for a specified number of workers, paid a recruiting fee, and SWANLA filled the orders.

ECONOMIC BOOM, U.K. INVESTMENT CAPITAL, AND U.S. MULTINATIONALS

What crystallized the labor recruitment monopoly and other control measures was an economic boom in Namibia that began during World War II and skyrocketed in the postwar period. What drove the boom was investment capital from South Africa, much of which originated in the United Kingdom, and the growing involvement of U.S. multinationals in base metal mining. Virtually everything foreign flourished. From 1935 to 1960 the total number of animals under white control doubled. Land possessed by whites increased from 25 million hectares in 1935 to 39 million in 1960. A fishing industry developed with South African capital. Base metal production, dominated by the U.S. controlled Tsumeb Corporation, increased in value from 3 million pounds in 1950 to 8 million pounds in 1960.

While capital fueled the boom, labor delivered it. Increased supplies of African labor, particularly Ovambo workers, made the dramatic development of the white economy possible. The number of Ovambo recruited through SWANLA rose from 25,712 in 1953 to 44,000 in 1955. By 1960 about 50,000 Ovambo, who made up almost 40 percent of the territory's total African labor force, went to jobs through SWANLA. Employment of all Africans in the mining industry, which led the unprecedented expansion, increased from 2,809 in 1946, to over 7,000 by 1953, and then peaked at 16,000 in the mid-1960s.

While almost everything foreign flourished, almost everything African suffered. As the greatest physical contributors to white expansion, the Ovambo found their own homeland worse off than before. The 50,000 Ovambo who made up almost 40 percent of the territory's total African labor force in 1960 also constituted over 80 percent of the employable adult male population of Ovamboland. Their prolonged absences in such numbers adversely affected what remained of indigenous economic activity and entrenched impoverishment and dependency on white wages.

All African workers found themselves enmeshed in a more intricate control web. The economy of labor mobilization was bringing together a force that might do things other than labor. In the 1950s the South African government tried to contain or repress that potential power in various ways. It prohibited strikes or the intent to strike in the Bantu Labor (Settlement of Disputes) Act of 1953. The government denied to Africans significant opportunities to advance and enhance their skills in the Mines, Works, and Minerals Ordinance of 1954. This legislation required that all administrative, supervisory, engineering, and surveying positions be reserved for white workers. The government attempted to limit the development of African trade unions in the Industrial Conciliation Act of 1956. This enactment did not forbid Africans from organizing unions, but the government recognized only all-white unions for the purposes of collective bargaining.

In other legislation the government struck further at the ability of Africans to organize their personal lives. The Natives Urban Areas Proclamation of 1951 was central to this endeavor. It mandated segregated compounds for African workers and restrictions that prevented African families from moving into urban areas with employed husbands. It required unemployed Africans to leave municipal areas for their reserves within seventy-two hours of job termination. This provision dealt with the destabilizing potential of a growing army of urban unemployed. It also forced the African back home where he might become a recruit for more labor. The urban African had to be employed, could not have his family with him, and earned low wages justified as covering the needs of only one person whose family was "supported" by a reserve.

While the labor that delivered the boom experienced growing personal and group repression, the capital that powered it continued unrestrained. As the leading sector of the post–World War II boom, the mining industry engineered a critical phase in the economic repression of colonial Namibia. This was the emergence of a mining-dominated, export-oriented economy in the years after World War II. The Tsumeb Corporation played a large role in this process.

THE TSUMEB CORPORATION

The Tsumeb Corporation, Ltd., was formally incorporated in South Africa in January 1947, but it was controlled by capital based in the United States. At its incorporation and for much of its legal life, two U.S. multinationals, the Newmont Mining Company and AMAX Incorporated (formerly American Metal Climax), held controlling interests. At incorporation Newmont and AMAX together held 65 to 70 percent of the Tsumeb Corporation. This tandem of majority control continued until 1982, when AMAX sold its interest in Tsumeb to GFSA, a subsidiary of Consolidated Gold Fields, Ltd., of the United Kingdom. The Tsumeb Corporation developed into a mining giant in Namibia and an important player in the economy overall. For a long time it accounted for about 80 percent of base metal production in Namibia, which contributed about 20 percent of the total value of all Namibian exports.

Through the production and export of base metals the Tsumeb Corporation further connected the Namibian economy with outsiders.   Foreign owned, managed, and oriented, the company tried to maximize the extraction and export of ore, as well as the repatriation of the great bulk of its profits. It aimed to take the most it could from the country as fast as possible. From 1949 to 1971 the three mines of the Tsumeb Corporation at Tsumeb, Kombat, and Matchless (near Windhoek) produced an average of 589,938 tons of ore every year, almost all of which was exported. The ore was refined at the mining sites, then shipped by rail to Walvis Bay, from where it was exported to overseas markets. Copper went mainly to Japan, while lead and zinc reached Belgium, Luxembourg, and the United Kingdom. Production declined in the 1970s, as world commodity prices fell and the quality of available mineral reserves diminished.

Mining as the Tsumeb Corporation and others did in Namibia constrained the country many ways. These capital-intensive firms imported their specialized machinery from the United States and other western nations. The mining companies did little or nothing to promote the development of local manufacturing capacity. Taxes on mining operations produced revenue for the South African government.   This money might have financed a broad development program for Namibia, but it went instead to "develop" the white minority. There were no government controls on profit repatriation, and Tsumeb channeled most of its returns to sources outside the country.

The corporation did reinvest but in a manner that reinforced its primary role as an extractor. By 1971 reinvestment over the previous decades had amounted to $70,894,000. This sum was only 6.6 percent of the total sales that Tsumeb realized from 1947 to 1971, which came to $1,073,960,075. Most of what was reinvested went to the company's own operations: Tsumeb built more smelters, ore refineries, and processing plants. The company was supply oriented and export geared.

Unrestrained dividend repatriation harmed the country. The principal beneficiaries of this transfer were Newmont and AMAX, the two major controllers of Tsumeb. Before its involvement in this corporation, Newmont's dividend income from domestic sources (U.S.A.) was about three times the amount derived from foreign operations. By 1951 its foreign earnings, drawn largely from Namibia, exceeded domestic dividend earnings. Tsumeb's emergence enabled Newmont to assume a position of major leadership in the mining industry. AMAX also benefited considerably from its participation in Tsumeb. From 1965 to 1971 dividends from the Tsumeb Corporation contributed an average of 9.1 percent annually to AMAX's net earnings. Both companies, using their Tsumeb earnings, expanded their operations elsewhere in Africa and outside the continent. Newmont participated in a number of major projects, two of which were in South Africa (Palabora and Highveld) and one in southern Peru. AMAX acquired interests in mining in Botswana, South Africa, and Zambia.

Tsumeb was not as generous to its African workers. In 1956 African laborers throughout the entire mining industry received wages that ranged from R(Rands)60 to R280 per annum, while white employees averaged R1,200 annually, along with a monthly cost of living bonus of about R25. By 1973 Africans working for Tsumeb got an average annual wage of R470, a nominal increase of more than 167 percent from the maximum black salary in 1956. But African increments have not kept pace with those paid to unionized white workers, whose average annual salary had risen to R5,208 in 1973. From 1956 through 1973 white compensation increased almost three and one-half times: divide 5,208 by 1,500 (1,200 + 300). In 1973 Tsumeb's white mineworkers, 22.5 percent of the total labor force, received 80 percent of total wages.

African workers were entrapped by more than their poverty-level wages. They were forced to live in compounds similar to those in the Windhoek and Walvis Bay areas. African housing was officially described as "dormitory style." In fact, Africans lived twelve to a room in compounds near their places of work. Mine compounds were very crowded and unhygienic. With high walls around them, they resembled prisons: anyone trying to escape was liable to be shot. The town of Tsumeb graphically represented what Namibia's dependency came to mean. The company ran the town: water, roads, food supply, the airfield, and other facilities. AMAX and Newmont may have spent about $13.5 million as a "community responsibility" for housing, recreational facilities, and town development, but African workers have largely been excluded from experiencing the benefits of this expenditure. White workers, by stark contrast, usually lived in private residences of five or six rooms each. They could live with their families, a right denied to African workers.

NAMIBIA IN THE INTERNATIONAL POLITICAL ARENA

The harsh victimization of Namibia and its peoples encountered international censure. The United Nations ended South Africa's mandate over the territory in 1966. The South African government had refused to acknowledge the transformation of the mandate into the trusteeship system, which occurred under the sponsorship of the United Nations after World War II. The South African government defended its continued administration of the territory by pointing out that the land was by prior international certification a Class C or "basket-case" mandate. As such it needed special very long-term administrative care. The United Nations rejected South Africa's case and was sustained by the International Court of Justice. On 21 June 1971, the court held that ongoing South African administration of Namibia was illegal.

In 1974 the United Nations moved to create an international legal framework for the protection of Namibia's resources. Decree No. 1 for the Protection of the National Resources of Namibia, approved by the General Assembly on 13 December 1974, was central to that endeavor. The Decree declared that "no person or entity, whether a body corporate or unincorporated, may research for, prospect for, explore for, take, extract, mine, process, refine, use, sell, export, or distribute any natural resource, whether animal or mineral, situated or found to be situated within the territorial limits of Namibia without the consent and permission of the United Nations Council for Namibia or any person authorized to act on its behalf for the purpose of giving such permission or consent" (Naqvi 1984: 35).

THE CONTINUED CORPORATE EXPLOITATION
OF NAMIBIA'S RESOURCES

Despite this decree and its reaffirmation in 1983, western-based multinational corporations and other interests, in collaboration with the government of South Africa, continued to exploit Namibia's resources. Western and other foreign economic involvement helped perpetuate the illegal South African occupation of the territory. Multinational corporations based in Canada, France, the Federal Republic of Germany, South Africa, the United Kingdom of Great Britain and Northern Ireland, and the United States of America were among those foreign economic interests that in 1984 still exploited Namibia and buttressed South African rule. The roster of U.S. businesses with interests in companies in Namibia then included, besides AMAX and Newmont, Alexander and Alexander Services, Inc., American Cyanamid Company, Dresser Industries, Inc., Firestone Tire and Rubber Company, Fluor Corporation, General Electric Company, General Motors Corporation, Joy Manufacturing Company, Kennecott Copper Corporation, Mobil Oil Corporation, Nord Resources Corporation, Phelps Dodge Corporation, Tenneco Incorporated, and the Black and Decker Manufacturing Company (Naqvi 1984: 39-40). Namibia never received the attention of the divestment campaigners that South Africa itself did.

THE END OF WHITE MINORITY RULE

The economy of labor mobilization ironically prepared the way for its own demise and the end of white minority rule over Namibia. As more Namibians, especially Ovambo, went to work for wages after World War II, an industrial labor force emerged that, as South Africans correctly feared, engaged in other activities besides wage labor. The Ovambo strike of 1971, which brought another massive application of military force by the white oppressors, demonstrated the disruptive potential of concerted industrial action. The existence of a politically strong and aware industrial labor force was one pillar of Namibia's drive for independence. A second came from the campaign of guerrilla warfare directed by SWAPO, the South West Africa People's Organization. Many Ovambo are deeply involved in SWAPO, from its high leadership through the ranks, but it is more than an Ovambo organization.

A third pillar was the series of negotiations among the principal parties that unfolded during the 1980s. Those taking part included the South African government, SWAPO, Cuba, and diplomats from the United States, especially Chester Crocker, the undersecretary of state for African Affairs. The major issue was Namibian independence, but South Africa's security was also critical. Cuba reportedly had over 45,000 troops in Angola, which is north of Namibia, and South Africa regarded this force as threatening. A Cuban promise to withdraw its forces was essential to the South African government's agreement to relinquish control over Namibia. The achievement of "flag independence" on 21 March 1990 did not end economic dependency, however.

The indepedent government worked to reform Namibia's relations with international businesses. In Rössing Uranium the government found a cooperative corporation, and their relationship shows that economic dependency can be transformed into economic reciprocity (*FT* 12 July 1991: 14).

13

Capitalism v. Socialism in Independent Africa: An Exclusive Dichotomy?

In much of Africa today the trend in economic development is apparently toward more reliance on market forces and less reliance on government action. This march parallels a retreat from Marxism, which had sometimes inspired or reinforced state-based economic development in many countries of independent Africa. Even in countries known for their doctrinaire and uncreative applications of Marxist ideology, the sacrosanct role of the state is crumbling. Mozambique, a former Portuguese colony in southeast Africa now grappling with a draining civil war and a crushing drought, opened the door in the early 1990s for the greater operation of market forces from the private sector. In October 1990, Mozambique's parliament approved articles in the country's new constitution that committed the previously Marxist state to political pluralism after fifteen years of one-party rule by Frelimo. In the same month the parliament also approved a clause in the new constitution that recognized private property and the role of market forces in the economy. The new economic order in Mozambique will be based on "appreciation of labour, market forces, initiative of agents, participation of all types of ownership and action by the state as a regulator and promoter of economic and social growth and development" (*FT* 23 October 1990: 4).

While this statement recognizes "initiative" and "all types of ownership," it reserves for the state a crucial role as "regulator and promoter of economic and social growth and development." The question for Mozambique, as it is for other African countries, may not be so much a switch from socialism to capitalism; rather, the challenge is to fashion an approach to development that combines elements of capitalism and socialism in public-private sector mixes distinctive to each country. For much of Africa capitalism and socialism do not represent totally opposed policy choices, but two major menus of approaches that are not exclusive of each other. One can select from both.

To understand why capitalism and socialism may be intersecting sets of possibilities and not contrary dogmas, one should appreciate what the colonial legacy has meant for Africa and how some African countries have dealt with development in the post-independence period. For Africa this time began in 1957, when the Gold Coast Colony obtained its independence from Great Britain as Ghana. Most of colonial Africa was decolonized by the late 1960s, but the struggle is not over in the former Spanish Sahara and South Africa. This case study first introduces the colonial legacy and then analyzes some post-independence attempts to define development, socialism, and capitalism in African contexts.

Tanzania receives special attention. It had an elegantly defined type of African socialism, inspirational leadership, ambitious goals, but flawed implementation. Experience there demonstrated in the 1970s that reliance on the state for all economic initiative and organization was a poor approach. The multiplication in Tanzania of *parastatals*, or agencies performing state-related functions, proved to be a bureaucratic nightmare, as paperwork and permissions throttled progress. During the early 1980s the Tanzanian government relaxed its opposition to a private sector. Toward the end of that decade it took positive steps to incorporate private initiative into a public-private sector mix that still retained the flagship notion of Tanzanian African socialism.

The experience of Tanzania and other countries in independent Africa demonstrates the need for prospective investors in Africa to look beyond the rhetoric. Zimbabwe illustrates how ideology is defined in actions and not just on paper. It remains a one-party state at a time when many other African countries are choosing pluralism in their political structures. It persists in a commitment to an Africanized version of Marxism at a time when Marxism is retreating elsewhere. It has recognized the necessity of foreign capital for its economic development and has promulgated and strengthened an investment code designed to attract foreign capital by specifying its rights and responsibilities. But in 1992 the Zimbabwean Parliament passed a law that permits compulsory acquisition of land with compensation but *without* the right to appeal the state's valuation of your confiscated property (*FT* 20 January 1992: 4). This law has sent chills through the international investment community and undermined the credibility of the country's investment code.

COLONIAL BACKGROUND

When each African territory achieved its legal, or "flag," independence, its new leaders inherited a range of problems. One was the existing bureaucracy. Colonial administrations were designed to promote stability, not economic development, an approach that was grounded in the situations the administrators faced. In the typical situation. several hundred European bureaucrats, assisted by thousands of co-opted "locals," attempted to manage populations in the millions. A key to effective administration was to preserve existing levels of localism and to encourage fragmentation where strategic, so as to never permit any entity to emerge that would be significant throughout an entire territory. The principle of divide and administer influenced colonial bureaucrats everywhere.

Only when Africans had organized themselves into "western-style" political parties with territorial stature were they able to challenge their European rulers within a system that the latter understood. But independence when granted was only "flag independence," to use the trenchant phrase of Julius K. Nyerere, one of Africa's greatest modern figures. "Flag independence" did not mean freedom from past structures of either international dependency or internal bureaucratic manipulation. The leaders of "flag independent" governments confronted the formidable tasks of how to deal with those twin sets of shackles.

DIFFERENT DEFINITIONS OF DEVELOPMENT

Their responses were not uniform. They differed considerably with respect to definition, rationale, and implementation.   Most "flag independent" governments at first proposed comprehensive definitions of development. They also located a major source of their problems in inequitable international economic relationships that are a legacy of formal imperialism.

A classic example of development broadly defined appeared in the preface to the Kenya Development Plan for the 1966–1970 period. Kenya received its "flag independence" from Great Britain in 1963. In that preface the late Tom Mboya summarized the many goals of government: "The aims of the Government are clear—to achieve high and growing per capita incomes, equitably distributed, so that all are free from want, disease, and exploitation, while at the same time ensuring and guaranteeing—(i) political equality in the full Kenyan traditional sense of a right which is independent of economic status and divorced from stern tests and discriminatory criteria; (ii) social justice; (iii) human dignity, including freedom of conscience; and (iv) equal opportunities, without discrimination by race, tribe or belief, but also without prejudice to remedying the inequalities inherited from the past." With so many objectives seemingly equal before it, no wonder the Kenyan government felt over-burdened. Other governments, whose visions of the future contained many specified but unranked components, also experienced difficulties in trying to reach so many ends simultaneously (McCarthy 1969: 7-8).

The Kenyan approach to development was advertised as *African socialism*. The government of Kenya took some actions to reduce barriers to educational and business opportunities. School fees for primary education were abolished in the 1960s, for instance. But socialism is more than government abolishing fees or giving money to people. It involves legal relationships that subordinate a small private sector to a larger public one. Sometimes private ownership of any kind of property is not recognized because the government asserts ownership of all land and everything on and under it within its borders. More often various types of usufructuary private property rights exist. That is, individual farmers, for instance, may not technically own the land they work, but they may have a property right to its product or usufruct. The approach of Kenya is socialist in rhetoric only. Its fundamental legal structures, on the level of the state, are capitalistic.

Some countries like Kenya have tried to promote development by relying on the entrepreneurial energies that privatized structures have historically nurtured. At the same time, they rhetorically invoke the communalism of earlier times through African socialism. This approach has proved congenial to international business, since governments with this outlook have taken a synergistic approach to foreign capital in their lands. International capital along with local entrepreneurship will, it is hoped, generate growth and development beyond what each working singly could achieve.

THE CASE OF TANZANIA

Other countries have tried to implement their own versions of an African socialism that was structurally socialist. Noteworthy among these, in terms of articulation of ideology and comprehensiveness of policy, has been Tanzania. Ideology has received more attention than implementation. Julius K. Nyerere, who led Tanganyika to independence and was president for almost a quarter century, is the foremost exponent of the Tanzanian version of African socialism. In 1963 he noted that "we are committed to a philosophy of African socialism and basic to it is the principle of human equality. The important question is how can we deal with income inequalities, given the present facts of our economic life. First, we must energetically pursue policies which will increase the amount of wealth produced in this country. Secondly, we must not allow the present income differentials to become sacrosanct." The generality of these two solutions informed the original formulation of the Tanganyikan Five-Year Plan for Economic and Social Development, written in 1964. It was not until the Arusha Declaration of January 1967 that a fuller ideological document emerged (McCarthy 1969: 8).

The Arusha Declaration, named after the northern Tanzanian town where the drafting conference convened, explained an African socialism that planners had devised for the Tanzanian environment. According to the declaration, TANU (the Tanganyikan African National Union) stood committed to policies of *socialism* and *self-reliance*. (TANU was the name of mainland Tanzania's only legal political party until 1977, when it merged with the Afro-Shirazi party of Zanzibar, also part of Tanzania, to become the *Chama cha Mapinduzi* [CCM], the Party of Revolution.) Socialism is understood as "a social situation which excludes exploitation of one man by another or of one class over another. The major means of production are to be under the control and ownership of the workers and peasants through the agency of the government and through cooperatives" (Bienen 1969: 545).

Exploitation, which is not precisely defined, supposedly originates in the actions of both persons and classes. In this respect the Tanzanian conception of socialism is selective. It borrows exploitation by class from a tradition that is strongly though by no means completely Marxist. It recognizes that people acting on their own can inflict harm on their fellow citizens. In this latter respect it partakes of an earlier strain of western liberalism in which the personality, rights, and responsibilities of the individual person were central.

The second part of the definition addresses the ownership of the means of production. The major means of production are at issue here. People may argue as to which means of production are major, but one fact is clear. The Tanzanian situation was never envisioned as one of complete public ownership in which there was no role for a private sector.

The "workers" and "peasants" (everyone is either one or the other) *de jure* (legally) own and control the major means of production. The government and its agencies, which include cooperatives, act on behalf of workers and peasants. This mediation role gives the government great power and has important implications for the sources of exploitation in such a society. The government and its associated agencies join classes and individual people as possible perpetrators of exploitation or harm.

Besides socialism, the second core concept in the Arusha Declaration is self-reliance. This is not the self-reliance that may be familiar to readers of Henry David Thoreau or other authors in the Transcendentalist school of U.S. literature. The "self" in Tanzania's conception of self-reliance is not so much the individual person depending on his or her own resources and able to go it alone. Rather, it is the country or nation itself. It is also the individual person working out his or her own personal identity through participation in the community on all its levels, from the family, through the village, up to the nation-state itself. In the context of development self-reliance means that the country must rely on its own resources, which are mainly agriculture, and depend less on outside sources of assistance.

The Tanzanian version of socialism exhibits the generic feature of a dominant public sector. But its conception of exploitation treats the person both as an individual and as a member of a class and, by implication, as an agent of an institution. In its emphasis on the major means of production, Tanzanian socialism opens the door wide for vigorous discussion as to just what is major and minor and thereby makes it possible for a significant private sector to emerge. In practice, the record until the mid-1980s showed the public sector, meaning the government and its agencies, multiplying itself and attempting to reduce the private sector. In the late 1980s the government shifted and gave greater recognition to "market forces."

The Tanzanian government began in the 1970s to implement systematically its version of socialism. Its endeavors included the reorganization of government, known as decentralization, which started in the early 1970s. Decentralization aimed to return more local decision-making autonomy to officials at the grass roots, whether they were government or party functionaries. In many cases, given the substantial overlap of state and party, the local party and government bureaucrat was often the same person. Decentralization achieved some measure of decision-making devolution within the structures of a one-party state that remained, on the whole, tautly organized from the center on substantive issues.

Besides decentralization, the Tanzanian government embarked during the 1970s on its world-famous experiment in rural reorganization known as *villagization*. Neither the term itself nor its implementation as policy was elegant. Villagization involved relocating thousands of Tanzanians into *ujamaa* villages. *Ujamaa* means "familyhood" in Kiswahili; the government translated it as "socialist." The roots of villagization are both near and remote. In the near term there had been scattered attempts in the late 1960s to organize rural life more efficiently. Efficiency meant then, as it would later on, the clustering of people in locations that would make the delivery of essential social, medical, and educational services more cost-effective.

It is crucial to note that the concept of efficiency uppermost in the minds of decision makers was bureaucratic. Though the government and the party were attempting to decentralize some structures of bureaucracy under the decentralization program, they found the rural population living in an excessively decentralized manner from their perspective. Most rural people lived too far part from one another to permit the effective delivery by the government of basic services. It seemed to make more sense to bring the people to the places deemed optimal for service delivery than to bring the services to where the people were then living.

How rural reorganization, not accomplished with an excess of voluntarism, would affect agricultural efficiency was not well thought out in advance. Total agricultural output declined in the early years of villagization from the mid-1970s on. Energies that might have been devoted to agriculture were absorbed in building the *ujamaa* villages. It would take time for people, familiar with their own land, to become as knowledgeable about the land at the disposal of their new village. The siting of these villages was not done with the quality of arable land as a crucial criterion. Therefore, for many Tanzanian farmers, the new land was not as suitable for what they were doing as was their former acreage.

Villagization evoked memories of the infamous Groundnut Scheme of the late 1940s and early 1950s in colonial Tanganyika. In that grossly bungled "development plan" British bureaucrats and business people undertook to have significant amounts of groundnuts produced in certain Tanganyikan locations. These had not been properly reconnoitered for their suitability in terms of soil content, precipitation patterns, or general desirability. The Groundnut Scheme relied on mechanization of an astonishingly inappropriate sort: over-sized machines on rugged terrain with no guarantee of replacement parts. Villagization was not as mismanaged as the Groundnut Scheme, but both demonstrate what can happen when decisions are made primarily with reference to remote goals and with insufficient local knowledge. The goal of villagization was the socialization of Tanzania as President Nyerere and his supporters wanted it. The Groundnut Scheme was designed to respond to the needs of British industry for commodities.

In the 1970s and into the early 1980s the Tanzanian government tried to reduce the private sector. This attempt drew strength not only from President Nyerere's vision of socialism, but also from historical grievances against the Indian community in Tanzania, which had been involved in business there for centuries. Some Africans accused Indian business people of unfair practices: the image of "the Indian" as the "exploiter" of "the African" was a powerful stereotype.   Indians were also viewed as part of the harmful legacy of imperialism and colonialism.   So the government moved to make private business activities difficult, if not impossible.

What the government tried to suppress it could not itself replace. The detailed local knowledge of commercial patterns and business practices, which generations of Indian families had accumulated in East Africa, was not in the possession of government bureaucrats, who were already struggling with an over-bureaucratization of the national economy. The delivery of basic goods and services, never problem free in the best of times, became more irregular. There were some things, the government had to acknowledge, that a private sector could perform more efficiently than a public one. The assault on private activities, which had weakened but not eliminated them, was abandoned as a misdirection of already scarce government energies and resources.   The Tanzanian government in the 1990s seeks to place more reliance on market forces. In addition, the ruling Revolutionary Party on 18 February 1992 decided to transform the country into a multi-party system (*Afrika* April 1992: 24).

BUSINESS OPPORTUNITIES IN INDEPENDENT AFRICA

Detailed local knowledge is necessary for every situation in Africa in which businesses contemplate activity. These opportunities can be grouped in three categories. There are countries, such as Kenya, that are rhetorically socialist but functionally capitalist. There are countries, such as Tanzania, that are ideologically and to some extent practically socialist but willing to work with international business on equitable terms. There are countries that articulate and practice capitalism. From Francophone Africa the two most successful examples, in economic terms, are the Ivory Coast and Cameroon, although both have experienced economic and political problems in the last several years. Both countries are still receptive to the presence of international capital and operate on the synergistic axiom concerning foreign involvement: international capital, local capital, and the state can accomplish more working together than separately. From Anglophone Africa, Nigeria and Sierra Leone are capitalistic in both ideology and practice. Nigeria, for all its problems, must be considered as a country of great business opportunities—a land of more than 70 million people whose buying power is not always monetized but that could be creatively tapped to support a variety of niche markets.

Each country must be examined on a case-by-case basis to determine what ideology means in theory and practice. While we have put countries in categories, many Africans do not view their choices in terms of an exclusive dichotomy: either capitalism or socialism. Their approaches to development are hybrids—trying to be "neither East nor West." Their approaches draw on other sources. One is the pre-colonial past. Theorists and planners attempt to translate past meanings of "community" and "extended family" on the local level into present motivating constructs on the national level.

DEVELOPMENT AS SHADOWED BY COLONIALISM

Development must deal with colonialism. This experience was in some respects capitalistic: the notion of private property was accepted *de jure* (legally) and *de facto* (actually) in certain areas. For instance, most Africans never owned the land that they farmed under pre-colonial or colonial legal patterns. In their "traditional societies," the chief or the group as a corporate body held the land in trust for all members, who owned the product of the land (the usufruct) and sometimes the trees, dwellings, and other equipment on it. Under formal colonialism the state or the colonial governor claimed the legal right to hold the land in trust for its inhabitants. The people retained the usufructuary rights, which most thought they had never given up.

Virtually all African countries today acknowledge some form of usufructuary right, but those societies inclined toward socialism place ownership of the land itself with the government. The ownership of the state is defended as necessary to achieve an egalitarian distribution of land among the people, most of whom are small-scale farmers. The case against state ownership of the land itself rests on the notion of *complete incentive*. The more private or privatized a process is, the more powerful is the incentive to use that process to pursue some maximum gain—whether output, financial returns, or some combination of the two. People who own the usufruct but not the land itself, according to this principle, are motivated but not as much as they would be if they owned the land itself. The principle, its adherents maintain, holds even within the domain of usufructuary rights. Those people who own only the product and not their dwellings, machinery, trees, or other improvements on or to the land do not experience the same degree of incentive as those who own everything except the land itself.

The colonial experience was in some respects also socialist or conducive to the creation of conditions necessary for socialism. The state or head of government as ultimate trustee of all land within a territory is important here. People can argue whether trusteeship implies legal ownership or means that the question of absolute ownership has been suspended. Whatever the case, the large state role in everyday life during the colonial period was a harbinger more of state socialism than of state capitalism (for more on state capitalism, see part V). The imposition of "western-style" bureaucracy on the many kinds of communalism (not to be confused with Marxist communism) exhibited by "traditional societies" has given leaderships inclined toward socialism the following argument. Their approach uses the already large role of the state in accord with "traditional" values that emphasize the individual person more in relation to the community than to himself or herself.

The fact that there is often a gross imbalance between an excessively bureaucraticized state and fading notions of "traditional community" undermines that argument. It is an over-bureaucraticized state that has contributed to the tainting of "traditional" values and been responsible for suffocating and distorting much needed entrepreneurial energies from people not in government. But a cure cannot be put so simply as downsizing the bureaucracy and reducing government regulation.

There are legitimate arguments for state action today that even the most laissez-faire business person must appreciate. Those who advocate minimal government intervention accept the necessity of state action to provide security, which is essential to the prosperous conduct of most business activity. The state can also provide a host of services to nurture economic activity in its incubation period. The state is needed as a referee should business interests harm the public. These positive aspects of state action are well known, although reasonable people can differ as to the degree of government involvement necessary to achieve those ends (part II, introduction).

What is not as widely understood is the role that African governments must play with respect to markets themselves in their countries. Some people in the West, when addressing Africa's current economic problems, argue that "market forces" must play a greater role. This argument rests on the assumption that there are "market forces" waiting to be unleashed in those areas where government intervention has predominated. There are compelling reasons to challenge this assumption. During the colonial period government bureaucracies damaged expressions of those "market forces" as well as the markets themselves. Various administrations manipulated prices, sometimes fixing them, in ways that undermined the capacity of price to function as an indicator of relative scarcity or abundance. Without price as a credible regulator of supply and demand, the "force" of the "market" is pretty weak.

Wages, which are both a cost of labor and an incentive to work, did not always function that way under colonial administration. They were a "cost of labor," but an incomplete one, since the vast majority of African laborers did not receive fair wages. Many African men sought wage labor because they needed it to pay the taxes that government levied on them. The incentive to work for money wages was less one of acquisition than avoidance—of working on "public works" if one defaulted on money tax. Wages, which some regard as mechanisms of exploitation under capitalism, were under colonialism entwined with another mode of extraction—that imposed by the state. So any concept of wage functioning as an indicator of supply and demand for various labor markets was seriously tainted. With such basic symbols as price and wage seriously distorted, "market forces" cannot express themselves with sufficient clarity.

Besides the symbols of market communication, colonial governments adversely affected the articulation of internal markets. The location of official market centers was often determined by administrative criteria, which blended supervisory and revenue concerns. Wider economic considerations—which locations would most benefit economic growth and development—received secondary emphasis, if these were taken into account at all. In some cases the siting of markets on administrative criteria may have coincided with where these should have been located for best economic effect. Evidence shows that official markets were, in the majority of cases, not sited in the best economic locations. There is a disturbing parallel between how colonial bureaucrats located official markets and how Tanzanian administrators sited *ujamaa* villages in the 1970s.

"Market forces" and markets themselves were not left alone by governments during the colonial period. The type and extent of damage inflicted by state action must be examined on a case-by-case basis: more research is needed. But it is clear that governments today may have to play various restorative roles with respect to "market forces" and markets. State action may be necessary for market revitalization and development.

GOVERNMENTS, BUSINESSES, AND "MARKET FORCES" TODAY

The kinds of restorative state action will vary according to particular cases. Some situations may require the gradual introduction of competition between or among private businesses. The state, in its role as referee, can regulate the restoration of competition. These "start-up" cases may need not only a referee, but also a supplier of resources. The state can provide incentives for both established and new businesses in these situations. The government can give or lease the land needed for operations. It can give grants or extend loans on favorable terms—with long repayment periods, low interest rates, and possibly a clause stipulating the forgiveness of the principal should certain mutually agreed upon goals be met within a certain time period. The government can furnish, or arrange for, free technical and legal assistance. Market restoration or creation requires that the government play a refined economic and business role. While intervening in certain aspects of activity as referee and resource supplier, the government may find it necessary to deregulate or revise regulation of other areas of behavior.

The government's capacity to communicate and persuade may be critical for the healthy emergence of "market forces" and markets in those situations where prior state action trampled and distorted them. There is one kind of market that a government can greatly affect in the short run—that for information. This set of markets is important, since the symbols of market communication—such as prices and wages—were abused by government bureaucracies during the colonial period. What strategies a government can employ to rejuvenate those essential symbols of market communication will depend upon consultation among media specialists, public relations personnel, government planners, the local citizenry, and involved business people. The irony is that for a government to cease acting as a market substitute it will have to intervene creatively in developing "market forces" and markets. Governments that acknowledge the utility of those forces and structures in economic growth and development must support rather than suffocate them.

Businesses contemplating ventures in Africa should consider all the main points analyzed in this case study: the hybrid nature of African development, ideology in theory and practice, and what openings a country's evolving public-private sector mix present, including crucial business roles in market restoration and development.

14

Vignette: International Business and Economic Integration in Africa

Contrasted with the progress of intercountry economic integration in Europe and North America, Africa is not doing as well as it could. The economic integration of East Africa is minimal and that of the continent as a whole remains another misty Pan-African dream. In West Africa significant progress has been made, but there the record is mixed.

The East African Community (EAC) was a customs union born during the colonial period of the three British territories of Kenya, Uganda, and Tanganyika. It was a ready-made nucleus for a common market in the post-independence period, which started for Kenya in 1963, Uganda in 1962, and Tanganyika in 1961. The EAC sponsored a common airline and other shared services such as ports and harbors for those three centuries (Tanganyika became Tanzania in 1964, as Tanganyika and Zanzibar combined). But the EAC disintegrated during the 1970s under the cumulative weight of national rivalries, contrasting approaches to development, and irreconcilable personality conflicts of its leaders. Kenya and Tanzania were pursuing sharply different development policies. Kenya was capitalist oriented and was criticized by many Tanzanians as materialistic and moneygrubbing. Tanzania was inclined toward its version of African socialism, which struck many Kenyans as impractical, excessively idealistic, even the product of a society that was "daydreaming" all the time.

When Idi Amin Dada seized power from Milton Obote in Uganda in 1971, all the destructive elements were in place to undermine the EAC. Idi Amin was a brutal dictator who savaged his own country and was only overthrown when Tanzanian troops intervened in 1979. During the 1970s his presence as the leader of Uganda intensified the tensions that had already been building between the men who headed Kenya and Tanzania at that time. Jomo Kenyatta, who played a crucial role in his country's independence movement against Great Britain, was president of Kenya from its independence until he died in 1978.

Julius K. Nyerere was president of Tanzania from its independence until the mid-1980s and party chairman into 1990. These men were more concerned with working out a vision of economic development for their own countries than they were with nurturing the economic integration of their region. Idi Amin's central purpose in life was cannibalizing his country. It is not hard to see why and how the EAC would unravel during the 1970s. The loss of this community as a nucleus for a regional common market, which could then act as a building block for promoting the economic integration of the continent, is inestimable.

In West Africa the situation is different. There two interlocked customs unions are functioning. The first is the Economic Community of West African States and contains both Anglophone (English-speaking) and Francophone (French-speaking) countries. The acronym for the English name of the community is ECOWAS; that for the French name is CEDEAO. Fifteen countries signed the ECOWAS treaty on 28 May 1975. It was formally ratified on 19 June 1975, but ECOWAS did not really get underway until 1977. A sixteenth country, Cape Verde, has since joined. The second community is the six-nation Francophone *Comunauté Economique de l'Afrique de l'Ouest* (CEAO) or Economic Community of West Africa. The members of this group are Ivory Coast, Mali, Mauritania, Niger, Senegal, and Burkina Faso. All are also members of ECOWAS, which means that CEAO is a subset of ECOWAS or CEDEAO.

The name—economic community—implies a common market. That apparently remains a very long-term goal for both communities. As far as ECOWAS is concerned, over the last fifteen years or so it has barely managed to achieve its more practical short-term objective of trade liberalization—reducing barriers to trade among its members. As journalist Ruby Ofori put it, the history of ECOWAS "has been rocked by border disputes, mass deportations and mini wars, not to mention the personal animosities between rival heads of state and deep seated rifts in anglo-francophone relations" (*West Africa* 28 May-3 June 1990: 882). CEAO has apparently made more progress in trade liberalization than ECOWAS (Asante 1985: 84-93).

ECOWAS contains some countries that were once formal colonies of Great Britain (Anglophone) and others that were under official French control (Francophone). The members of CEAO were all under French colonial rule. Francophone Africa, however, should not be equated with territories that France administered. In central Africa, Zaire, which Belgium administered from 1909 to 1961, has French as an official language and is part of Francophone Africa. Nor should Anglophone Africa be identified only with territories that Great Britain once colonized. Liberia, founded in West Africa by freed American slaves in 1822 and a member of ECOWAS, has English as an official language and was never an official colony of any European power.

In West Africa the cultural differences between former British and former

French countries are sometimes like chasms. The parallel existence of ECOWAS and CEAO demonstrates the continuity of the imperial division and colonial administration of Africa. The French-speaking countries of ECOWAS include the CEAO six, plus Benin, Togo, and Guinea. These nine nations have also constituted a special monetary grouping, known as the CFA zone, which is based on a monetary unit tied to the French franc. This zone is one example of a special relationship that France has maintained with its former colonial territories. This connection, which has a distinctive cultural intensity especially for Africans who have gone through French schools, has at times worked against the unity of ECOWAS. Bridging these differences, which includes working with and not against the CEAO, is one of the great challenges for ECOWAS (Asante 1985: 89-93).

Despite its problems, ECOWAS has survived as a combination of states seeking to become a customs union. ECOWAS can serve as a nucleus for the emergence of a West African common market. The difficulties that the European Community has encountered as it pursues unification and integration should console, not intimidate, ECOWAS. The problems that the EC endures as it struggles toward a single currency are relevant here. The EC shows how it can take decades for even a partial common market to emerge, but the process is well worth the effort.

ECOWAS has already proven itself in several ways. It has become a viable framework for modest trade liberalization, an agency for stimulating constructive thinking about the possible paths toward an economic community, and an instrument for facilitating business. ECOWAS, for instance, played a role in the emergence of an offshore banking network, Ecobank, which was launched by the Federation of West African Chambers of Commerce under Chief Adeyemi's chairmanship in 1980. In 1983 the federation received ECOWAS approval and substantial capital. The holding company, Ecowas Transnational Incorporated (ETI), has a Nigerian office set up in October 1989, and others in Togo and *Cote d'Ivoire* through affiliates; other locations are projected for Benin and Ghana (*West Africa* 28 May-3 June 1990: 884).

The sparseness of economic integration in Africa means numerous trade barriers. Because of these obstacles, both national and international businesses have missed many opportunities, and Africa as a whole continues to experience losses and distorted trade patterns. The experience of one African company, as described by Jane Perlez in *The New York Times*, demonstrates some of the obstacles to trade. The company is Obitsports, located in Nairobi, Kenya. The only Adidas franchise in sub-Saharan Africa, it manufactures a variety of sporting goods. Its products include rugby balls, soccer balls—all kinds of balls—dart boards, boxing gloves, and a wide range of sports clothing and leisure wear. Obitsports was founded after independence in 1963 by the Jumas, an Asian family that came to Kenya from Uganda.

Obitsports "is an African success story," though it has grown not because of its African sales, but because of exports outside the continent. Nizar Juma, the managing director, recounted that at the outset Obitsports did well on African business alone. The company's hand-stitched, top-of-the-line soccer balls command a lower price in Europe than in Africa. While price was an incentive to concentrate on building up its African sales, other problems multiplied that moved Obitsports to look for business away from Africa. One problem involves unpaid bills. Another comes from national jealousies. Even though a number of East African countries still have a preferential trade agreement—a remnant of the EAC—national jealousies are strong. Tanzania prefers to buy its sports equipment in Europe rather than "make Kenya rich," Juma noted. This attitude is costly: Tanzania pays 45 percent more for Adidas in Europe, not including freight, even though the products are made next door (Perlez 1990: C2).

A third problem is rooted in the outward-looking infrastructure of the continent, a legacy of the colonial period. "The idea of doing business across the continent—from Kenya in the east to the Ivory Coast in the west—makes Juma laugh. 'If I want to export to the Ivory Coast, it's often easier out of Paris,' he said. There is no direct flight to the Ivory Coast from Kenya." A fourth problem is corruption. Commodities destined for West Africa often pass through Lagos, Nigeria, perhaps Africa's most corrupt airport, where Juma estimates that about 75 percent of any shipment is likely to be stolen (Perlez 1990: C2).

Obitsports has done well outside Africa and has had problems in Africa outside of Kenya. In the Kenyan market it is thriving. The company provides about 90 percent of the country's sporting equipment. Yet Juma still sees the company's future in increasing exports outside Africa, perhaps to the United States, as "U.S. importers look for replacements for Asian products that are subject to quotas." Obitsports is well positioned to take advantage of the incentives that the Kenyan government is starting to offer to exporters. The government is establishing an export processing zone in the industrial park "not far from the Obitsports factory, where manufacturers will be able to import raw materials duty free as long as the finished product is exported" (Perlez 1990: C2).

Like businesses everywhere, African enterprises must make full use of what economic advantages they have. Much African labor is now relatively low cost. In 1990 about 500 Kenyans who worked for Obitsports received a basic 2,200 Kenyan shillings a month, or about $100 at the exchange rate of 22 shillings to the U.S. dollar, for a five-day, forty-hour work week with three weeks of paid vacation a year. Much African labor, including Obitsports' work force, produces high quality goods. The problem African businesses face is not so much product quality as the extent to which the labor force applies itself. Many African businesses experience high rates of absenteeism, which are sometimes a result of local customs. Obitsports does well in product quality and price, but its overall efficiency is poor in comparison with Adidas's Asian franchises. Part of the explanation is a tradition that workers go home to their rural villages the day after payday. On that day, there is 30 percent absenteeism (Perlez 1990: C2).

To put matters in historical perspective, other countries have encountered great difficulties in achieving a steady application of labor over the year. Jean-Baptiste Colbert, seventeenth-century finance minister to the French King Louis XIV, wanted to upgrade product quality and worker productivity as he implemented his version of mercantilism in France. The basic thrust of mercantilist policies was to use economic policies to strengthen the power and wealth of the state, but Colbert discovered that numerous days during the year were Roman Catholic feast days that required workers be given all or part of the day off. The removal of so many work days for religious reasons greatly hampered his efforts. Just as Colbert whittled away at the number of workdays lost for religious purposes, so also can public and private sectors work together in many African countries to reduce absenteeism and motivate more extended worker application. International businesses should remember that Africa may now hold a decisive advantage in the quality of some labor-intensive production techniques.

PART V. ASIA AND THE WESTERN PACIFIC

The western Pacific rim and its environs are experiencing the most dynamic economic growth of any area in the world. Japan has the most powerful economy in the region, but Taiwan, Korea, Singapore, Hong Kong, and Thailand have been remarkable success stories in their own right. Other countries have made significant strides in recent years in becoming more global business players. These include Indonesia, Malaysia, Australia, and New Zealand. Other nations, such as the Philippines and India, are striving for better economic performance. Some countries that have had serious internal problems, such as Vietnam and the People's Republic of China, are struggling to improve their climates for international business.

The more successful of these countries share one or more characteristics. Internationalization and state capitalism are two recurring factors in these success stories. *Internationalization* involves the activities of businesses in forming relationships with other countries and their peoples. The extent to which businesses from a country internationalize themselves is one key to understanding the dynamism of the most successful economies.

State capitalism is a concept sometimes used to explain the emergence of strong economies in Japan, Taiwan, Korea, and Singapore. State capitalism means a high degree of government intervention (the state part) in an economy that is based on private property (the capitalism part). Businesses from all four countries exhibit high degrees of internationalization, but the state has also played key roles in guiding and nurturing the expansion of all four economies.

The notion of state capitalism has struck some as contradictory. Since capitalism rests on private property and requires a strong private sector, the fact of significant state involvement suggests to some the suffocation not salvation of capitalism. This impression is wrong. While preponderant state ownership of the means of production, distribution, and exchange would mean socialism, other types of state involvement in an economy can help capitalism. In Japan, Taiwan, Korea, and Singapore the state has been a significant coordinator, investor, promoter, and regulator of economic activity occurring in a capitalistic framework.

Others have objected to the label of state capitalism as exaggerating the role that government has in fact played in the economies of Taiwan, Korea, Singapore, and especially Japan. The essence of their complaint is that state capitalism directs too much attention to the government and not enough to the thriving private sectors in these four economies. From this perspective, the argument can become which sector—the public or the private—was more responsible for the stunning economic success which these countries have accomplished? Put this way, the debate will be interesting but never over because it was and is the synergy of public-private interaction—the two producing more together than singly—that marks the evolution of all four economies. As economists and children remind us, joint products are sometimes difficult to disentangle: who was responsible for what is hard to separate.

While state capitalism is an appropriate concept, it must never become a stereotype. State capitalism describes capitalistic environments in which the state shoulders significant responsibilities for an economy or undertakes some functions that the private sector might itself have performed sooner or later. Yet within the category of economies associated with state capitalism there are differences. There are different degrees and patterns of government involvement in state capitalism. There are, in other words, various mixes of public and private sectors.

State capitalism is a major theme of the first case study in this part, which examines Japan. Taiwan, Korea, and Singapore have all evolved their own brands of state capitalism and these deserve mention here. To appreciate the distinctive approaches of each country one needs to know some basic facts.

These three countries, though culturally and linguistically different, share some common characteristics. In each Confucian philosophy exerts great influence. Confucius (551-478 B.C.) was a Chinese philosopher and teacher who was very concerned with elaborating the principles of proper conduct. According to his teachings, one should treat others as one wished to be treated. Confucius emphasized loyalty and intelligence. One should strive, he taught, for the fullest development of the individual person in the five key relationships of life: ruler and subject; father and son; elder and younger brother; husband and wife; and friend and friend. These attitudes toward life in general have significant implications for business behavior in particular. Relations between supervisors and their subordinates, when imbued with the spirit of Confucianism, should be based much more on cooperation than conflict. This approach makes for an attractive working environment.

Besides aspects of a common ethics, each country shares with the others an exploited colonial past. The Japanese ruled Taiwan (Formosa), an island off the southeast coast of mainland China, from 1895 to 1945. China itself, after the defeat of Japan in World War II, governed Taiwan from 1945 to 1949. Taiwan then became an independent country in 1949, when Chiang Kai-shek and his nationalist army fled the Chinese mainland after their defeat by the communists. South Korea was also a Japanese possession from 1910 to 1945; it became a republic in 1948. Singapore remained a British colony until 1965. Upon independence it chose to form a federation with the Malaysian states, but eventually it went its own way in 1969.

All three countries experienced about two decades of booming economic growth. Between 1964 and 1984 the national economies of Taiwan, South Korea, and Singapore expanded by an average of 9 percent every year in terms adjusted for inflation. The United States, by contrast, managed only about 3 percent real economic growth per annum during that same period. All three countries have workers who practice their own version of a work ethic. During those two decades people in Taiwan, South Korea, and Singapore worked between 2,100 and 2,350 hours a year, while in the United States the average was 1,860 and in West Germany, 1,635. In all three countries pay was well below that in much of the West. In 1983 hourly wages in these three Asian nations averaged $1.61; in the United States, the figure was $12.18 and in West Germany, $10.73. All three countries built their economic success on exports, which depended heavily on the U.S. market. Taiwan exported about 50 percent of its manufactured goods to the United States, South Korea 45 percent, and Singapore 25 percent (Yates 1986a: 3A).

All three countries began to lose economic impetus in 1985, but their downside was neither long nor evenly shared. Singapore was hardest hit. In 1985 its manufacturing output declined 7 percent, export demand fell 2 percent, and real gross domestic product contracted by minus 1.8 percent. In 1986 Singapore struggled back into positive growth, as its real GDP climbed 1.9 percent. Both Taiwan and South Korea recovered from their 1985 slump in forceful fashion. Taiwan experienced an annual rate of GDP growth of 10.8 percent in 1986, even greater than the 10.4 percent registered for 1984.

One final similarity that used to characterize all three countries was a crucial imbalance between economic and political change. Economic change was occurring much faster than political change. During those two decades of booming growth, from 1964 to 1984, strong middle classes that were economically empowered but politically disenfranchised appeared in all three countries. As the 1980s went by, the middle classes in Korea and Taiwan were no longer willing to accept dividends from economic growth as a substitute for direct participation in politics at the national level. When added to other local factors, this imbalance between economic and political change created volatile situations. Korea in particular experienced the physical violence that the frustrated ignited. In the late 1980s both Taiwan and Korea had national elections that provided ways for those who felt left out to take part in the political system.

Of these three countries only the government of Singapore has so far resisted significant political change. Prime Minister Lee Kuan Yew maintained an iron grip on Singapore's official politics by stifling free speech during his tenure, which ended in November 1990. So worried was he about the contamination of Singaporean society by "alien forces" that he restricted sales of the Asian edition of *The Wall Street Journal*. Whether he fashioned an effective long-term apparatus for the political disenfranchisement of important elements of Singapore's prosperous middle and upper classes remains to be seen. His handpicked successor, Goh Chok Tong, has not been in office long enough to make a judgment about his policies, although he has introduced some cosmetic changes to make Singapore a "happier" place.

State capitalism has acquired a distinctive character in all three countries. On the whole, Taiwan and South Korea have experienced a magnitude of government intervention that surpassed what was occurring in Singapore, although the "hands on" style of Prime Minister Lee was a force in its own right. In South Korea, which has some of the leading construction multinationals in the world, the activities of the late President Park Chung Hee, who was assassinated in 1979, illustrate an aggressive state capitalism. In 1976 Kim Woo Chong, founder and chairman of the multinational Daewoo Group, which now takes in over $8 billion a year, received a call from President Park. The president asked him to take over a state-owned machinery plant that had been losing money for thirty-seven years. Kim recalled that he told the president at the time that Daewoo was only a trading company with no experience in heavy industry. The president insisted that his company take on the plant. "I know you can do it," he supposedly said. And "Kim did it. Within nine months, the plant was making a profit and turning out more diesel engines than it ever had." His action saved thousands of jobs and Daewoo Heavy Industries was born (Yates 1986b: 1A).

Several years later, Park called Kim again on an urgent business matter. He ordered Daewoo to take over a huge government shipyard that was deeply in debt and still not completed. Kim refused, but when he was out of the country on a business trip, Park announced the takeover anyway (Yates 1986b: 1A). These two episodes show a particular type of state capitalism in action: a government forcefully privatizing state businesses by getting highly qualified private entrepreneurs to take them over.

The reactions of all three countries to their downturn in the mid-1980s give a fuller portrait of the similarities and differences that characterize their versions of state capitalism. This slump produced much soul-searching about future economic and political strategies. Known for years as venues of inexpensive labor that turned out low-cost, high quality manufactured goods such as textiles, steel, shoes, leather goods, and electronics, all three countries saw their competitive edge over the United States and Europe dwindle in the first half of the 1980s. Their own domestic wages almost doubled, and other nations have retaliated against them with laws designed to protect home industries allegedly endangered by floods of less expensive Asian imports. Companies in the United States and Europe adopted more efficient and productive manufacturing technologies, often involving robotics, which further eroded the labor advantage Taiwan, Korea, and Singapore had long enjoyed. Many economists had seen the storm brewing, but when the boom actually went bust in 1985, many people in those countries were still shocked. Many asked, what next? The era of mega-growth seemed over; competitive advantage had apparently shrunk; and the U.S. market, so central to the export-led growth of the three, was no longer as easy to penetrate or as lucrative as before (Yates 1986c: 4A).

Before the end of 1985, advice was pouring in. Diversify markets.

Emphasize high-tech industries more.   Expand domestic spending with government projects. These suggestions were all provocative, but leaders had to confront first the issue of export-propelled growth.   To what extent should exports continue to lead the way? Japan has decided to shift in some degree away from the fundamentally export-oriented economy it has had since the end of World War II and to devote more attention to expanding its domestic markets. Japan, with a population of over 120 million active consumers who enjoy a per capita annual income of $11,000, could embark on such a strategy with significant support for a domestic market already in place. Taiwan, South Korea, and Singapore found themselves in a different situation in that regard. They had a collective population barely half of Japan's and an average per capita income of $3,790 ($6,620 in Singapore, $2,740 in Taiwan, and $2,010 in South Korea) (Yates 1986c: 4A).

With lower population and income thresholds, the strategy of domestic market expansion as a way to sustain economic growth was not so immediately inviting. Export-led growth would remain the single most important source of economic expansion for these three countries, but there clearly was a critical need to redesign the specifics of an export strategy. The central decision was to move away from labor-intensive and into brain-intensive industries. In practice, these meant high-tech industries, but not every aspect of high-tech manufacturing. The aim, as Chairman Chen Li-an of Taiwan's National Science Council put it, was to find "windows in high tech" and then take the risk and seize those research and market opportunities (Yates 1986c: 4A).

Not all three countries implemented a high-tech export strategy in the same way, and these differences further show various approaches to state capitalism. The government of Taiwan has played a crucial role in developing the first industrial park in Asia exclusively for high-tech industries. Known as the Hsinchu Science Park, this 5,000-acre complex stands on the outskirts of Taipei, the capital, and maintains laboratories and offices used by 4,000 of the nation's top scientists and researchers. Unlike Japan's Tsukuba Science City, which is primarily a research center with no manufacturing, Hsinchu actively promotes research, development, and manufacturing. About fifty domestic and foreign companies, many of them from the United States, have taken up quarters at Hsinchu, where they are conducting research in biochemical engineering, electronics, precision instruments, and energy science. Besides Hsinchu, which has put an Asian nation other than Japan on a leading edge of innovation, the government of Taiwan has assisted in creating what amounts to a national brain trust. A network of computer stations, designed to collect and process research data, links the nation's top universities and research facilities (Yates 1986c: 4A).

The brain-intensive approach to high-tech exports from Taiwan appears strikingly in its expanding electronics industry. The strength of Taiwanese manufacturers is less and less in standard, high-volume consumer products, where they are in danger of being overtaken not only by the Koreans but also by the mainland Chinese and the Thai. The Taiwanese have been quietly developing a substantial presence in data processing and ASICS (application specific integrated circuit) chip design. These two areas provide some "windows in high tech" through which Taiwan can gain some specialized competitive edges (*FT*, "Asia's Pacific Rim," 30 June 1988: VI).

Taiwan has no large conglomerates like Korea's Samsung. Its biggest electronics groups, Tatung, Sampo, and Teco, are a fraction of the size of their Korean competitors. Yet Taiwanese companies, in seeking to build those "windows in high tech," have strengths upon which they can draw. The government has strongly supported research in microelectronics and the training of engineers. The government research institute, Industrial Technology Research Institute (ITRI) and its electronics subsidiary, the Electronics Research and Service Organization (ERSO), have made that commitment concrete. In 1988 ITRI had 2,600 engineers doing post-graduate research (*FT*, "Asia's Pacific Rim," 30 June 1988: VI).

This emphasis carries over into the structures of Taiwan's corporations. Multitech, which has changed its brand name to Acer, exemplifies that dedication to research and development. Founded by its current head, Stanley Shih, in 1976, Acer had about 400 engineers on its payroll in mid-1988 and planned to double that number by the early 1990s. Acer can redesign entirely a computer to lower its cost, improve its performance, and add new features. This redesign capacity distinguishes Acer from companies that simply assemble standardized components made by others (*FT*, "Asia's Pacific Rim," 30 June 1988: VI). It also lays an essential foundation for seizing or creating those "windows in high tech."

South Korea, which lags behind Taiwan and especially Singapore in personal income, is just about even with them in technological expertise. Like Taiwan and Singapore, South Korea has the capacity to produce complex computer memory chips. In 1986 it became the second Asian nation after Japan to export cars to the United States, but unlike Taiwan and Singapore, which also has its own version of a science park, South Korea is following an approach to technological change that accords the private sector a greater role. This stance makes Korea closer to the United States in this respect. Rather than building an ambitious science park, South Korea is allowing private multinational corporations such as Samsung, Daewoo, Hyundai, and Goldstar to create tomorrow's technological breakthroughs. The South Korean version of state capitalism has undergone a major transformation from the days of President Park's personal interventions. The government is willing to let its major multinationals, whose earlier development and current large size come partly from aggressive state nurturing, now carry the torch in crucial areas (Yates 1986c: 4A).

This change does not mean that South Korea has abandoned state capitalism.

To the contrary, the government presence remains important in many areas, including research and development. The South Korean government supports the Korean Development Institute, a think tank for developing economic and industrial policy. In 1991 the government unveiled a new plan to increase industrial specialization and international competitiveness. Under this approach the highly diversified conglomerates that dominate the country's economy—the *chaebol*—each to select three subsidiaries, which they will develop as core businesses. The government will provide credit incentives to concentrate on fewer businesses (Ridding 1991: 4).

State capitalism, as exemplified in different ways by Taiwan, Singapore, South Korea, and Japan, is the central theme of part V; yet, other subjects deserve consideration. Two of these focus the last two case studies in this part. The second case study, after Japan, examines the legal implications of the chemical tragedy that befell Bhopal, India, in December 1984 when a Union Carbide subsidiary there leaked lethal methyl isocyanate gas, which killed thousands of people and injured thousands more. The ensuing litigation involved a number of different concepts of liability. Central to the case study is the concept of *multinational enterprise liability*, which was a pillar of the government of India's case.

The final case study turns to the People's Republic of China and assesses the implications of economic reform in that country for international business. It considers major episodes of economic reform in China since the Communist party seized power in 1949. Given special attention are the Chinese government's first twelve years in power (1949–1961) and the decade of the 1980s. In the first period the government tried and rejected central planning based on a Stalinist model (Joseph Stalin was the dictator who ruled the Soviet Union for several decades until his death in 1953). China also attempted a "Great Leap Forward" from 1958 into 1961, which fell short of its ambitious goals.

In the 1980s China experimented with lessening state involvement in the economy. A general goal was to make the Chinese economy less dependent upon state commands and more responsive to the operation of market forces. This period of partial debureaucratization coincided with an acceleration of political ferment. The open expression of this tumult culminated in the events surrounding Tiananmen Square in June 1989. The brutal repression of political protest led to a significant reduction of international business activity in that country. The history of China, even before its communist period, exhibits cycles of openness and repression, which make the country a high-risk investment venue even when it seems politically stable. Nonetheless, these risks may be worth taking, since there are over 1 billion Chinese, about one fifth of the world's total population, and many of these may be potential customers.

15

State Capitalism and the Emergence
of International Business in Japan

Japan's version of state capitalism has served as both model and inspiration. Some have marveled at how far an extensive archipelago has come with a limited natural resource base. Others have pondered the bases of Japanese labor productivity. Still others have been struck with the working relationships that have developed over the years between the public and private sectors. These relationships have featured an increasing role for the private sector, although the state has retained and refined its roles in economic coordination and enhancement.

Whatever facet of the Japanese experience proves most compelling, most business people and government leaders in the world today would acknowledge that Japan should be studied for two reasons. The first is to appreciate the significance of the Japanese achievement in its own terms. Understanding it in this way relates to the second reason: determining its relevance for other situations. Some may decide that one or another aspect can serve as a model, though rarely do the thoughtful simply mimic what has occurred elsewhere without introducing some variation into it. This possibility blends into the next. More often, those who examine Japan yesterday and today come away with the sense that its record doubtlessly contains guidelines for others. But what those guidelines are and how they can be adapted to other situations without losing their effectiveness are tough questions for policy makers.

This case study introduces the reader to some essentials of the Japanese experience, starting with a brief summary of the Tokugawa period, which lasted from 1603 to 1868. This was a time of dynastic rule by a family that was far more interested in maintaining itself in power than in promoting economic expansion. During the latter decades of the Tokugawa period, however, national markets began to emerge for some commodities, which had a positive impact on business people and consumers.   The national government built on this preliminary movement and nurtured the emergence of a strong national economy during the Meiji period, which lasted from 1868 to 1912.   The first part of the Meiji (pronounced Mayjee) period, from the overthrow of the shogun to the financial crisis of 1881, is sketched.   During these twelve years, the deep foundations for Japan's state capitalism were laid.   The government undertook a comprehensive reform program, which touched on many aspects of economic and business life.   Despite the ups and down of subsequent decades, which are briefly noted, the core of Japan's state capitalism—a comprehensive involvement by government in economic and business matters—remains intact.

The greater part of this case study spotlights the emergence of Japanese international business within our comparative emergence model.   It considers the *zaibatsu*, which can denote both the great industrial families of Japan and the large economic combines they put together, and the *keiretsu*, the interlocked corporate groups that distinguish Tokyo-style capitalism.   The *sogo shoshas*, general trading companies that constructed important international networks of business contacts, are noted as crucial to the emergence of Japanese multinationals.   Japan's evolving strategies of business internationalization, which take a very long view but are open to short-run refinements, complete the case study.

THE TOKUGAWA PERIOD, 1603–1868: A THUMBNAIL SKETCH

The major objective of the House of Tokugawa was preservation of its rule. Its founder, Ieyasu Tokugawa, set the themes for the period after he established his power militarily in 1603.   He wanted nothing of the world outside Japan—for himself, his family, and other Japanese.

While the Tokugawa period is sometimes stereotyped as static, important developments unfolded, especially in the later Tokugawa period, with great significance for the subsequent commercial history of the country.   There was considerable market formation on the national level.   Despite tolls and other restrictions imposed on trade, national commodity markets emerged in indigo, sugar, paper, and rice.   The needs of many for credit, especially among the peasant and samurai classes, stimulated the growth of financial markets (Scott, Rosemblum, and Sproat 1980: 21-22).

Two other important developments came in urbanization and education.   Two related factors spurred a clustering of population in certain centers.   For one, the concentration of administration in the castle towns of the territorial lords required the presence there of more members of what was becoming a bureaucratic bourgeoisie.   For another, the shogun or leader permitted territorial lords from all over the country to maintain residences in the three great metropolitan centers of Kyoto, Osaka, and Edo, which became modern-day Tokyo (Moriya 1990: 99). Merchants could with these centers more effectively organize large-scale production of such commodities as rice wine, earthenware, and sugar (Scott, Rosemblum, and Sproat 1980: 22).

As to education, it has been estimated that 40 percent of the boys and 15 percent of the girls were in some kind of school during the Tokugawa era (Scott, Rosemblum, and Sproat 1980: 22). This was not widespread education for either gender, especially for women, but it was an important start in the direction of more widespread educational opportunity. Putting resources into education is investing in a society's human capital. All these developments—market formation, rapid urbanization, and the beginnings of education—were laying the foundation for what was to come. During the Tokugawa period "the dramatic development of commercial capital" took place, "which provided a stable foundation for the creation of industrial capital following the Meiji Restoration" (Sakudō 1990: 165).

As it entered the 1850s, the House of Tokugawa encountered problems that would threaten its control over the country. The internal situation was not promising. There was insufficient productive investment. The territorial lords faced financial problems. Most ominously, the House of Tokugawa found its own finances deteriorating: the central bureaucracy was bloated, cost-ineffective, and specialized in mismanagement.

From the outside came the challenge of western penetration. On 8 July 1853, Commodore Matthew C. Perry led a squadron of United States ships into Tokyo harbor and initiated a process that would have great historical consequences. The shogun, who governed Japan, eventually maded unbalanced concessions to some western powers. By 1858 he granted the five principal powers interested in Japan—the United States, Great Britain, Russia, France, and the Netherlands—rights to set up diplomatic missions and trade in some ports. By 1865 the shogun had entered into other agreements that inflicted enormous political damage on a House that still claimed the right to say what was best for Japan. He accepted a severe limitation on one of the government's most cherished rights—to control foreign trade. The Japanese government could not by treaty levy import duties of more than 5 percent *ad valorem*: on the value of anything coming into the country. By this action the House of Tokugawa, hard pressed financially, reduced the revenue it might have obtained from foreign commerce. The House also sealed its fate. As the West had made no parallel concessions, this set of treaties became known as the "unequal treaties" (Scott, Rosemblum, and Sproat 1980: 20). Criticism of the shogun intensified, and he was removed in a coup d'état in 1868.

THE MEIJI PERIOD, 1868–1881: AN OVERVIEW

Japan's version of state capitalism acquired some distinctive underpinnings during the first twelve years of the Meiji period. The new leadership, which consisted essentially of the victorious territorial lords, the emperor's advisers, and the emperor himself in that order of power, adopted the concise slogan of "Rich country, strong army."

But the new leadership recognized that military reform was, by itself, not enough. Japan had to become strong in other senses as well. The country had to acquire economic power, which required state-of-the-art technology. The country, given its limited natural resources, had to pursue economic strength with an efficiency that was comprehensive. Japan already possessed formidable strengths in its people and their values, such as the centrality of the family, the great emphasis placed on loyalty, and the individual person's importance more to society as a whole than to himself or herself. All these tenets lent themselves to the pursuit of strength in an ethical framework that supported group activities dedicated to improving communities and the whole country. These values would underpin a team approach to economic betterment.

This substructure of values was the foundation upon which the Meiji leaders and their successors after 1912 would build. The Meiji leadership had a legacy from the Tokugawa period of market formation, urbanization, and education to manipulate as it thought best. It inherited a tradition of central government from the House of Tokugawa, which, if fraught with financial and military weaknesses toward the end of the shogunate, was embedded in Japanese political life. The new leadership found this tradition useful, if not essential, to the implementation of its comprehensive reform program.

The new leadership moved on virtually all fronts. It revised government on all levels and class structures. Three classes—an open nobility, the ex-samurai (warriors), and everyone else—replaced the long-standing four-class division that had rigidified society. The government eliminated numerous restraints on economic activity. It abolished restrictions on personal movement. It empowered all individuals with the rights to buy and sell land. It abolished labor guilds and other constraints on labor (Scott, Rosemblum, and Sproat 1980: 27).

The Meiji government, which until 1890 ruled Japan with little popular participation in its decisions, moved in other areas: technology, education, and infrastructure. From its earliest days, the Meiji government had as one of its goals not to oust the West, but to "out-West" the West on its own terms. Nowhere is this clearer than in technology. Before one surpassed western technology, one first had to get it and get to know it. The Meiji introduced western technology in several ways. The Japanese bought strategic goods from western factories. They relied on the movement of people—their own nationals and foreigners—to gain information. Students, assisted by government subsidies, went abroad to take courses at foreign universities. Japanese business people and government officials traveled frequently to the West. Japan imported technical assistance in the form of personnel (Scott, Rosenblum, and Sproat 1980: 28).

The Meiji leadership knew that education was crucial to economic improvement. During the Tokugawa period a preliminary framework for educational opportunity had emerged. The Meiji built on this foundation and in 1872 dedicated themselves to a four-year system of free, compulsory schools. They changed the curriculum that had prevailed during the Tokugawa era, which emphasized the teachings of the Chu Hsi School of Confucianism. This school emphasizes loyalty in the key relationships of life. The Meiji leadership directed that the curriculum reflect a practical bent. Their reforms here affected primary or elementary education (Scott, Rosenblum, and Sproat 1980: 29). There is a strong relationship between spreading basic skills in reading, oral and written expression, and the greater abilities of a population to participate in economic growth and development. The Meiji, expanding a Tokugawa tradition, were positioning Japan very well in this respect.

The Meiji government dealt with another essential ingredient of economic advance—the infrastructure. It decided to make a swift expansion of the telegraph industry its second most pressing priority after the military. The telegraph was essential to permit the rapid mobilization for national defense, but it also facilitated the spread of ideas and information unrelated to military matters. By the early 1880s the national telegraph system of Japan extended over 2,000 miles in length (Scott, Rosenblum, and Sproat 1980: 29).

The Meiji wished to develop indigenous shipping capacity. Besides its knowledge dependency, Japan was also harmfully reliant upon western companies and western ships for most of its coastal trade. The emergence of a powerful Japanese shipping industry during the Meiji period shows what state capitalism can mean in practice. The modern Japanese shipping industry originated in a distinctive combination of state support and energetic private initiative. The founding private entrepreneur of the Japanese shipping industry was Yatarō Iwasaki, who began his company in 1870 by leasing three steam ships from a territorial lord and who bought them the following year. From these "three ships of the Orient" came the firm that dominated the Japanese shipping industry—the Mitsubishi Company.

Mitsubishi benefited from military action. To support its invasion of Taiwan in 1874 the Japanese government purchased thirteen steam ships and placed them under Mitsubishi's control. The company later got them for nothing. During the famous Satsuma rebellion of the samurai in 1877, the government gave Mitsubishi some $700,000 to buy steamers and expand its business. Even before the rebellion started the company was hard pressed to meet government demands to transport and supply troops. Iwasaki played for keeps. In 1875 he pressured a rival firm out of business and took over its eighteen steamers. During the 1870s the Mitsubishi Company achieved a near-monopoly in its field. This dominance resulted from Iwasaki's entrepreneurial daring and considerable government support. In its first decade the company apparently received from the government about 8 million yen, about half of which was a subsidy and half a loan, repayable in ten to fifteen years almost without interest (Scott, Rosenblum, and Sproat 1980: 30).

When Iwasaki died in 1885, he thought his achievements made him "The Man of the Far East." He was one of the greatest Meiji entrepreneurs and perhaps the most daring. His great-grandchild, Kikuko, is married to Minoru Makihara, who became president of the Mitsubishi Corporation in 1992 (Sanger 1992: C3). Whether Yatarō Iwasaki was "Man of the Far East," the patterns of behavior interlocking the government and private business he helped fashion during the last fifteen years of his life laid the foundation for state capitalism in Japan.

The first ten years or so of the Meiji period were a time of considerable activity with consequences for the long-term future of Japan. The essentials for a framework of state capitalism came into existence. Depending on the situation, the government would assist, sponsor, or create economic opportunity. The government, in explicit, evolving, and institutionalized relationships with businesses, would not only draw the outlines of the country's future but also specify some of its particulars. The framework, most of which had emerged by 1880, did not immediately produce dramatic economic gains.

In fact, Japan underwent its own cycles of often moderate economic growth and ocassional recession and crisis. In 1880 and 1881 the country experienced a severe financial crisis, marked by inflation, intensifying balance-of-payments problems, and deepening debt. The government responded with a belt-tightening strategy, which produced deflation. Between 1900 and 1911 the country faced a resurgence of inflation and a worsening imbalance in its balance-of-payments accounts. World War I produced significant short-term gains for the Japanese economy in overseas market penetration, territorial acquisition, and a rising demand for war materials.

Realizing Japan's full economic potential had to wait until the decades after World War II. A "radical right," which emerged in the 1920s, gained more power during the 1930s and made Japan's international stance more militaristic and its domestic situation more militarized. The Second World War devastated Japan. Its comeback is one of world history's most dramatic episodes. The revival of its democratic institutions in a more stable framework is as gripping as the unprecedented economic growth it would experience, especially in the 1950s and 1960s. Cradling its "economic miracle," which by 1970 had pushed the country ahead of Great Britain, France, and West Germany in terms of gross national product, was a more intricate version of the state capitalism that had taken root in the early Meiji period. Business and government, in varieties of partnerships, tapped with striking effectiveness the economic potential that a cultural ethos of hard work, discipline, and loyalty within an extended family tradition possessed.

THE EMERGENCE OF JAPANESE INTERNATIONAL BUSINESS: THE ZAIBATSU

The concept of partnership, both between and within the public and private sectors, has played a crucial role in Japanese national as well as international business history. Within the private sector the *zaibatsu* exemplify partnership in their formation, expansion, and business dealings. The term *zaibatsu* (which stands for either the singular or the plural) refers both to the great industrial families of Japan and to the large economic combines that they put together. Partnership drew special strength from the kinship nature of the *zaibatsu*, and partnership characterized the fashioning of those large economic combines that the families energized.

Partnership also marked relations between some *zaibatsu* and foreign business interests that wished to invest in Japan. During the first three decades of the twentieth century, foreign direct investment in Japan, while not large in aggregate terms, was important, in part because of its structure (Mason 1987: 105-6). Much of it entered the country in the form of joint partnerships with some *zaibatsu*, which joined with foreign interests to establish firms in Japan. Before World War II, at least eight *zaibatsu*, including Sumitomo, Mitsui, and Mitsubishi, participated in major domestic joint ventures with direct foreign investment. Numerous Japanese companies, including Mitsubishi Electric, American-Japan Sheet Glass, and Dunlop Rubber (Far East), emerged as the result of these joint ventures (Mason 1987: 101-4).

These alliances between *zaibatsu* and foreign companies, which produced those new Japanese firms, benefited both parties. Foreign investors needed the local knowledge, contacts with government and business, and size and power of the *zaibatsu* in order to penetrate a market that posed enormous obstacles to those operating with little knowledge, few connections, and on a small scale. Participating *zaibatsu*, for their part, sometimes used their joint ventures with foreign direct investors as ways to compete more effectively with other domestic manufacturers (Mason 1987: 103).

THE EMERGENCE OF JAPANESE MULTINATIONALS: DOMESTIC BEGINNINGS

These joint ventures with foreign direct investment, which could begin only after treaty revisions from 1899 gave foreigners the explicit right to invest directly in Japan outside the so-called Treaty Settlements, were instrumental in preparing the way for the emergence of a major Japanese multinational presence abroad. As other case studies have shown, the articulation of a country's multinationals begins with what did or did not happen to the corporation at home and what it did or did not do there. So also in Japan did the process of becoming a multinational begin at home.

Joint ventures with foreign partners in Japan, which through the early 1980s included at least seven in which Mitsubishi Rayon joined, were integral seams in a tapestry of educational foreign contact. From the early Meiji days there has been a sustained effort to learn as much as possible about non-Japanese technology and management. This endeavor encompasses such techniques as study abroad, productivity missions, foreign factory visits, intense reading of foreign publications, and technology licensing (Franko 1983: 60).

Those joint ventures proved to be valuable lessons in the school of internationalization and globalization. They amounted to "domestic multinational operations" (Franko 1983: 60). The Japanese partners could learn from on-the-spot experience how or how not to manage multinational enterprise. These were lessons learned locally with important international transferability: from their domestic involvement in multinational enterprise the Japanese gained useful knowledge about how to manage operations that involved foreign managers and employees outside of Japan itself. The relative ease with which Japanese firms have managed relationships with foreign sales agents, sales forces, plant managers, and work forces outside of Japan is rooted directly in the domestic learning experiences that those joint ventures provided (Franko 1983: 60). Internationalization at home constitutes one key to understanding the subsequent emergence of Japanese multinationals abroad.

THE EMERGENCE OF JAPANESE MULTINATIONALS: THE SOGO SHOSHA

A second key resides in the international mindedness of the past and the institutions it created. Foremost among these organizations are the general trading companies, or *sogo shosha*, and the international networks they have constructed. The *sogo shosha* have rich histories. Some, like Mitsui, can trace their origins back to the early seventeenth century and various commercial operations. Others came into existence after World War II, such as Sumitomo trading (Franko 1983: 61). The *sogo shosha*, by their numbers, influence, and longevity, have come to occupy important positions in both domestic and international trade. Whatever their background or power, they all exemplify partnership in the best Japanese business tradition.

The *sogo shosha* perform numerous functions for their *keiretsu*, or brethren, within their group as well as for others. Especially important have been their roles as gatherers of information and facilitators of market penetration. Because two barriers that can hamper international business—language and distance—obstructed Japanese business overseas with special force, there is a crucial need for marketing expertise. The *sogo shosha* have met this challenge. Their knowledge of international business affairs and their marketing networks have proved to be invaluable in the ongoing internationalization and globalization of Japanese business.

The *sogo shosha*, marketing specialists, have greatly assisted Japanese manufacturing companies in their activities abroad. Their support has helped manufacturers as they try to establish themselves as exporters. Some companies have drawn on the expertise of the *sogo shosha* as they set up their own manufacturing facilities overseas. This collaboration reinforces the links among the international mindedness of yesterday, today, and tomorrow. "The marketing knowledge built up over time," Lawrence Franko writes, "is thus retained within the Japanese multinational information grid" (Franko 1983: 61).

The *sogo shosha* pioneered in the creation of an efficient market network linking both domestic and international markets. They themselves articulated parent-subsidiary structures that are one hallmark of multinational enterprise. They, along with other multinational Japanese businesses, have organized themselves to preserve and reinforce the culture of Japanese business abroad. Despite a number of joint ventures in production overseas initiated by Japanese businesses that give to locals significant ownership, the vast majority of the foreign commercial subsidiaries of the *sogo shosha* remained wholly Japanese owned. In the early 1980s most of the rest were Japanese majority-owned and controlled businesses (Franko 1983: 61). Retention of total and majority legal control over subsidiaries protects that business culture.

The structures of Japan's long-standing commercial internationalism, embodied par excellence in the *sogo shosha* and their pervasive business networks, have greatly influenced more contemporary multinational articulation. Those trading companies, especially the "Big Nine," have made possible and facilitated the multinationalization of small- and medium-sized Japanese firms, in addition to some operating on a larger scale. The roles of small- and medium-sized firms in the internationalization of Japanese business have made that process distinctive. From a global perspective, a far larger proportion of both Japanese exports and Japanese foreign direct investment in manufacturing has involved small- and medium-sized firms than has occurred in the multinational experiences of the United States and European countries.

This record contrasts sharply with the predominance of largeness in the multinational thrusts abroad of U.S. and European business. The preponderant share of U.S. exports of manufactures comes from large firms, while significant U.S. multinational direct investors are almost always the giant and super-giant firms. The largest European industrial firms, with some significant exceptions, make up the ranks of European exporters and multinational enterprises (Franko 1983: 60-63). Since Japanese manufacturing firms contemplating more business abroad already had international trading networks in place with experience, knowledge, and a capacity to deliver, they did not themselves need to have or develop fully international scanning and marketing functions. They could, as Lawrence Franko puts it, "'hook on' to the trading company networks by forming multi-party joint ventures abroad, in which ownership would be often split between a small- to medium-sized Japanese manufacturing firm, a trading company, perhaps the bank related to the trading company and last, but not least, a local Thai, Korean, Indonesian, or Brazilian joint venture partner" (Franko 1983: 63; and Tsurumi 1976: 141-48). By contrast the multinational experiences of the United States and Europe usually reveal that only those industrial firms that themselves had a "large critical mass of personnel and contacts" could articulate the scanning and marketing functions necessary for effective operation abroad (Franko 1983: 63).

While multinationalization at home, the *sogo shosha*, and small- to medium-sized businesses play important parts in the internationalization of Japanese business, there are still other factors that power that process. Some Japanese manufacturing multinationals have built their own international distribution networks. After some initial help from the *sogo shosha*, the larger and more powerful Japanese exporters and overseas investors all set up their own distribution and investment networks overseas (Franko 1983: 64).

The trading companies were able to help some manufacturers more than others. This specialization of assistance resulted both from the nature of the *sogo shosha* and the product an organization wished to market. More accustomed to selling than intensive market development, the *sogo shosha* have been effective in helping firms that sell clothing, textiles, or other less complex products. The trading companies have been important more as procurement agents for Japan than as export or manufacturing agents (Franko 1983: 64).

When the exports were automobiles and home electronics, the *sogo shosha* had limited roles. Manufacturers themselves articulated their own international distribution networks. Sony developed its own network from the beginning. Matsushita was also an early starter in this regard. By the early 1980s many more Japanese manufacturers in the electronic and electrical industries had their own sales subsidiaries abroad (Franko 1983: 64). Some manufacturing multinationals worked out a division of labor with some *sogo shosha*. This arrangement featured a manufacturer that developed its own distribution system in its major markets abroad but contracted a *sogo shosha* to represent it in markets regarded as secondary or peripheral. In the 1960s and early 1970s Toyota let Mitsui handle its sales in Canada, although from 1971 it had taken a shareholding in the Mitsui-owned Canadian dealership. All the while, Toyota refined its own distribution network in the U.S. market (Tsurumi 1976: 143-44).

The internationalization of Japanese business has depended at times on the domestication of its exports under foreign brand names in their respective home markets. To a much greater extent than U.S. or European businesses in their international expansion, Japanese companies have employed "OEM" or "private label" distribution agreements with foreign distributors. These contracts legalize the sale of Japanese products under western importers' brand names. Sanyo television sets reached U.S. customers under the familiar name of Sears Roebuck. Mitsubishi automobiles were sold for a time under the Chrysler or Dodge name in the United States. In Germany, Fujitsu computers had a Siemens label, while Fujitsu facsimile machines appeared under that of Burroughs. Hitachi computers in Italy carried the Olivetti name (Franko 1983: 64-65). Japanese businesses capitalized on the potency for market penetration inherent in identification with brand names well known in their local markets. They demonstrated that business internationalization can at times utilize product domestication as represented by name changes as an effective tool for market expansion.

THE MULTINATIONALIZATION OF JAPANESE BUSINESS AND THE COMPARATIVE EMERGENCE MODEL

The multinationalization of Japanese businesses has combined the three factors of external markets, technological change, and factor scarcities and qualities in our comparative emergence model in a distinctive fashion. As far as overseas production is concerned, Japanese multinational activity into the 1980s concentrated in the newly industrializing "Third World" countries (NICs) of Asia and Latin America. These Japanese manufacturing sites in the NICs are oriented toward export markets, much more so than those of their European and U.S. counterparts. The Japanese elected to multinationalize production more in the mature sectors of industry rather than in intensively high-tech areas.

These strategies of product multinationalization placed Japanese subsidiaries abroad in highly competitive domestic industries in which Japan was actually losing its own competitive advantage. So much of their overseas manufacturing production in Asia and Latin America was concentrated in areas where Japanese edges in efficiencies were hard to translate into decisive competitive advantages. The Japanese clustered their product multinationalization in NICs in highly competitive industries that produced standardized or traditional goods, like textiles and metal products, or less complex product lines of electrical appliances, like batteries and radios, and of chemicals, like paints and plastics (Ozawa 1979: 28-29).

At first glance this strategy seemed a likely boomerang. Why locate where some of your most formidable weapons, such as high technology, are neutralized or marginally effective? The answer to this question demonstrates the importance that the Japanese assigned to a particular mix of factor qualities in shaping the multinationalization of their production. By locating so much of their overseas production in the NICs of South Korea, Hong Kong, Brazil, Singapore, and Malaysia, Japanese firms gained several advantages simultaneously. The first concerned labor. In those countries, through the early 1980s, labor was both, on the whole, low cost and highly productive. The cost advantage has since eroded in some countries.

The second benefit related to markets. The countries just mentioned have been among the fastest growing markets in the world, as measured in average annual growth rates of real gross domestic product. Those Japanese firms were strategically positioned in another sense. Japan itself contained the fastest growing market of all the industrialized countries in average annual growth rates of real gross domestic product. Both at home and abroad Japanese multinationals were plugged into powerful sources of market growth. These dual engines of market expansion accounted for a major part of the gains made by Japanese firms in their shares of world markets during the 1970s, especially in electrical equipment and electronics (Franko 1981).

During the 1980s the Japanese refined their strategies of localizing production abroad. While they kept a significant presence in the NICs, they developed considerable production capacity in the United States and Europe. Numerous factors prompted this shift. Some NICs were losing a competitive advantage as wages rose, and Japan was under great pressure to reduce a large surplus (over $50 billion yearly) in its balance of trade with the United States. Goods produced in the United States could help the surplus problem in two ways. Fewer commodities would have to come from Japan itself and Japanese products made in the United States could also be exported. There was an important public relations benefit from locating more production in a host market: some products, like cars, became so commingled that people wondered whether a product was more from Japan or the United States. This ambiguity helped the Japanese for it made targeted criticism of their presence in the United States more difficult.

Japan has also been positioning itself to take advantage of the economic groupings emerging in the world. Localizing production in Canada, Mexico, and the United States is designed to be on the inside of an emerging free trade area encompassing the western hemisphere. Likewise, internalizing more production in Europe is aimed at EC92 and other moves towards continental economic integration.

Japanese businesses have defined their opportunities at home and overseas with precision, perspective, and power. As to the first, Japanese businesses usually have refined market perceptions. Much has been written about the unimaginative market horizons of some western businesses. To the contrary, the Japanese have demonstrated creative acuteness in defining market segments that have lent themselves to targeted and profitable production. Because of the characteristics of their home market, many Japanese firms have developed smaller, lower-priced versions of products first introduced in the West. Low production costs made possible by the economies of scale available within the huge Japanese home market have given Japanese firms a natural competitive advantage in those market segments abroad. Most Japanese business people would never use the distinction between "up-market" and "down-market" in a disdainful way, if they construed their potential customers that rigidly. While too many western businesses operating abroad neglected what they perceived as down-scale market segments and aimed for the up-scale, Japanese businesses as a whole have avoided such a costly conceptual trap.

Much has been written about the narrow time horizons of many western businesses. The importance of taking a longer view of the future is essential for sound business strategy. A critical area for business planning is that of research and development. Another major source of strength for Japanese businesses consists of substantial expenditures on research and development structured over a much longer term than is customary for many western enterprises. Without an important R & D component, a business is flying into the future with a crucial piece of equipment missing.

The internationalization of Japanese businesses has flourished in meeting challenges with the precision of market definition, the perspective of business operating abroad for the long haul, and the power of substantial research and development funding. These factors join with those explained earlier—the government as economic enhancer and coordinator, multinationalization at home, the long-standing structures of Japan's commercial internationalism, the roles of small- to medium-sized firms abroad, the vertical integration overseas of many larger multinationals in terms of distribution networks, the domestication of exports under foreign brand names, and the distinctive combination of external markets, technology, and factor scarcities and qualities—to explain the long-term process of Japanese business internationalization and its more modern phase of multinationalization.

This long list of factors can be described another way. The internationalization and multinationalization of Japanese businesses abroad represents the outward thrust and expression of a cultural ethos of hard work, discipline, and loyalty within an extended family tradition. Partnership, a core concept for Japanese businesses both at home and abroad, embodies loyalty among members of a structured business "family" as it develops from the hard work and discipline of all participants.

Here lies the major lesson of the Japanese experience for outsiders. One must build on, not try to reform or change, the basic strengths of one's people, whatever their assets may be. One can import machines, ideas, people, money, and other commodities from the outside, but unless these are all integrated in an approach anchored in the strengths of a population, the best laid plans of not only mice, men, and women, but also businesses and government developers, will go awry.

16

India: The Green Revolution, Bhopal, and Multinational Enterprise Liability

On 3 December 1984, poisonous gas leaked from a plant in Bhopal, India, killed at least 3,000 people, and injured tens of thousands. By early 1992 more than 4,000 victims had died and at least 200,000 survive with injuries because of the explosion, according to the Indian government. The plant was controlled by an Indian subsidiary of the Union Carbide Corporation, a U.S. multinational headquartered in Danbury, Connecticut. The gas was methyl isocyanate, which is used in the production of pesticides. Union Carbide had located a subsidiary in India to meet the demand for chemicals that had escalated in connection with the "Green Revolution." This "revolution" occurred during the 1960s and 1970s, when yields from Indian agriculture increased substantially. Increased chemical use by Indian farmers was a major factor in increasing those yields.

The disaster at Bhopal stands as a tragic counterpoint to decades of progress in Indian agriculture. This achievement was made possible by the very agency that destroyed and maimed so many human lives in one terrifying display of the costs that chemical use sometimes brings. Chemicals, along with rural reorganization, the willingness and ability of Indian farmers to adapt technologies in an appropriate fashion, and other government policies, have all catapulted Indian agriculture into a position of generating surpluses for export. For a number of years India has been a net exporter of wheat. Indications are that agriculture can continue to make positive contributions to that country's international balance of payments by earning precious foreign exchange. The Bhopal tragedy unfolds in a wider developmental context in which chemicals have played beneficial roles. The local manufacture of chemicals for agriculture had, before Bhopal, produced enormous short-run benefits for a vast country that is still struggling to ensure that all its citizens participate in those gains.

India occupies much of the great subcontinent that thrusts south from Asia into the Indian Ocean. The British had unified India during their centuries of colonial rule and partially dissected it as they legally exited in 1947. Then they partitioned the country into Pakistan, which had two separate parts, and an India that while huge was not quite so gigantic. India is one of the world's largest countries in terms of both land mass and population; it has 853.1 million citizens, ranking it second behind China's 1.139 billion people (United Nations Population Fund, 1990). It is also one of the areas on the globe most bitterly racked by religious and cultural differences. India continues to endure somehow as a fascinating endeavor in human organization beset by complex problems but spurred on by rich possibilities. A country unified in pain and given its "flag independence" in pain has experienced the pain coming from history's worst industrial accident to date.

This case study focuses on the litigation that unfolded in the aftermath of the Bhopal tragedy. In arguing that the Union Carbide Corporation itself was responsible for the actions of its Bhopal subsidiary, the Government of India advanced a number of traditional legal theories. These included absolute liability, strict liability, negligence, breach of warranty, and misrepresentation. The Indian government also introduced a novel legal doctrine—that of *multinational enterprise liability*. The thrust of this doctrine is that the multinational parent—headquarters—is responsible or liable for the action or inaction of its offspring—its subsidiaries. The legal demonstration of this doctrine requires an analysis of the multinational corporation based on many of our essentials for the historical study of international business.

Multinational enterprise liability has an uncertain legal future, but it raises important questions about relations between headquarters and subsidiaries. These inquiries involve the degree of decentralization of power in those areas related to the act(s) for which headquarters is allegedly liable. How does one define decentralization and what constitutes degrees of it? What are the connections between official structures and unofficial ways of doing things? How does one prove contentions based on these notions—decentralization and its extent, official structures, and unofficial practices—in courts of law in different legal jurisdictions?

The least impractical solution to these problems may be, as *The Economist* has suggested, an international treaty concerning business responsibilities based on *absolute liability*. In 1986 India's Supreme Court made a decision, with Union Carbide in mind, that a multinational corporation engaged in hazardous activity in that country is "absolutely liable" for damages for an accident. In other words, a company is liable whether or not the accident was caused by negligence (as was claimed by lawyers representing Bhopal victims) or sabotage (as was claimed by Union Carbide). A precedent on the personal level, *The Economist* noted, comes from Great Britain: in *Rylands v. Fletcher* (1868) it was upheld that a person is *prima facie* (at first glance) liable for the damage done even by accidental release of any substances that the person has accumulated on his or her land (*Econ* 18 February 1989: 70).

MULTINATIONAL ENTERPRISE LIABILITY: A CRITIQUE

On 8 April 1985, the Government of India filed a lawsuit against the Union Carbide Corporation in Federal District Court in Manhattan. This action sought compensation for the victims of the gas leak at Carbide's Bhopal pesticide plant on 3 December 1984. It requested punitive damages "in an amount sufficient to deter Union Carbide and any other multinational corporation from the willful, malicious and wanton disregard of the rights and safety of the citizens of those other countries in which they do business" (*NYT* 9 April 1985: 1). In the lawsuit the Indian government attempted to recover damages for the cost of its emergency aid and relief to the victims of the Bhopal disaster. Under the category of emergency aid and relief the government specified medical treatment, food, and rehabilitation.

The Government of India rested its case on the central contention that Union Carbide as a multinational corporation was responsible for what happened at Bhopal. The question of responsibility was one major issue in the litigation. Lawyers representing Union Carbide alleged that only its Indian subsidiary, not the parent corporation, should figure in the determination of who was, or was not, responsible for the disaster. To demonstrate that Union Carbide as an international corporate entity was responsible for the actions of its Indian subsidiary, the Government of India advanced the theory of multinational enterprise liability. Based on expanding concepts of product liability in the United States, this theory provides a framework in which a parent company can be held responsible for the actions of its subsidiaries. The Indian government did not base its case only on multinational enterprise liability. It invoked a number of traditional legal theories, which included absolute liability, strict liability, negligence, breach of warranty, and misrepresentation.

In its complaint the Government of India cited a number of actions that allegedly made the parent and subsidiary together liable. The parent company designed the Bhopal plant, wrote the performance specifications, and trained technical personnel in the United States. The parent company also "warranted that the design was based upon the best manufacturing information available and that the drawings and design instructions were sufficiently detailed and complete so as to enable competent technical personnel to detail, design, erect, commission and operate the Bhopal plant" (*NYT* 9 April 1985: 30).

Multinational enterprise liability deserves a critique from the perspective of international business history. First of all, while multinational enterprise liability as a package concept may appear of recent origin, some of its elements have a much longer international business history. Discussion of the Medici Bank indicated that its structures, which featured a combination of partnerships, were apparently sufficient to shield the apex partnership in Florence from litigation initiated against any subsidiary partnership. While Florence exerted considerable control over its subsidiaries, the fact that each offspring had its own distinctive legal personality based on its operating jurisdiction created an autonomy that the law recognized as decisive.

Though Florence had by the Medici articles of association the powers to determine overall policy and implement it, with rights to inspect and supervise, the subsidiaries were not marionettes dancing on Florence's strings. There were crucial forces of decentralization at work within the Medici Bank. Each branch had its own style, capital, books, and management, which worked to establish a distinctive legal personality for each branch or manufacturing establishment within the Medici Bank itself.

There was a critical imbalance between what the law recognized and what the Medicis had created. The Medicis had supervised the establishment of branches that were separated, in some ways but not totally, from the apex partnership in Florence. They had not brought into existence institutional offspring that were completely separable from their corporate parent in an institutional manner. The Medici Bank raises a core problem that proponents of multinational enterprise liability must face: what happens to related concepts as they move back and forth between the disciplines of law and institutional analysis? Can one prove the *legal significance* of *institutional linkages*? Medici subsidiaries were autonomous, not independent institutionally but separate legally.

Multinational enterprise liability, in its present formulation, stands on stereotypes of the multinational corporation. As it appears in the Government of India's complaint, the multinational corporation is large, complex, has enormous power that can produce adverse consequences, and is one entity with a global purpose that the actions of all its parts support. Moreover, only the multinational corporation as a corporate whole, not as one or more of its components, has the capacity to guard against or prevent major disasters.

Many multinationals are large, none are simple, and most have power of some sort, but whether all multinationals have the capacity to "take actions that can result in industrial disasters of catastrophic proportion and magnitude" is arguable (*NYT* 9 April 1985: 30). Multinationals that manufacture chemicals actually or potentially dangerous to the environment and its inhabitants, as does Union Carbide, are candidates for inclusion in this generalization. Some produce military items that can cause other disasters, but not all multinational enterprises are so involved.

The buck does stop at the top. But what is the top for multinational enterprises operating in multiple legal jurisdictions? The Government of India insisted in its legal brief that the multinational corporation is one entity carrying out "global purpose through thousands of daily actions" (*NYT* 9 April 1985: 30). The multinational corporation is "one entity" in one or more institutional senses. The table of organization, at least on paper, indicates divisions and functions arranged in hierarchical fashion, with the source of ultimate decision-making power residing in the apex.

Major problems arise when one attempts to describe that singular entity as carrying out "global purpose" through thousands of daily actions. Global purpose is an ill-specified concept. "Thousands of actions" do occur within an entire corporation on a daily basis, but whether these all support a global purpose that has a sharper focus than the clichés of survival and expansion is doubtful. Case studies of multinational corporate behavior both at home and abroad, such as those concerning International Harvester and Singer, show how personnel can have different formulations of the general goal of expansion. Plant managers can understandably want to increase the physical size of their domains, while those in sales may strive to maximize market share and/or market size. Internal stuggles over resource allocation can arise from those contrasting conceptions. These observations highlight the necessity of investigating what table of organization and its companion notion of chain of command mean for specific enterprises in practice.

The Government of India, and other proponents of multinational enterprise liability, place responsibility both for what happens and what should not occur in the multinational enterprise as one entity. In the Indian government's brief it is only the overall entity that can guard against or prevent major disasters. The crucial phrase is "overall entity." This construct is ambiguous. The overall entity is both a collectivity and the sum of its parts. The perspective depends on the situation. The Government of India relied on collectivity. It is easier to take that route. An approach that views the multinational corporation as the sum of its parts must define what table of organization and chain of command mean in practice. It is less difficult to invoke complexity and assert that it is not possible to pinpoint responsibility and liability.

The essential problem for multinational enterprise liability remains as follows. While from the perspective of institutional analysis a multinational corporation can be both a collectivity in some ways and the sum of its parts in others, from a legal standpoint it is the sum of its parts. More accurately, it is the disjointedness of its parts because national laws are, in the main, more influential than any international law pertaining to international enterprise. The emergence of community law for such economic groupings as the European Community will temper but not negate the preceding statement. The only solution may be an international treaty concerning business behavior based on absolute liability.

LITIGATION AND NEGOTIATION

Key parties attempted to avoid the strain and cost of prolonged court proceedings and had apparently worked out an out-of-court settlement in the first part of 1986. But this agreement unraveled (*NYT* 23 March 1986: 1 and 7). On 12 May 1986, Judge John F. Keenan, a federal judge in the Southern District of New York, sent the cases to India for trial. In the third week of November 1986, Union Carbide filed an affidavit in India that blamed its own Indian subsidiary and the national and Madhya Pradesh state governments for the Bhopal disaster. In that document the company again denied any liability for itself. The company further charged that former employees and one supervisor were covering up possible sabotage that could have caused the world's worst industrial disaster. The Indian government, partly in response to this affidavit, declared on 22 November 1986, that it would seek a minimum of $3 billion from Union Carbide as compensation for the Bhopal tragedy.

Throughout 1987 and 1988 efforts continued to reach an out-of-court settlement. A report by the Associated Press, attributed to unnamed sources at Union Carbide and the Indian government, indicated in November 1987 that the chemical company had offered a settlement package that amounted to $500 million, with most of the money to be paid over ten years to victims of the disaster. Company officials denied that a final agreement had been reached (*NYT* 18 November 1987: 31). This offer eventually proved significant, but the immediate road was uncertain. On 1 December 1987, two days before the third anniversary of the tragedy, the Government of India filed criminal charges against Union Carbide, which included culpable homicide, injury to people, and the killing of animals. A company spokesperson called the criminal charges "completely unfounded" (*Associated Press* 1 December 1987).

Finally, in February 1989, the Government of India reached an out-of-court settlement with Union Carbide, which amounted to $470 million. The agreement was challenged in the Indian Supreme Court, so not until 3 October 1991 did the Indian Supreme Court give its assent to the $470 million settlement. The court also said that the former chairman of Union Carbide, Warren M. Anderson, as well as Indian officials with the company, could be tried on criminal charges arising from the Bhopal disaster (*NYT* 4 October 1991: C4).

POSTSCRIPT

On 14 April 1992, Union Carbide announced that "it would sell its last holdings in India to raise as much as $17 million to build and operate a hospital in Bhopal." Carbide is to sell its 50.9 percent stake in Union Carbide India Ltd., India's largest producer of consumer batteries. The company has "complained that Indian courts have been too slow to start compensating victims from the funds it supplied in 1989.   Tens of thousands of victims began receiving payments of $12 a month" in 1990, "but huge numbers of the 500,000 Bhopal residents classified as eligible have not been paid" anything as of mid-April 1992 (*NYT* 15 April 1992: C1 and C19).

17

Implications of Economic Reform
in China for International Business

China has for centuries experienced periods of political turbulence and stability. Since the Communist party seized power in 1949, these cycles have been especially interwoven with attempts at economic reform. The country today is a potentially vast market with over 1 billion people, but it is still experiencing aftershocks from the government's brutal repression of the pro-democracy demonstrations, which peaked in the first part of 1989. The events associated with Tiananmen Square in May and early June 1989 seemed to end the tentative debureaucratization of economic life that had been slowly occurring since the early 1980s. But in March 1992, the Chinese Communist party committed itself without reservation to economic reform. This was a victory for the country's long-lived paramount leader Deng Xiaoping, who initiated the process in the 1980s (*FT* 13 March 1992: 1).

This program advertises price reform, upgrading management and business skills, and dealing with China's bloated and inefficient state industry (*FT* 13 March 1992: 4). It holds great promise for the Chinese people as well as for international businesses interested in the Chinese market. These reforms, along with such other programs as the Great Leap Forward (1958–1961), illustrate how fundamental economic change in China is never easy or harmonious. China is both a market of enormous potential and a venue of high-risk investment. It should help students of international business, in evaluating the degree of risk attached to any future dealings with China, to appreciate these episodes of economic reform against the wider background of politics in China from 1949 to the present.

BACKGROUND

China has long fascinated the world. In earlier times the interest that western countries and their nationals had in China did not always take benign forms. China received gross abuse over the centuries from external forces. In the nineteenth century western powers aggressively intruded into China in an attempt to open it up to the outside world. Japan experienced the same thrusting but largely escaped the physical harms inflicted upon China by western military forces.

China did suffer and lose much. Between the fall of the Manchu Dynasty in 1911 and the conquest of mainland China by the People's Liberation Army in 1949, Russia, China's Eurasian neighbor, supposedly stole about $2 billion worth of machinery and equipment from Manchuria (Ashbrook 1968: 18). This sum constitutes only a portion of the levy that the forces of imperialism forcibly collected from China and its residents.

THE FIRST CHINESE REVOLUTION

The country was also torn apart by internal conflict and disaster. The struggle between the forces of Mao Zedong and those of Chiang Kai-shek, which solidified in the 1930s and escalated in the 1940s, severely damaged the country's infrastructure. The contending armies severed and then cut again rail lines; dams, irrigation systems, and canals broke down. Money deteriorated; a ruinous inflation undermined whatever confidence remained in the country's monetary system. By 1949, when Chiang Kai-shek fled and established his government in exile on the island of Taiwan, the people on the mainland had sustained numerous casualties from disasters both human and natural. Many were in physical and mental disarray—fatigued, hungry, and disoriented (Ashbrook 1968: 18).

The reforms that began in the 1980s must be appreciated against the historical background that the leadership of the victorious Chinese Communist Party experienced before it came to power and confronted once in control. Though internal problems had sapped the population and destroyed a major part of the country's infrastructure, the foreign factor appeared as the poison that harmed China the most. Defined from the ideological perspective of the Chinese Communist party, the foreign factor stood for capitalist imperialism or, in the evocative phrase of the late Chairman Mao, "the running dogs" of capitalism (Mao Zedong 1972: 82). Imperialism was largely identified with western capitalism, even though Russian imperialism had pillaged Manchuria and other locations.

MOBILIZATION AND COMEBACK

Once in power, the leadership mobilized the country to meet the great demands of reconstruction. From 1949 through 1952 China made a striking comeback. The new government during its first several years in power "ended large-scale brigandage, starvation, inflation, epidemics, and corruption" (Ashbrook 1972: 16). These all added up to an outstanding accomplishment. China's gross national product (GNP) for this preliminary period suggests the extent of rehabilitation and recovery. China's GNP increased from $36 billion in 1949 to $59 billion in 1952. This growth translated into a substantial per capita or per person increment. During that same period per capita GNP rose from $67 to $104 (Ashbrook 1972: 17).

China's substantial recovery resulted mainly from a more efficient use of existing resources. There was no significant growth in the amount of productive resources available within China itself (McCormick 1980: 2). The comeback took place within a framework of partial ideological penetration of the economy. The state took over such core industries as railroads, steel, and banking. It seized foreign capital owned by supporters of the defeated Nationalists. It initiated major land reform, which resulted in over 300 million peasants gaining land. During this rebuilding, the government did not attempt a complete nationalization of either industry or agriculture (Wheelright and McFarlane 1970: 33).

THE FIRST FIVE-YEAR PLAN

By 1953 the leadership believed that the country was ready for more directed economic growth and development. Ironically, in light of their stormy past, China greatly depended upon the Soviet Union for intellectual guidance and material assistance in the implementation of its first five-year economic plan. The Soviet Union partly drafted that plan, which was heavily influenced by the Stalinist development model. This approach, associated with the Soviet leader who applied its principles in his country through the 1930s, 1940s, and until his death in 1953, exhibits the following features. The state occupies the central roles as economic planner and executor. Heavy industry, viewed as the foundation for future economic growth and development, receives the most substantial share of available investment funds. Agriculture continues as the servant of the rest of the economy: it is to provide the bulk of the surplus necessary for capital accumulation. All these elements characterized China's first five-year plan. Economic power was centralized and a vertical chain of command established. Heavy industry received the greatest amount of investment. Agriculture was squeezed to generate most of the surplus essential to future economic growth.

Though Chinese leaders relied heavily on agriculture they did so in a less heavy-handed manner than had their Soviet counterparts. Chinese agriculture was collectivized but without the blood spilled when Stalin and his associates collectivized Soviet agriculture in the 1930s. The Chinese, perhaps having learned a lesson from the Soviet experience, proceeded more gradually and met less resistance from the rural population. The Chinese leadership designed the details of its collectivization to give rural reorganization a congruence with human needs and aspirations, which Stalinist abruptness and force never displayed in practice.

In China collectives at that time were in theory only more structured cooperatives (McCormick 1980: 4). The distribution of after-tax income preserved some material incentives for the individual producer but in an environment that was becoming increasingly bureaucratized. "Ad hoc mutual aid teams" of six or seven families pooling their labor during the harvest evolved into "permanent mutual aid teams," which formed the bases for the creation of "agricultural producers' cooperatives of the less advanced type." These in time combined to form "agricultural producers' cooperatives of the more advanced type." Twenty to thirty of these organizations were joined together to form particular communes. Within this communal structure, which exemplified the centralization of economic power through the establishment of a tight vertical chain of command, some name changes occurred. The more advanced cooperatives became known as production brigades, while the less advanced were only production teams (Eckstein 1977: 68-74). New names did not change the hierarchical decision making that collectivization implies.

More penetrating bureaucratization did not, at least in the beginning, retard or choke off completely agricultural productivity. Rural reorganization, assessed in gross quantitative terms, was an initial success. Measured in 1952 prices, the gross value of agricultural output increased by 24.7 percent during the first five-year plan (Wheelright and McFarlane 1970: 39). Such substantial growth apparently resulted from a number of factors. Greater organization produced a more efficient use of available resources. Reorganization had not proceeded so far as to bring negative returns. Cooperatives, even of a more structured type, can produce economic advantages until a chain of command becomes top heavy and unresponsive. Cooperatives can mobilize surplus labor in the off season for work on such infrastructure projects as irrigation. They can facilitate the pooling of member savings, more efficient use of land by combining small fragmented plots, and the emergence of various kinds of insurance to protect members in their active and retired years (Wheelright and McFarlane 1970: 37-38). All these advantages coupled with the zeal of a successful revolution's early years in power help explain the initial success of rural reorganization.

Agriculture was doing its duty by Stalinist logic. It was generating part of the investment in heavy industry, which itself grew significantly during the first five-year plan. From 1952 to 1957 Chinese steel output rose from 1.35 to 5.35

million metric tons (MMT); oil production, from .44 to 1.46 MMT; cement, from 2.9 to 6.9 MMT; and electric power, from 7.3 to 19.3 million kilowatt-hours (KWH) (King 1969: 187).

Agriculture was doing its duty with a relatively small investment in material and money (physical and liquid capital). During the first five-year plan agriculture received only 6.2 percent of the total investment allocated by the state. This modest input testifies to the strength of reorganization allied with human capital in generating that agricultural surge. The magnitude of the initial Chinese agricultural accomplishment did not hypnotize the leadership into an unquestioning acceptance of the status quo. China's leaders knew that the gains from structural reorganization and labor productivity motivated by the exciting early years of making a new country would or had run their course. They realized that agricultural output would continue to increase substantially only if investment in agriculture rose considerably.

QUESTIONING THE APPLICABILITY OF THE STALINIST MODEL

This conclusion emerged during intense questioning of the applicability of the Stalinist development model to China. Agriculture was so central to the Chinese economy that it made no sense to treat it in the Soviet fashion as an abused and unrewarded family member. Chinese agriculture had to perform with great vigor all the functions that development theorists assign to agriculture. Chinese agriculture had to feed a huge population growing at high rates and continue to generate a surplus critical for capital accumulation. Chinese agriculture was helping industry in other ways. About 50 percent of all industry depended upon agriculture for raw materials (Magdoff 1975: 31). Thus, a bottleneck in farming could cripple the entire economy. With these facts before them, the Chinese leadership found it impossible to rely on a development model that explicitly minimizes the importance of rural development and takes an essentially exploitative stance toward agriculture in general.

The Stalinist-inspired first five-year plan was creating or intensifying other problems in China. The investment favored by that imported model—in heavy industry—was very capital-intensive in terms of physical and liquid capital. This capital-intensity meant jobs for workers was a secondary concern. Such an approach slighted the necessity of generating sufficient employment for the population, especially people living in urban locations. In fact, capital-intensive industrial investment during the first five-year plan was not creating enough jobs.

Unemployment, particularly in the cities, was becoming a serious problem. It mocked the ideological commitment of the leadership to providing jobs for the working class. It enlarged a potential cadre of restless and discontented people in central locations, where they might threaten the regime. Rising unemployment increased the waste of human resources and magnified inefficiencies in the utilization of human capital. A model that already had one strike against it—its lack of appreciation for agriculture—missed again in a major way by insufficiently linking the nature of investment with ideology, stability, and economy.

But there was a third and even fourth strike against a Stalinist-inspired approach. The new industrial investment directed by the first five-year plan did not occur on a blank slate. There was already an industrial infrastructure in place in certain areas. About 90 percent of the modern industry inherited by the communists was located in five coastal cities: Shanghai, Tientsin, Tsingtao, Peking, and Nanking (Magdoff 1975: 32). The configuration of existing industry determined in large measure the trajectory of new investment under the first five-year plan. This continuity had adverse consequences for the emergence of a stable national economy. The less vibrant areas within China, which included the majority of its land mass and citizenry, were becoming more stagnant.

The direction of new industrial investment under the first five-year plan did not introduce regional or other disparities to China. Economic imbalances between or among different areas of the country have characterized China throughout its history. But new investment, largely following the contours of past investment, entrenched those locational inequalities and inequities. This intensification deeply bothered Chairman Mao and his associates.

More directed development of an intensely centralized sort—the essence of planning inspired by Stalinism—brings the growth of bureaucracy. Administration can increase in terms of personnel, structures, or both. The degree to which an administration manipulates or penetrates the objects of its concerns can intensify. Bureaucratization was growing in all these ways, which greatly concerned Chairman Mao. The entrenchment of bureaucracy associated with a Soviet style of development was underpinning the emergence of a new elite. This contradicted Mao's vision of a more progressively egalitarian society. For all these reasons—the slighting of agriculture, investment inadequately linked to job creation, greater regional imbalances, and a bureaucratization that mocked ideology—China canceled its second five-year plan in 1958, almost as soon as it had begun. The short-lived second plan yielded to the program popularly known as the Great Leap Forward.

Chinese disenchantment with Soviet-style central planning contains important clues for understanding the nature and implications of the reforms begun in the 1980s. How external military and economic forces had harmed China gave its revolutionary leadership a fierce determination to build a new country on the hard work of their own people and the efficient use of all their resources in a framework that promoted their own ideological goals. How an imported development model generated adverse local consequences reminded the Chinese leadership of the importance of selectivity and adaptability.

China's disillusionment with central planning inspired by Stalinism meant that future experiments with other outside approaches would be well considered.

China would, with care and deliberation, adapt those aspects of the experiences of others that seemed to hold the greatest promise for furthering the goals of the current leadership. A central question in China would become whether adapting aspects of an economic system associated with a certain ideology would bring the intrusion of other premises and forces in that ideology.

THE GREAT LEAP FORWARD

While the implementation of highly centralized planning in China in the early 1950s produced another example of an unadapted import gone awry, the Great Leap Forward would provide another and different set of historical memories to guide the present. The experience of the Great Leap, from 1958 into 1961, furnishes an intriguing case study because the lessons to be learned were not as straightforward as some have made them. The Great Leap Forward was aptly named. It was an attempt, never tried before on such a scale in China, to mobilize the population for progress in many areas: agriculture, industry, handicrafts, communication, transport, commerce, science, technology, and culture. Liu Shao-ch'i officially described the Great Leap Forward as the "simultaneous development of agriculture and industry" (Liu Shao-ch'i 1958, quoted by Eckstein 1977: 56). The leadership aimed to mobilize on a massive scale what it regarded as an underemployed surplus in agriculture. It took the view that the skills of many people in agriculture were not employed as efficiently as possible and that they were, therefore, underemployed.

The leadership tried to rely more on production based on its version of technological dualism. In China technological dualism, which became known as "walking on two legs," meant a shift in various ways. China tried to move away from reliance on large-scale operations with state-of-the-art technology toward the greater utilization of enterprises of more modest sizes that employed technology described as "traditional" or "intermediate." China attempted to replace one-person factory management with a team-oriented approach, from party committees and production teams. It appealed more to notions of social responsibility than to material incentives as it motivated the workers and farmers. It tried to relax the pervasiveness of central command decision-making control and locate more authority in the local masses (Magdoff 1975: 36-37). The premises of the Great Leap Forward made it distinctive. Bigger was not necessarily better, more recent was not necessarily more appropriate, and more centralized was not necessarily more effective.

A major thrust of the Great Leap Forward was adaptability. Relying on smaller, less expensive factories dispersed throughout the country, instead of on costly and large industrial complexes in fewer locations, would increase and broaden the capacity of Chinese industry to meet local needs. The Great Leap tried to tailor its resource requirements to prevailing abundances and scarcities.

In a country that was capital short in terms of money and material, it was imperative to use the relatively abundant factor—labor—as creatively and as efficiently as possible.

The aim was to economize on capital as material and money and to emphasize the human dimensions of capital or, as some might put it, the capital aspects of labor. Labor can, within limits, through learning by doing and formal education, upgrade its contribution to production and substitute for capital as material and money. Small-scale industries dispersed throughout the country were designed to utilize available local raw materials, to meet more effectively local demands, and to mobilize surplus labor in a way that maximized its ability to substitute for capital as material and money.

THE GREAT LEAP FORWARD: CRITICS

The Great Leap Forward lacked neither critics nor problems. Some observers, especially those in the West, contended that the small industries associated with the Great Leap were inefficient and that their output was of relatively lower quality and higher cost. It is easier to make these assertions than to substantiate them with logic and evidence. As to logic, the Great Leap Forward was consistent with neoclassical economic theory in the following central axiom. When one factor is relatively abundant and another relatively scarce, decision makers should design projects that more fully utilize what is abundant and conserve what is scarce. China was wrestling with a capital shortage in money and material and mobilizing labor that was relatively abundant but underutilized (McCormick 1980: 8).

The inefficiency charge also falters in the context of the infrastructure. Despite the rebuilding that had gone on since 1949, transport within China was inadequate over longer distances. To bypass this constraint, the small industries connected with the Great Leap employed local resources where possible. Localization of production economized on transport that was in short and uncertain supply. Communes, as well as decentralized smaller factories, efficiently tapped surplus labor in the countryside. While those factories provided closer opportunities for work for people in agriculture part-time or with no jobs at all, communes mobilized many laborers for such projects as dam and irrigation construction. On several major counts the inefficiency indictment of the Great Leap Forward collapses.

Whether the output of the smaller factories was more costly and less well made is open to dispute. Many are still operating today because they meet local needs. They process local agricultural output, produce and repair agricultural implements, make fertilizers, and fabricate construction materials (McCormick 1980: 8). Their continued existence and responsiveness do not in themselves prove quality or cost-effectiveness. However, even if a local factory incurred production costs that were higher than those involved in making a similar product in a larger complex, the savings from reduced transportation costs and time between production and final distribution may compensate. The issue of quality is more elusive, but in some cases, if there were no local manufacturing, goods would not be available at all.

THE GREAT LEAP FORWARD: PROBLEMS

The Great Leap encountered serious problems. Its immediate impact was positive in terms of increased output. The gross national product rose from $82 billion in 1957 to $95 billion at its highwater mark in the 1958–1960 period; per capita GNP increased from $128 to $144; grain production rose from 185 million to 200 million tons; and steel output increased from 5.35 million to 13 million tons (Ashbrook 1972| 23). Then the Great Leap Forward ran into nature. From 1958 to 1961 China suffered through natural disasters that rank among the most severe in its long history. Floods, droughts, typhoons, and pests ravaged the country and reduced agricultural output to the danger point. During both 1959 and 1960, drought or flooding affected over half of all cultivated areas (Wheelright and McFarlane 1970: 54). Nature and the Great Leap greatly stressed the population. The reduction in the food supply, caused by nature, and the extra hours of work necessitated by the Great Leap, exhausted the labor force. China escaped a nationwide famine by efficient rationing procedures, but there was little food to spare (McCormick 1980: 9).

The Great Leap Forward also ran into a Soviet rebuff. In 1960 the U.S.S.R. withdrew its technicians as a response to Chinese rejection of Soviet planning techniques. When the technicians left, they took with them blueprints for about 150 unfinished industrial complexes. The U.S.S.R. also refused to ship parts that China needed to keep other Soviet-built factories in operation (McCormick 1980: 10).

China reeled under the double blows from nature and the Soviet Union. By the end of 1961 gross national product had declined to $72 billion, per capita GNP to $103, grain production to 160 million tons, and steel output to 8 million tons (Ashbrook 1972: 23). These represented, when contrasted with the highwater marks reached in all four categories during the 1958–1960 period, declines of 24.2 percent, 28.5 percent, 20 percent, and 38.5 percent, respectively. Chronological coincidence is, especially in the domain of politics, sometimes mistaken for causality. Because this sharp reversal occurred during the time the Great Leap Forward was in operation, enough people concluded that the plan was somehow responsible for these failures.

Whether the Great Leap Forward deserved to be brought into total disrepute is another matter. There is no doubt that in practice the Great Leap was too ambitious, lacked consistent planning, and harmed the country's natural resources and population (McCormick 1980: 11). It left China with little or no margin of safety when faced with uncontrollable setbacks, which nature provided in abundance. But the extent to which it had made the mobilization of human and natural resources more efficient contributed to China's comeback, since the rationing program that averted widespread famine piggybacked on existing bureaucratic structures. The outcome might have been different had nature not crippled and the Soviet Union not tripped China during the Great Leap's crucial early years.

While implementation was seriously flawed structurally and made too intense by an excess of "revolutionary zeal" in some quarters, the premises of the Great Leap Forward were sound. Bigger is not always better; more contemporary is not always more efficient; and more controlled is not always better implemented. Tapping creatively and effectively a "developing" country's relatively abundant factor(s) makes common economic sense, no matter what one's ideology. The most recent technology may not always be needed, especially when most of your resources are in short supply.

Above all, the Great Leap must be viewed in its preeminent ideological guise. Chairman Mao fervently believed that an authentic Marxist-Leninist state must reduce the three great differences in society: between rural and urban areas, between workers and peasants, and between agriculture and industry (Sweezy 1979). Had not disaster floored the Chinese economy, the Great Helmsman might have continued with the Great Leap, perhaps in a modified fashion. In 1961 the leadership announced a "New Economic Policy" for China, which was a more realistic and less stressful approach to planning. The New Economic Policy did not return to the status quo before the Great Leap Forward. It did not reinstate a Stalinist model; it recognized and fostered Chinese agriculture.

The legacy of the Great Leap Forward has proved consequential. As far as economic planning is concerned, the legacy has become structural. Small-scale industries have continued to fulfill local needs from local resources with local labor. There are other continuities as well. The emphasis on agriculture, the thrust for regional self-sufficiency or at least a reduction in regional imbalance, and the efficient utilization of surplus labor—all these remain key elements of Chinese policy. The success of the Chinese economy since 1961 comes partly from the preservation of this structural legacy.

THE GREAT PROLETARIAN CULTURAL REVOLUTION

In an ideological context the legacy was not so benign. Some speculate that the failure of the Great Leap to reduce significantly those three great differences in society—between rural and urban areas, workers and peasants, and agriculture and industry—may have led to the Great Proletarian Cultural Revolution. This upheaval, which wracked China from 1966 through 1976, was a more radical endeavor than the Great Leap to deal with the oppression of humankind as analyzed in Marxist constructs. As did the Great Leap, so did the Great Proletarian Cultural Revolution emphasize the importance of liberating people from class structures. There was a recognition in both phases that ideological salvation might mean a temporary setback in development.

The Great Leap sought to improve China's economy and egalitarianism; the Cultural Revolution specialized in ideological purification. The Great Proletarian Cultural Revolution is captured in pictures of crowds waving copies of the red book containing quotations from Chairman Mao. This period of prolonged turbulence was not conducive to the economic development that might have reduced or at least transformed those three great societal differences. Once again, the Chinese leadership received a forcible reminder that zeal can begin as benefit, evolve as benefit and bane, and end up as burden.

THE REFORMS OF THE 1980s AND 1990s: A SECOND CHINESE REVOLUTION?

Against this historical background the reforms started in the 1980s gain perspective. The Chinese economy, especially agriculture, had performed well over the years. Agriculture was meeting the basic nutritional requirements of a growing population. Yet the Chinese leadership, under the guidance of Deng Xiaoping, was not satisfied with the economy and its labor force. With a vision of the future as panoramic as the country itself, Deng Xiaoping and his associates began to engineer in the early 1980s what some called China's second revolution. They were determined to restructure fundamental relationships in order to give the Chinese economy what it needed to achieve the level of the advanced countries by the middle of the twenty-first century.

The following analysis considers the goals and impact of the 1980s phase of the "Second Chinese Revolution." As this book went to press, it is too early to tell what the 1990s will mean for reform. One general objective for part of the 1980s was to restructure relations between bureaucracy and economy. Reorganizing these connections involved not so much reducing the size of the bureaucracy as lessening its involvement in core areas of the economy.

ENLIVENING STATE-OWNED ENTERPRISES

Deng Xiaoping believed that one key to economic revitalization was to enliven state-owned enterprises. These numbered over a million, employed about 80 million workers, and accounted for 80 percent of state revenues. State enterprises were to receive more decision-making autonomy, more economic responsibility, and more motivated managers and workers (Ji: 1985: 8).

As envisioned on paper these three characteristics were to result from the following actions. To grant more decision-making autonomy, the government was to have withdrawn from directly managing state enterprises and was to have concentrated on its administrative roles, a category never fully specified. State enterprises were to gain autonomy not only from the downsizing of a state operational role but also from the assignment of economic responsibility. Each enterprise was to achieve a quasi-corporate status as it became a legal person with rights and duties. Each enterprise was to be responsible for its own profits and losses. Greater motivation was to flow from restructuring the company chain of command and distribution of pay. Workers and staff were to receive the right to participate in a management of the enterprise that was to be more "democratic." Everyone's pay was to be directly linked to the performance of their enterprise in order to "mobilize their initiatives" (Ji 1985: 8-9).

Projected internal reforms in state enterprises were not seen as sufficient to trigger their revitalization. To facilitate relations among enterprises, the leadership planned to deregulate some prices to make them more effective communicators of relative scarcities. The range of inflexible prices was to have shrunk and the scope of floating prices, within limits, was to have increased (Ji 1985: 9).

DEBUREAUCRATIZING AGRICULTURE

The leadership aimed to release agriculture from the tight grip of central planning. The goal was to make already productive Chinese agriculture more efficient. Extra efficiency was to come from a greater synchronization of agriculture with the rest of the economy. The leadership, as it proposed for state enterprise, wanted to transform agriculture by decentralizing decision-making authority, more precise targeting of economic responsibility to specific collectives and groups of workers, and intensifying motivation of all agriculturists. The debureaucratization of agriculture was to rest on the deregulation of some prices and the apparent encouragement of market-based economic activity within a controlled framework (Ji 1985: 9).

Economic debureaucratization had to occur in a manner that did not threaten stability. The concern with stability is overriding. Deng and his supporters were trying to achieve a more stable management of investment, the money supply, and the food supply; but stability also means preservation of the leadership's version of public order. The tensions, discontent, and misdirected zeal that reform on a grand scale, such as the Great Leap Forward and the Great Proletarian Cultural Revolution, generated in the past provided a haunting background against which these reforms were implemented and then slowed.

IMPLEMENTATION PROBLEMS

Implementation was uneven. Because of political turbulence in the late 1980s associated with student demonstrations, implementation became more hesitant and then stopped. What emerged was essentially a dual economy in more than one sense. The first came from the fact that state planning and distribution systems endured alongside a variety of "unofficial" marketing networks based on free and floating prices (Delfs 1986: 70). A second dualism was sectoral. Agriculture, which accounts for about three fourths of the economy, underwent gradual debureaucratization as it was slowly freed from central planning. The industrial one quarter remained tightly controlled (*Econ* 24 January 1987: 34). There were two spheres existing in several overlapping and uneasy ways.

In 1986 important industrial reform did occur. China's first stock market since 1949 opened in Shanghai on September 26, and shares of stock are now traded. Individual companies were empowered to hire and fire workers, which departed dramatically from the long-held orthodoxy of guaranteeing every worker a job. Statistics on those hired and fired are hard to come by, so the power may have remained largely theoretical. Yet there were reports that at least one company was allowed to fail, under the justification of individual enterprise assuming more economic responsibility for its operations. Even with these changes, there was still a major difference between the extent of change in agriculture and that in industry. There was as well a substantial contrast between the areas of greater and lesser regulation within the entire economy, but especially in agriculture. These imbalances created tensions. Regulated economic activity still accounted for most of what took place.

The difficulties of reform were easy to spot. The uneven change between agriculture and industry turned the terms of trade against the countryside. This area had been the major source of strength for the Communist party's first revolution in China. The *People's Daily* noted in 1986 that "state price rises for farm produce in recent years have been mostly wiped out by the rapidly rising cost of manufactured goods sold in the countryside" (*Econ* 24 January 1987: 34). This state of affairs was not surprising. Agricultural produce, from the more reformed sector of the economy, was in abundant supply, while manufactured goods, from the less reformed sector, were scarce. The forces of supply and demand had worked their way. The government in 1986 decontrolled prices on some of the most sought after consumer products, such as bicycles, black-and-white television sets, and sewing machines. Abolishing price controls for these products should over time have increased their supply, but in the near term it simply boosted prices (*Econ* 24 January 1987: 34).

The unevenness of change within agriculture also generated problems. While decision making was decentralized and central planning reduced, the bureaucracy still played a considerable price-setting role for commodities. About 90 percent of the grain harvest was bought at a price that the government largely controlled. Some structures changed—a system of contracts with local authorities replaced that of fixed quotas—but the outcome—governmentally administered prices—remained substantially the same. The government was reluctant to deregulate grain trading further for political reasons. In markets left to themselves grain prices would probably double. In 1985 the free retail price for grain, according to the government's own figures, was 88 percent higher than the state-controlled price (*Econ* 24 January 1987: 34). Deregulating grain prices would adversely affect the standard of living for urban consumers. The government correctly fears the potential for destabilization that aggrieved urban dwellers represent. The unrest of 1989 strengthened this concern. Discontent and pro-democracy demonstrations accelerated in the wake of a spike in inflation that hit 30 percent in cities (*IHT* 23-24 February 1991: 12).

INTERNATIONAL BUSINESS AND GOVERNMENT BUREAUCRACY IN CHINA TODAY

Many people insufficiently analyzed the reforms of the 1980s and jumped to conclusions about the "capitalist tilt" of China's socialism. From the bureaucracy's perspective, China is not turning capitalist but undergoing another phase in its socialist transformation. From the author's perspective, reforming state industries, prices, and management practices do not add up to capitalism or necessarily represent "capitalistic tendencies." That China today is undergoing another phase in its socialist transformation should make international investors cautious but not passive. A foreign business presence in China can grow if investors remember the lessons of Chinese economic reform as a historical phenomenon, which this case study has illustrated.

Whatever the ongoing nature of reform, the government bureaucracy itself will remain a fact of life for all Chinese and all foreign business people. The bureaucracy is the ultimate guarantor of the stability of the economic environment in China. The government may have modestly deregulated certain areas of the economy, but it has not yet downsized itself. It remains the directing agent of economic transformation and the custodian of ideology and public order. The excesses of zeal associated with the Great Leap Forward and the Great Proletarian Cultural Revolution strengthen the motivation of the Chinese Communist party to control a bureaucracy with the power to repress threatening behavior. The theme of excess offers a final caution to all outsiders but pointedly to foreign business people already in China or those contemplating involvement. One's own plans must be deliberate, gradual, implemented in a manner that does not trigger or strengthen such excesses, and put into practice in a fashion that respects culture, bureaucracy, the people, and their history.

18

Vignette: International Business and Economic Integration in Asia and the Western Pacific

Economic integration has made a modest and controversial start in the western Pacific and Asia. In 1989 Bob Hawke, then Australian Prime Minister, proposed a forum for trade and economic cooperation that would embrace at least twelve nations. These include the six members of the Association of Southeast Asian Nations (ASEAN): Brunei, Indonesia, Malaysia, the Philippines, Singapore, and Thailand. Other participants in the forum are Australia, Japan, Korea, New Zealand, Taiwan, and the United States. This is a loose economic grouping, which now emphasizes cooperation among its members rather than the structural integration of their economies. It spans the Pacific littoral, with countries from the northern, southern, and eastern Pacific among its ranks. It includes countries with economic interests that sometimes sharply diverge, such as the United States and Japan. It can therefore function as a forum for both cooperation and reconciliation.

In December 1990, the Uruguay round of the GATT (General Agreement on Tariffs and Trade) talks stalled in Brussels, Belgium. This organization of 108 members is dedicated to reducing barriers to trade among its members. It is the largest organization concerned with trade liberalization in the world. The Uruguay round, named after the host country, ran aground on the issue of agricultural subsidies. The United States and other countries asked the European Community (EC) to reduce significantly subsidies to its farmers, but the EC refused. The collapse of the GATT talks reinforced concerns that the world was moving away from free trade and toward an arena of competitive and protectionist trade blocks. The GATT talks revived in 1991, and in 1992 the EC made possibly important concessions on the question of agricultural subsidies, which could break the deadlock. The final fate of the Uruguay round is not known at this writing. What is known is that its temporary failure spurred the emergence of a proposal for a tighter economic grouping of trading countries from the Pacific littoral than the forum represents.

After the GATT negotiations collapsed in late 1990, Malaysia proposed a new East Asian economic group. The Malaysian prime minister, Mahathir Mohamad, is a principal sponsor of this proposal. In a February 1991, interview with Michael Richardson of the *International Herald Tribune*, Rafidah Aziz, the Malaysian minister of international trade and industry, had these thoughts about the proposed group (*IHT* 23-24 February 1991: 12). It would be "consistent with GATT. While promoting regional trade, we should not stop or divert trade with nations outside the region. It would be like the U.S.-Canada free trade agreement, which enhances trade between the United States and Canada but is not detrimental to other trading partners."

Malaysia's proposal did not at first win a warm reception from Japan, China, and Indonesia. The Japanese are wary of anything that would intensify friction with the United States. An East Asian economic community, which could serve as a counter-block to an emerging free trade area in the western hemisphere, might further antagonize the United States. The minister insisted that an "East Asian economic grouping will not be protectionist, inward-looking or a negative trade block." So there could be "no reason why there should be any hesitation in supporting the proposal."

There is also considerable concern that the Malaysian grouping would be exclusionist. A strength of the forum is that it includes both Japan and the United States. In its initial formulation the proposed East Asian economic grouping seemed exclusionist: the suggested core was ASEAN. The minister believed that all its members "have agreed to the concept" of a new economic grouping. As to "which countries is Malaysia proposing should join the group," the minister said, "we do not have an exclusion list. We think that ASEAN should decide the membership. Initially, we see ASEAN as the core and its East Asian neighbors the most logical additional members. Later on, if other countries want to join, why not."

Japan's possible role in this new grouping raises questions. Japan's economic power could dominate, but the minister asserted that all members "would be equal partners." While an "equal partner," Japan would have a major "leadership role." As a member of both the East Asian economic grouping and the G-7 group of leading industrial nations, Japan "could act as a conduit between us and the G-7 countries." This would be a change from the past, as "East Asian countries have not been able to bring their concerns to the G-7 before." The G-7, or group of seven, is Japan, the United States, Canada, the United Kingdom, France, Germany, and Italy.

The move for a more cohesive economic grouping in East Asia comes from the same principles that motivate the evolution of the European Community and the emergence of a possible western hemisphere free trade area. The minister spoke about the grouping as a way to "synergize our economic potential. We could develop strategies to enhance regional trade and investment. We could harmonize some of our foreign investment laws so that we no longer undercut each other in bidding for funds."

An East Asian economic grouping might do for the region what some of its prospective ASEAN members are attempting to do among themselves. In February 1991, Singapore proposed an economic tie linking itself, Indonesia, and Malaysia. This plan expands an existing agreement between Singapore and Indonesia. In December 1989, those two countries entered into memoranda of understanding for exchanging material and personnel in broadcasting and information. Singapore's 1991 proposal aims to create an economic growth "triangle." This plan involves Singapore, the southern Malaysian state of S. Johore, and the Riau Islands of Indonesia. Its central principle is locating business activity where the factors of production are most favorable. Singapore faces a major labor shortage and wants to encourage foreign companies doing business within its borders to relocate their labor-intensive operations to S. Johore and the Riau Islands (*IHT* 19 February 1991: 11). This "triangle" hints at the possible synergies that a wider economic grouping might unleash.

In late January 1992, the six members of ASEAN signed a mutual tariff reduction agreement and indicated that they wanted an ASEAN free trade area within fifteen years (*FT* 29 January 1992: 7). The thoughts of Minister Rafidah Aziz may contain clues as to the evolution of the group in other respects. In the meantime, international businesses need strategies for dealing with economic integration in Asia and the western Pacific, no matter what turns and twists occur.

Japanese actions in Asia and the western Pacific should be studied. Japanese business has for decades situated production within countries that can serve as major markets for those products or as convenient re-export locations. This strategy—the localization of production—is a global approach that takes into account many local factors; for example, local wages. During the 1960s and 1970s Japanese businesses located many manufacturing outlets in such countries as Taiwan and Korea in order to capitalize on their market potential and relatively low wages. As wages in these countries rose in the 1980s, Japanese businesses shifted more manufacturing within East Asia to those countries that still have low wages but also considerable market potential.

Thailand, which since the late 1970s has experienced a major economic boom, is one such country. A ride from the international airport in Bangkok to the city center reveals the intensity of that investment: numerous Japanese manufacturing outlets dot the urban landscape. While Thailand was a vanguard market for Japanese businesses in the 1980s, Vietnam may become another cutting edge location in the 1990s. Many western businesses did not get as early a start in Thailand as the Japanese did.

Why many western business people missed or underestimated Thailand's economic potential speaks volumes about the competitive situation in world markets today. They were occupied with opportunities closer to home. They did not penetrate the stereotypes that sometimes surround "exotic" Thailand. About 95 percent of Thailand's population is Buddhist. It is easy to stereotype Buddhism as a religion of resignation, infer that all Buddhists are passive in every aspect of their lives, and to conclude that a work force of Buddhists could never be sufficiently productive. How wrong such judgments are.

Thailand has been a constitutional monarchy since 1932. Numerous coup attempts by the armed forces have occurred over the years. Elective government had apparently made some progress in the late 1980s, but the military overthrew the government of Prime Minister Chatichai Choonhavan on 23 February 1991. Deadly street demonstrations in May 1992 showed the frustration of thousands of Thais with the current political situation. Many western business people, especially those from the United States, associate political stability with democracy. They also regard military intervention in politics as destabilizing economic growth—both short-sighted impressions. The Japanese were able to seize the initiative in Thailand because they have global strategies, an appreciation of how religion can strengthen not weaken a work ethic, a keen understanding of how making a product can serve as an incentive to get what is needed to buy it, and long-term viewpoints. This longer view places short-term "political instability" in proper perspective: it works against changing an investment plan because of some near-term political turbulence, such as the May 1992 demonstrations and military repression in Thailand. The Japanese have also been able to appraise business opportunities shorn of biases about what is the best political system for economic advancement. All these characteristics and the localization of production strategy lead Japanese business to Vietnam in the 1990s.

Vietnam has a labor force with a strong work ethic that now receives relatively low wages. Because the country is serious about economic growth, the government is introducing market-oriented reforms in an effort to spur growth. Vietnam is a major opportunity for international business (*FT* 10 September 1992: 7). But many western investors are focusing on the European Community and Eastern Europe. Vietnam carries hostile historical memories and, like Thailand did, images of impenetrable eastern mysteries that seem incompatible with crisp capitalist efficiency. One Japanese business person recently remarked, "That's how you [U.S. business] missed Thailand in the early 1980s."

For international businesses wishing to anticipate East Asian economic integration or just be advantageously positioned no matter what happens, Thailand and Vietnam represent two strategic bases. Thailand is already a member of ASEAN, which as noted plans to become a more cohesive economic grouping. Investment there carries with it the advantage of being on the inside of an emerging economic community. Vietnam is not now a member of

ASEAN, but it seems a likely candidate for membership. Investment in Vietnam requires not only the abilities to transcend historical memories, penetrate cultural stereotypes, and control one's political and ideological biases. It must also be placed within the context of a very long-term global investment strategy. Many U.S. businesses are aware of the opportunities in Vietnam but cannot proceed because of a trade and investment embargo that the U.S. government maintains against Vietnam. The embargo was relaxed in April 1992 to permit the installation of more telephone links between the United States and Vietnam, but it has not been abolished.

Suggested Readings

PART I. EUROPE

Rondo Cameron, *A Concise Economic History of the World: From Paleolithic Times to the Present* (New York: Oxford University Press, 1989). Chapters 7, 8, 9, and 10 are especially good.

CHAPTER 1

Vincent P. Carosso, *The Morgans: Private International Bankers, 1854–1913* (Cambridge, Mass.: Harvard University Press, 1987), and Ron Chernow, *The House of Morgan: An American Banking Dynasty and the Rise of American Finance* (New York: Atlantic Monthly Press, 1990) have given the Morgan family expert scholarly attention.

A highly readable non-specialist work is Frederic Morton, *The Rothschilds: A Family Portrait* (New York: Atheneum, 1962). A short but fascinating essay on the recent history of the French branch of the Rothschild family is "How the Rothschilds Took Their Revenge," *Financial Times*, 14 February 1991, special section on European Finance and Investment: 4. This analysis tracks the emergence of *Compagnie Financière* as a major financial force.

See also Michael Field, *The Merchants: The Big Business Families of Arabia* (London: John Murray, 1985).

CHAPTER 2

The literature on multinationals is extensive. A valuable anthology is Mira Wilkins, ed., *The Growth of Multinationals* (Brookfield, Vt.: Ashgate Publishing Company, 1991), which is Volume 1 in *The International Library of Critical Writings in Business History*, Geoffrey Jones, general editor. Another essential book is Alfred D. Chandler, Jr., *Scale and Scope: The Dynamics of Industrial Capitalism* (Cambridge, Mass.: Harvard University Press, Belknap Press, 1990), which contrasts the industrial development of Great Britain, the United States, and Germany in the decades after 1870. Another comparative work all students should consult is Mansel Blackford, *The Rise of Modern Business in Great Britain, the United States, and Japan* (Chapel Hill: University of North Carolina Press, 1988). A fascinating comparative paper is Robert Locke, "The Reaction of German, British, French, and Japanese Higher Education to the Professionalization of American Management After World War II," Business History Conference, Baltimore, Maryland, 25 March 1991. See his *Management and Higher Education* (Cambridge, England: Cambridge University Press, 1989).

A valuable work that addresses topics in the "transnational debate" and other concerns of this book is Richard Tanner Pascale, *Managing on the Edge* (London: Viking Penguin, 1990).

More specialized essays can be found in Martin Chick, ed., *Government, Industries and Markets: Aspects of Government-Industry Relations in the UK, Japan, West Germany, and the USA* (Brookfield, Vt.: Gower, 1990). A book likely to provoke discussion is Alex Rubner, *The Might of the Multinationals: The Rise and Fall of the Corporate Legend* (New York: Praeger, 1990).

Worthwhile collections are Alice Teichova, Maurice Levy-Léboyer, and Helga Nussbaum, eds., *Historical Studies in International Corporate Business*, (Cambridge, England, and New York: Cambridge University Press; Paris: *Éditions de la Maison des sciences de l'homme*, 1989) and *Multinational Enterprise in Historical Perspective* (same publishers, 1989).

Other useful studies are Geoffrey Jones, ed., *British Multinationals: Origins, Management, and Performance* (Brookfield, Vt.: Gower, 1986); Alfred D. Chandler, Jr., and Herman Daems, *Managerial Hierarchies: Comparative Perspectives on the Rise of Modern Industrial Enterprise* (Cambridge, Mass.: Harvard University Press, 1980); and Julien Savary, *French Multinationals* (London: Frances Pinter, 1984). Savary's book is a translation of his *Les Multinationales françaises*. The wider internal economic background for German international business is lucidly portrayed in "D-Mark Day Dawns: The New Germany," *The Economist*, 30 June 1990: special survey, 1-22.

An excellent short essay is "Swedish Multinationals: A Hard Act fo Follow," *The Economist*, 1 August 1987: 63-5. A highly readable analysis of the present and future of Saab Automobile, the Swedish automobile manufacturer, is Kevin Done and Robert Taylor, "Skid on Road to More Productivity," *Financial Times*, 11 February 1991: 12.

A helpful introduction to multinationals in the "Third World" is Sanjaya Lall, *The New Multinationals: The Spread of Third World Enterprises* (New York: Wiley, 1983).

CHAPTER 3

The literature on the European Community is growing. An essential introduction is John Mole, *Mind Your Manners: Culture Clash in the European Market* (London: The Industrial Society Press, 1990). Other useful works are Collin Randlesome, William Brierly, Kevin Bruton, Colin Gordon, and Peter King, *Business Cultures in Europe* (Oxford: Heinemann Professional Publishers, 1990), Alex Roney, *The European Community Fact Book: A Complete Question and Answer Guide* (London: Kogan Page in association with the London Chamber of Commerce and Industry, 1990, updated yearly), Hellen Wallace, ed., *The Wider Western Europe: Reshaping the EC/EFTA*

Relationship (London: Pinter Publishers for the Royal Institute of International Affairs, 1991), and William Wallace, *The Transformation of Western Europe* (London: Pinter Publishers for the Royal Institute of International Affairs, 1990). An excellent brief analysis, with a historical overview, is "At the Top of the Slope: Reshaping the EC," *The Economist*, 8 December 1990: 17, 18, and 22.

General Electric's relationship with the Tungsram Company, with special emphasis on the president of the Hungarian operation George Varga, is examined in Steven Greenhouse, "Running on Fast-Forward in Budapest," *The New York Times*, 16 December 1990: Section 3, pp. 1 and 8. See also Michael Porter, "Don't Collaborate, Compete: Europe's Companies after 1992," *The Economist*, 9 June 1990: 17-19. Porter argues that much of the energy invested in creating mergers and alliances in preparation for EC92 would be better spent in increasing the ability of individual companies to compete. A succinct essay, which also has relevance for U.S. and Japanese multinationals, is Michael Skapinker, "The Fashionable Place To Be Seen," *Financial Times*, 26 March 1991: 10. He analyses the invasion of Europe by U.S. and Japanese chip companies.

Two essays likely to stimulate discussion are Susan Lee, "Are We Building New Berlin Walls?," *Forbes*, 147, No. 1, 7 January 1991: 86-89, and a companion piece by David Stix (p. 89) on "A Lesson From History." She points to the protectionist tendencies allegedly inherent in the world's emerging mega-trading blocks. He tries to draw an analogy for today from the operation of the Commonwealth trade preferences, which emerged from the Ottawa Conference of 1931 and used to apply to the British Commonwealth.

For an article that introduces the author's next projected book, see "International Business and Economic Integration: Comparative Business Strategies Past and Present," *Business and Economic History*, Second Series, Vol. 21, 1992: 237-46.

PART II. NORTH AMERICA

For the wider economic environment in which U.S. business emerged, the best single modern introduction is Jonathan R. T. Hughes, *American Economic History*, 3d ed. (Glenview, Ill.: Scott, Foresman and Company, 1990). In *A History of American Enterprise* (Englewood Cliffs, N.J.: Prentice-Hall, 1988) John M. Dobson concisely presents the basics of U.S. business history. A penetrating work is Glenn Porter, *The Rise of Big Business, 1860–1920*, 2d ed. (Arlington Heights, Ill.: Harlan Davidson Inc., 1992). An insightful book is Richard Tedlow, *New and Improved: The Story of Mass Marketing in America* (New York: Basic Books, 1991). A work with significant classroom value is Mansel G. Blackford and K. Austin Kerr, *Business Enterprise in American History*, 2d ed. (Boston: Houghton Mifflin Company, 1990).

CHAPTER 4

See Mira Wilkins, *The Emergence of Multinational Enterprise: American Business Abroad from the Colonial Era to 1914* (Cambridge, Mass.: Harvard University Press, 1970), *The Maturing of Multinational Enterprise: American Business Abroad from 1914 to 1970* (Cambridge, Mass.: Harvard University Press, 1974), and *The History of Foreign*

Investment in the United States to 1914 (Cambridge, Mass.: Harvard University Press, 1989).

A classic study, presenting the "inside story," is Wayne G. Broehl, Jr., *Cargill: Trading the World's Grain* (Hanover, New Hampshire: University Press of New England, 1992).

CHAPTER 5

President Juan José Arévalo of Guatemala, predecessor to Jacobo Arbenz Guzmán, wrote the *Shark and the Sardines* (trans. June Cobb and Raúl Osegueda, New York, 1961), which attacked the U.S. government and powerful American companies for their shabby treatment of Latin Americans. See his obituary in *The New York Times*, 8 October 1990: C11. The role of the Central Intelligence Agency in fomenting "uprisings" in Guatemala and elsehwere is examined in the documentary *Intervention*, which is available as a PBS video (1988), Alexandria, Va. See also Thomas P. McCann, *An American Company: The Tragedy of United Fruit* (New York: Crown Publishers, 1976) and Stephen C. Schlesinger and Stephen Kinzer, *Bitter Fruit: The Untold Story of the American Coup in Guatemala* (Garden City, N.Y.: Doubelday, 1982).

CHAPTER 6

An excellent introduction is "For Want of Glue," *The Economist*, 29 June 1991, special survey on Canada: 1-18. For further reading and research, an invaluable document is E. Willard Miller and Ruby M. Miller, *United States Trade, United States, Canada, and Latin America: A Bibliography* (Monticello, Ill.: Vance Bibliographies, 1991). See also the essays in *Prospects for Canadian–United States Economic Relations Under Free Trade*, which is Volume 8 (1990) of *Research in International Business and Finance*, William Milberg and Philip F. Bartholomew, eds.

PART III. CENTRAL AMERICA, SOUTH AMERICA, AND THE CARIBBEAN BASIN

Peter Ashdown's *Caribbean History in Maps* (New York: Longman Group Ltd., 1979) is an enjoyable way to learn some basics about the Caribbean and its littoral. A provocative study of "transnational corporations" in the Caribbean is Tom Barry, Beth Wood, and Deb Preusch, *The Other Side of Paradise: Foreign Control in the Caribbean* (New York: Grove Press, 1989). See also Tom Barry, et al., *Dollars and Dictators: A Guide to Central America* (London: Zed Press, 1983), and Ransford W. Palmer, *Caribbean Dependence on the United States Economy* (New York: Praeger, 1979). A concise survey of the Caribbean is "Backyard Beauty," *The Economist*, 6 August 1988, special survey: 1-20.

CHAPTER 7

A valuable companion to the three mining case studies in the book is "Bougainville

Copper Ltd." in Raymond Vernon and Louis T. Wells, Jr., *Manager in the International Economy*, 4th ed., (Englewood Cliffs, N.J.: Prentice-Hall, 1981): 260-85. This case study shows the errors made by the copper company as it took a decidedly non-contextual approach to its environment. This island, part of Papua New Guinea in the southwestern Pacific, has been the scene of violence in recent years as groups campaign for the independence of the island. This turbulence has shut down the copper mines.

A useful sequel to the Cerro de Pasco case study is Elizabeth Dore, *The Peruvian Mining Industry: Growth, Stagnation, and Crisis* (Boulder, Colo.: Westview Press, 1986), which tracks the industry into recent times. A valuable article is Richard L. Garner, "Long-Term Silver Mining Trends in Spanish America: A Comparative Analysis of Peru and Mexico," *The American Historical Review*, Vol. 93, No. 4 (October 1988): 898-935.

CHAPTER 8

A book-length treatment of issues presented in this case study is Harvey F. Kline, *The Coal of El Cerrejón: Dependent Bargaining and Colombian Policy-Making* (University Park: Pennsylvania State University Press, 1987).

CHAPTER 9

The wider economic background can be found in Anthony Thompson, *An Economic History of the Bahamas* (Nassau, Bahamas: Commonwealth Publications, 1979).

CHAPTER 10

For a positive assessment of Mexico's economic prospects, see Matt Moffett, "Long-Sickly Mexico Has Investment Boom as Trade Hopes Grow," *The Wall Street Journal*, 24 May 1991: A1 and A8. For additional readings on trade see the Miller and Miller bibliography listed under Chapter 6 above.

PART IV. AFRICA

The historical evolution of the economic environment is ably traced in Ralph A. Austen, *African Economic History: Internal Development and External Dependency* (Portsmouth, N.H.: Heinemann, 1987). Dennis M. P. McCarthy presents a panoramic introduction to relations between government bureaucracies and businesses during the colonial period in "Bureaucracy, Business, and Africa During the Colonial Period: Who Did What to Whom and with What Consequences?," *Research in Economic History*, Vol. 11, 1988: 81-152. See also the annual journal *African Economic History* for 1983, Peter Wickins, *An Economic History of Africa from the Earliest Times to Partition* (Cape Town, South Africa: Oxford University Press, 1981), and John E. Flint, *Sir George Goldie and the Making of Nigeria* (London: Oxford University Press, 1960). A valuable historical work on poverty in Africa is John Iliffe, *The African Poor: A History* (Cambridge, England: Cambridge University Press, 1987). Another book worth consulting is Thomas J. Biersteker, *Multinationals, the State, and Control of the Nigerian Economy* (Princeton,

N.J.: Princeton University Press, 1987). An introductory chapter lucidly examines various analytical approaches to relations among business, dependency, and development. See also Richard L. Sklar, *Corporate Power in an African State: The Political Impact of Multinational Mining Companies in Zambia* (Berkeley: University of California Press, 1975). This book has comparative relevance for the mining case studies in this book. A valuable research essay in this regard is Raymond E. Dumett, "Sources for Mining Company History in Africa: The History and Records of the Ashanti Goldfields Corporation (Ghana), Ltd.," *Business History Review*, 62 (Autumn 1988): 502-15.

A key journal article, with global and comparative dimensions, is Ann M. Carlos and Stephen Nicholas, "'Giants of an Earlier Capitalism': The Chartered Trading Companies As Modern Multinationals," *Business History Review*, 62 (Autumn 1988): 398-419. An excellent study, which covers other areas of the world in addition to Africa, is Philip D. Curtin, *Cross-Cultural Trade in World History* (Cambridge, England: Cambridge University Press, 1984). This work has historical depth and a clear presentation that would help readers with little or no background in history.

CHAPTER 11

A fascinating examination of South Africa's future is "After Apartheid," *The Economist*, 3 November 1990, survey: 1-28.

A historical perspective on the involvement of U.S. business in South Africa is Richard Hull, *American Enterprise in South Africa: Historical Dimensions of Engagement and Disengagement* (New York: New York University Press, 1990). Valuable historical works are Leonard Monteath Thompson, *History of South Africa* (New Haven, Conn.: Yale University Press, 1990); Richard Elphick and Hermann Giliomee, *The Shaping of South African Society, 1652–1840* (Middleton, Conn.: Wesleyan University Press, 1990); and Colin Bundy, *The Rise and Fall of the South African Peasantry* (Berkeley: University of California Press, 1979).

CHAPTER 12

An informative series of articles on post-independence Namibia appeared in *The Christian Science Monitor* during September 1990. See, for instance, John Battersby, "Namibia's Combatants Seek New Role in Society," *The Christian Science Monitor*, 17 September 1990: 6. A factual article on Consolidated Diamond Mines opencast mine in Namibia is Kenneth Gooding, "Material Benefits: Consolidated Diamond Mines," in the *Financial Times* survey "Opencast Mining," 20 March 1990: III. "Nowhere in the world does the mining industry harness economies of scale to the degree seen at CDM's mine in Namibia (survey, I)."

Useful historical works are *Namibia, A Struggle for Independence: A Collection of Articles, Documents, and Speeches*, compiled by Y. Gorbunov (Moscow: Progress Publishers, 1988); Jon M. Bridgman, *The Revolt of the Hereros* (Berkeley: University of California Press, 1981); and Helmut Bley, *South-West Africa Under German Rule, 1894–1914* (Evanston, Ill.: Northwestern University Press, 1971).

CHAPTER 13

A useful overview of recent political changes in Africa, which highlights moves toward multiparty political systems, is Kenneth B. Noble, "Despots Dwindle as Reform Alters Face of Africa," *The New York Times*, 13 April 1991: 1 and 3.

For Tanzania relevant works are Andrew Coulson, *Tanzania: A Political Economy* (New York: Oxford University Press, 1982), Dennis M. P. McCarthy, *Colonial Bureaucracy and Creating Underdevelopment: Tanganyika, 1919–1940* (Ames: Iowa State University Press, 1982), and Paul Collier, Samir Radwan, and Samuel Wangwe, *Labour and Poverty in Rural Tanzania: Ujamaa and Rural Development* (New York: Oxford University Press, 1986).

An analysis of how and why the Ivory Coast's economic prospects soured during the latter 1980s is "Worn Out," *The Economist*, 24 March 1990: 45-46.

CHAPTER 14

A work that considers most attempts at economic cooperation in Africa is Ralph I. Onwuka and A. Sesay, eds., *The Future of Regionalism in Africa* (London: Macmillan, 1985). This book treats the East African Community (EAC), the Economic Community of West African States (ECOWAS), *Communauté économique de l'Afrique de l'Ouest* (CEAO/Economic Community of West Africa), the Central African Customs and Economic Union (UDEAC), and the South African Customs Union (SACU).

See also Ralph I. Onwuka and Olajide Aluko, eds., *The Future of Africa and the New International Economic Order* (New York: St. Martin's Press, 1986) and "ECOWAS at 15," *West Africa*, No. 3796, 28 May-3 June 1990: 882-902.

PART V. ASIA AND THE WESTERN PACIFIC

A helpful introduction is Brian Kelly and Mark London, *The Four Little Dragons* (New York: Simon and Schuster, 1990). A concise examination of Taiwan's strategy of seeking high-tech niches is Sheryl WuDunn, "Taiwan Aims for High-Tech Niches," *The New York Times*, 26 November 1990: C1 and C3. See also "Asia's Emerging Economies," *The Economist*, 16 November 1991: survey, 1-20.

An entertaining and educational booklet is Jean Currie, *"Export Avoidance" in Asia (or How Not To Do Business in Asia)* (Nr. Cardiff, Wales: CSP Economic Publications Ltd., 1989). This short work, complete with cartoons, explores "the cultural aspects of business with Hong Kong, Singapore, South Korea and Taiwan." See also Peter Wickenden, "Thoroughly, Exasperatingly, Delightfully, Chinese," *Financial Times*, 13 February 1991: 11. This article is about "doing business in Taiwan" and "explains the paradoxes of working within the system." A concise essay that contrasts the development paths taken by Taiwan and Korea is "Two Paths to Prosperity: Taiwan and Korea," *The Economist*, 14 July 1990: 19-20, 22.

CHAPTER 15

An extensive literature examines the strengths and limitations of Japanese business and its overseas activities. Some of the more valuable recent sources follow. An interesting essay on problems encountered by Japanese business is Guy Jonquières, "Industry Hits a Cultural Barrier," *Financial Times*, 5 December, 1990: 17. A worthwhile study of Japanese corporate governance is W. Carl Kester, *Japanese Takeovers: The Global Contest for Corporate Control* (Boston, Mass.: Harvard Business School Press, 1991). A fascinating analysis of how Japanese business took over the D-Ram industry from U.S. producers is David T. Methé, *Technological Competition in Global Industries: Marketing and Planning Strategies for American Industry* (New York: Quorum Books, 1991). D-Ram memories are mass-produced microchips used in products ranging from personal computers to Patriot missiles. See also Duane Kujawa, *Japanese Multinationals in the United States: Case Studies* (New York: Praeger, 1986), Max Eli, *Japan Inc.: Global Strategies of Japanese Trading Corporations* (New York: McGraw Hill, 1990), and Shintaro Ishihara, *The Japan That Can Say No: Why Japan Will Be First Among Equals* (New York: Simon and Schuster, 1991).

CHAPTER 16

A valuable study of the Green Revolution is Francine R. Frankel, *India's Green Revolution: Economic Gains and Political Costs* (Princeton, N. J.: Princeton University Press, 1971). A thoughtful essay on the legal implications of the Bhopal tragedy is "The Ghosts of Bhopal: Union Carbide's Settlement Reveals a Gap in International Law," *The Economist*, 18 February 1989: 70. An excellent survey of India is "Caged," *The Economist*, 4 May 1991: special section, 1-19.

CHAPTER 17

The essential first work on China is Jonathan D. Spence, *The Search for Modern China* (New York: Norton, 1990). Complementing Jean Currie's *"Export Avoidance" in Asia (or How Not To Do Business in Asia)* (Nr. Cardiff, Wales: CSP Economic Publications Ltd., 1989) is Scott D. Seligman, *Dealing with the Chinese: A Practical Guide to Business Etiquette* (London: Mercury, 1991). An analysis of the 1980s that focuses on international business is Richard W. T. Pomfret, *Investing in China: Ten Years of the Open Door Policy* (Ames: Iowa State University Press, 1991). A cautious return to China by international business is examined in Angus Foster, "A More Cautious West is Knocking on China's Door," *Financial Times*, 14 December 1990: 6. The tentative comeback of Shenzhen, a south China city and special economic zone in Guangdong province, as an attempt at "fusing socialism and capitalism" is tracked by Sheryl WuDunn, "China Revives Its Test of Capitalism," *The New York Times*, 23 May 1991: C1 and C15.

CHAPTER 18

Useful sources are Tan Loong-Hoe and Narongchai Akrasanee, eds., *ASEAN-U.S.*

Economic Relations: Changes in Economic Environment and Opportunities (San Francisco: Asia Foundation, Center for Asian Pacific Studies; ASEAN Economic Research Unit, Institute of Southeast Asia Studies, 1988) and K. S. Nathan and M. Pathmanathan, eds., *Trilateralism in Asia: Problems and Prospects in U.S.-Japan-ASEAN Relations* (Kuala Lumpur, Malaysia: Antara Book Co., 1986).

An article on Thailand's future economic plans, which remains useful even after the coup of 23 February 1991 and the violence of May 1992, is Helen E. White, "Thailand Plans for Slower, Stabler Growth," *The Asian Wall Street Journal*, 11-12 January 1991: 1 and 19. An essay that is haunting to read after the coup is "Divorcing the Army, Thai-style," *The Economist*, 15 December 1990: 33. A discussion of how one multinational piggybacked on local networks in Thailand is Jonathan Sikes, "Amway Discovers Thai Society Offers Built-In Sales Network," *Investor's Daily*, 20 November 1989: 11.

See also the essays in *Asia-Pacific Economies: Promises and Challenges*, which constitute Parts A and B of Volume 6 (1987), *Research in International Business and Finance*, M. Dutta, ed.

Sources

Abbreviations

CSM	*The Christian Science Monitor*
Econ	*The Economist*
*FT	*Financial Times*
IHT	*International Herald Tribune*
NYT	*The New York Times* (national edition, except for 1954)
WSJ	*The Wall Street Journal*

*With the exception of the period 15 January 1991 through 20 March 1991, all references are to the international edition of the *FT* printed in the United States. For those two months references are to the British edition.

INTRODUCTION

Works Cited:

Leavitt, Harold J. "Educating Our MBAs: On Teaching What We Haven't Taught." *California Management Review*, Vol. 31, No. 3 (Spring 1989): 38-50.
Rada, Juan. *FT*, 10 July 1989: 29.

CHAPTER 1

Works Cited:

de Roover, Raymond. *The Rise and Decline of the Medici Bank, 1397–1494*. Cambridge, Mass.: Harvard University Press, 1968.
Ehrenberg, Richard. *Capital and Finance in the Age of the Renaissance: A Study of the Fugger and Their Connections*. New York: Harcourt Brace and Co., 1928.

Powers, Joel. "The House of Rothschild: The Family and Capital Formation in Historical Perspective." Unpublished paper, Iowa State University, Spring 1982.

Works Consulted:

de Vries, Jan. *The Economy of Europe in an Age of Crisis, 1600–1750.* Cambridge, England: Cambridge University Press, 1976.
Lopez, Robert. *The Commercial Revolution of the Middle Ages, 950–1350.* Englewood Cliffs, N.J.: Prentice-Hall, 1971.
Miskimin, Harry A. *The Economy of Early Renaissance Europe, 1300–1460.* Englewood Cliffs, N.J.: Prentice-Hall, 1969.
_____ . *The Economy of Later Renaissance Europe, 1400–1600.* Cambridge, England: Cambridge University Press, 1977.

CHAPTER 2

Works Cited:

Bartlett, Christopher A., and Ghoshal, Sumantra. "Managing Innovation in the Transnational Corporation." In *Managing the Global Firm*: 215-55. Edited by Christopher A. Bartlett, Yves Doz, and Gunnar Hedlund. London, England: Routledge, 1990.
Behrman, Jack N. *National Interests and the Multinational Enterprise: Tensions Among the North Atlantic Countries.* Englewood Cliffs, N.J.: Prentice-Hall, 1970.
Chandler, Jr., Alfred D. *The Essential Alfred Chandler: Essays Toward A Historical Theory of Big Business.* Edited and with an introduction by Thomas K. McCraw. Boston, Mass.: Harvard Business School Press, 1988.
_____. "The Growth of the Transnational Firm in the United States and the United Kingdom: A Comparative Analysis." *The Economic History Review* 33 (August 1980): 396-410.
Dunning, John H., and Archer, Howard. "The Eclectic Paradigm and the Growth of U.K. Multinational Enterprises 1870–1983." *Business and Economic History*, Second Series, Vol. 16, 1987: 19-49.
Econ, 4 February 1984: 76; "Swedish Multinationals: A Hard Act to Follow," 1 August 1987: 63-65.
FT, "Sweden—a Model or Warning?," 21 September 1987: 20; 8 February 1991: 12; 11 February 1991: 12; 11 May 1992: 19.
Goold, Michael, and Campbell, John. *Strategies and Styles: The Role of the Centre in Managing Diversified Corporations.* Oxford, England: B. Blackwell, 1987.
Kocka, Jürgen. "The Rise of the Modern Industrial Enterprise in Germany." In *Managerial Hierarchies: Comparative Perspectives on the Rise of Modern Industrial Enterprise*: 77-116. Edited by Alfred D. Chandler, Jr., and Herbert Daems. Cambridge, Mass.: Harvard University Press, 1980.
Levitt, Theodore. *The Marketing Imagination.* New York: The Free Press, 1983.
_____ . *The Marketing Imagination: New, Expanded Edition.* New York: The Free Press, 1986.

Lévy-Leboyer, Maurice. "The Large Corporation in Modern France." In *Managerial Hierarchies: Comparative Perspectives on the Rise of Modern Industrial Enterprise*: 117-60. Edited by Alfred D. Chandler, Jr., and Herbert Daems. Cambridge, Mass.: Harvard University Press, 1980.

Nye, John Vincent. "Firm Size and Economic Backwardness: A New Look at the French Industrialization Debate." *The Journal of Economic History* 47 (September 1987): 649-69.

Porter, Michael. *The Competitive Advantage of Nations*. New York: The Free Press, 1990.

The author has spent time in Europe during 1969, 1970, 1973, 1977, and 1991.

CHAPTER 3

Works Cited:

Cameron, Rondo. *A Concise Economic History of the World: From Paeolithic Times to the Present*. New York: Oxford University Press, 1989.

"The Commerbank Report on German Business and Finance," No. 7/90. In *Econ*, 21 July 1990: 62.

Econ, 9 November 1991: 60; 23 November 1991: 58; 7 December 1991: 63.

FT, 20 November 1989: 25; 1 December 1989: 1 and 41; 11 January 1990: 1; 18 April 1990: 1; 19 June 1990: 18; 28 November 1990: 1; 16 January 1991: 21; 16 December 1991: 1; 29 January 1992: 1; 4 February 1992: 2; and 26 March 1992: 19.

NYT, 7 November 1989: 25; 31 July 1990: C1 and C5; 23 October 1991: A1 and C18; 10 December 1991: A1 and A6; and 12 December 1991: A1 and A8.

Works Consulted:

Econ, "A Survey of the European Community," 7 July 1990: 12 and 15.

FT, 4 October 1991: 21; and 12 December 1991: 5.

PART II. NORTH AMERICA

Works Cited:

LaFeber, Walter. *The New Empire: An Interpretation of American Expansion, 1860–1898*. Ithaca, N.Y.: Published for the American Historical Association by Cornell University Press, 1963.

Vernon, Raymond. "The Role of U.S. Enterprise Abroad." In *The American Business Corporation: New Perspectives on Profit and Purpose*: 129-49. Edited by Eli Goldston, Herbert C. Morton, and G. Neal Ryland. Cambridge, Mass.: The MIT Press, 1969.

Works Consulted:

Carstensen, Fred V. *American Enterprise in Foreign Markets: Singer and International Harvester in Imperial Russia.* Chapel Hill: University of North Carolina Press, 1984.

Davis, Lance E., Easterlin, Richard E., Parker, William N., et al. *American Economic Growth: An Economist's History of the United States.* New York: Harper and Row, 1972.

Hughes, Jonanthan R. T. *American Economic History,* 3rd ed. Glenview, Ill.: Scott, Foresman and Co., 1990.

North, Douglass C., and Davis, Lance E. *Institutional Change and American Economic Growth.* Cambridge, England: Cambridge University Press, 1971.

Robertson, Ross, and Walton, Gary. *History of the American Economy.* New York: Harcourt Brace Jovanovich, 1983.

Schmidt, Louis Bernard. "Internal Commerce and the Development of a National Economy Before 1860." *The Journal of Political Economy,* Vol. 47, No. 6 (December 1939): 798-822.

Ver Steeg, Clarence L. "The American Revolution Considered As an Economic Movement." *The Huntington Library Quarterly,* Vol. 20, No. 4 (August 1957): 361-72.

The author has taught United States economic history since 1972.

CHAPTER 4

This case study draws heavily from Fred V. Carstensen, *American Enterprise in Foreign Markets: Singer and International Harvester in Imperial Russia* (Chapel Hill: University of North Carolina Press, 1984), especially pp. 96-103 and 225-34. I am deeply grateful to the author and the University of North Carolina Press for permission to use this material.

CHAPTER 5

Works Cited:

Dulles, John Foster. News conference transcript, 8 June 1954. In *United States Department of State, American Foreign Policy, 1950–1955, Basic Documents,* Vol. I (parts I-IX, pp. 1-1707): 1310. Washington, D.C.: U.S. Department of State, 1957.

Eisenhower, Dwight D. *The White House Years: Mandate for Change, 1953–1956.* Garden City, N.Y.: Doubleday, 1963.

Geneen, Harold. *Managing.* Garden City, N.Y.: Doubleday, 1984.

Immerman, Richard H. *The CIA in Guatemala: The Foreign Policy of Intervention.* Austin, Texas: University of Texas Press, 1982.

May, Stacy, and Plaza, Galo. *The United Fruit Company in Latin America.* New York: National Planning Association, 1958.

NYT, 14 March 1954: 27.

Phillips, David Atlee. *The Night Watch.* New York: Atheneum, 1977.

Villanueva T., Benjamin. "An Approach to the Study of the Industrial Surplus: The Case of the United Fruit Company in Central America." Research Paper No. 40. Madison, Wisconsin: Land Tenure Center, University of Wisconsin, 1969.

Wemhoff, Linda. "United Fruit in Guatemala and Its Connection with the U.S. CIA." Unpublished paper, Iowa State University, Spring 1984.

Works Consulted:

Douglass, Patti. "The Multinational Corporation: Its Relation to the Third World and Its Development." Unpublished paper, Iowa State University, Fall 1977.

Farnsworth, Clyde H. Article on Overseas Private Investment Corporation (OPIC). *NYT*, 25 April 1982: F6.

O'Neill, Daniel J. "United Fruit Company in Costa Rica." Unpublished paper, Iowa State University, Spring 1982.

CHAPTER 6

Works Cited:

CSM, 13 February 1990: 8-9.

NYT, 8 October 1989: F4; 16 April 1990: C1 and C2; 15 June 1991; 17 and 21; 18 February 1992: A1 and C6; 7 March 1992, 17 and 19; and 16 May 1992: 17 and 24.

Works Consulted:

Owen, David. "A Withering Maple Leaf." *FT*, 10 April 1990: 20.

Simon, Bernard. "A Free Trade Disagreement." *FT*, 13 March 1992: 13.

Vincent, Bob. "New Baby is Causing Concern: U.S.-Canada Free Trade Agreement Assessed." *FT*, 9 November 1989: special survey on Canada, IV.

The author visited Canada in 1978, 1979, 1984, and 1986.

**PART III. CENTRAL AMERICA, SOUTH AMERICA
AND THE CARIBBEAN BASIN**

Work Cited:

Evans, Peter B. *Dependent Development: The Alliance of Multinational, State, and Local Capital in Brazil.* Princeton, N.J.: Princeton University Press, 1979.

Works Consulted:

Cutler, Clinton. "The Capitalist World-System: A Sampling of Theories." Unpublished paper, Iowa State University, 1981.

Richards, Donald Gordon. "Construction of a Synthetic Measure of Dependency and Its Uses in Testing Some Hypotheses." Ph.D. dissertation, 1983, University of

Connecticut.

CHAPTER 7

This case study draws heavily from Paul M. Kramer, "Silver Mining at Cerro de Pasco, Peru, 1630–1897." M.A. thesis, 1979, Iowa State University. I am deeply grateful to the author for permission to use his material.

CHAPTER 8

Works Cited:

Angel, Clara Roselina, and Navia, Rodrigo. "A Colombian Experience." Unpublished paper, Iowa State University, Spring 1983.
Kline, Harvey F. "The Coal of 'El Cerrejón': An Historical Analysis of Major Colombian Policy Decisions and MNC Activities." *Inter-American Economic Affairs*, Vol. 35, No. 3 (Winter 1981): 69-90.
_____. "The Colombian Debates About Coal, Exxon and Themelves." *Inter-American Economic Affairs*, Vol. 36, No. 4 (Spring 1983): 3-28.

CHAPTER 9

This case study draws heavily from Peter W. Deveaux-Isaacs, "The Hawksbill Creek Agreement: A Case Study in 'Development,'" unpublished paper, Iowa State University, Spring 1980. I am deeply grateful to the author for permission to use his material.

This author visited Freeport, Grand Bahama Island, in 1979 and Ocho Rios, Jamaica, in 1980.

CHAPTER 10

Works Cited:

FT, 30 January 1991: 4; 26 March 1991: 18; 25 April 1991: 3; 12 June 1991: 2; 6 November 1991: 24; 19 December 1991: 6; 13 March 1992: 13; 11 June 1992: 5; and 15 June 1992: 4.
LaValley, Gary. "The Andean Pact: An Experiment in Economic Integration." Unpublished paper, Iowa State University, Spring 1983.
Newsweek, 11 October 1971: 77.
NYT, 2 November 1989: 23; 29 March 1990: C1; 20 May 1991: C9; 14 September 1990: C1 and C6; and 25 September 1990: C1 and C2.

Work Consulted:

Douglas, Patti. "The Multinational Corporation: Its Relation to the Third World and Its Development." Unpublished paper, Iowa State University, Fall 1977.

PART IV. AFRICA

Works Cited:

Clarence-Smith, W. G. "Business Empires in Equatorial Africa." *African Economic History*, No. 12, 1983: 3-11.

McCarthy, Dennis M. P. "Bureaucracy, Business, and Africa During the Colonial Period: Who Did What to Whom and With What Consequences?," *Research in Economic History*, Vol. 11, 1988: 81-152.

Wickins, Peter. *An Economic History of Africa from Earliest Times to Partition.* Cape Town, South Africa: Oxford University Press, 1981.

Works Consulted:

Ascherson, Neil. *The King Incorporated: Leopold II in the Age of Trusts.* New York: Doubleday, 1964.

Dike, K. O. *Trade and Politics in the Niger Delta, 1830–1885.* Oxford, England: Oxford University Press, 1956.

Flint, John E. *Sir George Goldie and the Making of Nigeria.* London: Oxford University Press, 1960.

Johnston, Sir Harry H. *The Story of My Life.* Indianapolis, Ind.: Bobbs-Merrill Co., 1923.

CHAPTER 11

Works Cited:

de Villiers, René. "Afrikaner Nationalism." In *The Oxford History of South Africa*, Vol. 2: *South Africa, 1870–1966*: 365-423. Edited by Monica Wilson and Leonard M. Thompson. New York: Oxford University Press, 1971.

FT, 13 September 1990: 3; 14 February 1992: 24; and 19 March 1992: 1.

Thompson, Leonard M. (1969a) "Co-operation and Conflict: The Zulu Kingdom and Natal." In *The Oxford History of South Africa*, Vol. 1: *South Africa to 1870*: 334-90. Edited by Monica Wilson and Leonard M. Thompson. New York: Oxford University Press, 1969.

_____ . (1969b) "Co-operation and Conflict: The High Veld." In *The Oxford History of South Africa*, Vol. 1: *South Africa to 1870*: 391-446. Edited by Monica Wilson and Leonard M. Thompson. New York: Oxford University Press, 1969.

_____ . (1971a) "The Subjection of the African Chiefdoms, 1870–1898." In *The Oxford History of South Africa*, Vol. 2: *South Africa, 1870–1966*: 245-88. Edited by Monica Wilson and Leonard M. Thompson. New York: Oxford University Press, 1971.

_____ . (1971b) "Great Britain and the Afrikaner Republics, 1870–1899." In *The Oxford History of South Africa*, Vol. 2: *South Africa, 1870–1966*: 289-324. Edited by Monica Wilson and Leonard M. Thompson. New York: Oxford

University Press, 1971.

_____ . (1971c) "The Compromise of Union." In *The Oxford History of South Africa*, Vol. 2: *South Africa, 1870–1966*: 325-64. Edited by Monica Wilson and Leonard M. Thompson. New York: Oxford University Press, 1971.

Wilson, Monica, and Thompson, Leonard M., eds. "Preface." In *The Oxford History of South Africa*, Vol. 1: *South Africa to 1870*: v-xiii. New York: Oxford University Press, 1969.

Works Consulted:

Des Moines Register, "Drug Giant Merck to Sell South African Unit," 1 December 1987: 8S.

Inskeep, R. R. "The Archaeological Background." In *The Oxford History of South Africa*, Vol. 1: *South Africa to 1870*: 1-39. Edited by Monica Wilson and Leonard M. Thompson. New York: Oxford University Press, 1969.

Katzen, M. P. "White Settlers and the Origin of a New Society, 1652–1778." In *The Oxford History of South Africa*, Vol. 1: *South Africa to 1870*: 183-232. Edited by Monica Wilson and Leonard M. Thompson. New York: Oxford University Press, 1969.

Kuper, Leo. "African Nationalism in South Africa, 1910–1964." In *The Oxford History of South Africa*, Vol. 2: *South Africa, 1870–1966*: 424-76. Edited by Monica Wilson and Leonard M. Thompson. New York: Oxford University Press, 1971.

McCarthy, Dennis M. P. "The Economic Factor in the Origins of the Boer War: A Study in Multiple Points of View." Unpublished paper, Yale University, January 1968.

Thompson, Leonard M. *Survival in Two Worlds: Moshweshwe of Lesotho, 1786–1870*. Oxford, England: Oxford University Press, 1975.

_____ . *The Unification of South Africa, 1902–1910*. Oxford, England: Oxford University Press, 1960.

Wilson, Monica. "Co-operation and Conflict: The Eastern Cape Frontier." In *The Oxford History of South Africa*, Vol. 1: *South Africa to 1870*: 233-71. New York: Oxford University Press, 1969.

CHAPTER 12

Most of this case study draws heavily from Timothy Joseph O'Rourke, "From Black to White: The Underdevelopment of African Namibia," honors thesis in the Special Scholars Program, Corcoran Department of History, University of Virginia, Spring 1978, Joseph C. Miller, Advisor. I am deeply grateful to the author for permission to use his material.

Other Works Cited:

FT, 12 July 1991: 14.

Naqvi, Ali Sarawar. "Foreign Enterprise and Labor Exploitation in Namibia: A Report of the U.N. Council for Namibia." *Issue: A Journal of Africanist Opinion* 13, 1984: 35-40.

NYT, 21 March 1990: 1.

CHAPTER 13

Works Cited:

Afrika, April 1992: 24.
Bienen, Henry. "An Ideology for Africa." *Foreign Affairs*, Vol. 47, No. 3 (April 1969): 545-59.
FT, 23 October 1990: 4; and 20 January 1992: 4.
McCarthy, Dennis M. P. "Contrasting Development Plans: Kenya, Uganda, and Tanzania." Unpublished lecture and paper, New Haven, Conn., Summer 1969.

Works Consulted:

Bienen, Henry. *Tanzania: Party Transformation and Economic Development*. Princeton, N.J.: Princeton University Press, 1967.
Coulson, Andrew. *Tanzania: A Political Economy*. New York: Oxford University Press, 1982.
Econ, "On the Road to Somewhere: A Survey of East Africa," 20 June 1987: special survey, 1-20.
FT, 8 January 1992, III: Survey of Kenya.
Hogendorn, J. S., and Scott, K. M. "The East African Groundnut Scheme: Lessons of a Large-Scale Agricultural Failure." *African Economic History*, No. 10 (1981): 81-115.
McCarthy, Dennis M. P. "The Bureaucratic Manipulation of Indigenous Business: A Comparative Study in Legal Imposition from Colonial Africa." *Business and Economic History*, Second Series, Vol. 19, 1990: 123-32.
_____ . "Bureaucracy, Business, and Africa During the Colonial Period: Who Did What to Whom and with What Consequences?" *Research in Economic History*, Vol. 11, 1988: 81-152.
_____ . *Colonial Bureaucracy and Creating Underdevelopment: Tanganyika, 1919–1940*. Ames: Iowa State University Press, 1982.·
McHenry, Jr., Dean E. *Tanzania's Ujamaa Villages: The Implementation of a Rural Development Strategy*. Berkeley: University of California, Institute of International Studies, 1979.
Shivji, Issa G. *Class Struggles in Tanzania*. New York: Monthly Review Press, 1976.
Wood, Alan. *The Groundnut Affair*. London: Bodley Head, 1950.
The author conducted research in Tanzania in 1973.

CHAPTER 14

Works Cited:

Asante, S. K. B. "ECOWAS/CEAOI Conflict and Cooperation in West Africa." In *The Future of Regionalism in Africa*: 84-93. Edited by Ralph I. Onwuka and A. Sesay. London: Macmillan, 1985.

Perlez, Jane. "Obitsports." *NYT*, 24 August 1990: C2.

West Africa, No. 3796, 28 May-3 June 1990, "ECOWAS at 15": 882-902.

PART V. ASIA AND THE WESTERN PACIFIC

Works Cited:

FT, "Asia's Pacific Rim," 30 June 1988: special section, I-XII.

Ridding John. "S Korea's Industry Giants Pick Their Core Businesses," *FT*, 23 April 1991: 4.

Yates, Ronald E. Three articles on Asia's "Little Tigers." Published in the *Chicago Tribune*. Reprinted in the *Des Moines Register*:

> 1986(a) 11 May 1986: 3A;
> 1986(b) 12 May 1986: 1A and 9A;
> 1986(c) 13 May 1986: 4A.

Works Consulted:

Lohr, Steve. "East Asia: The Face of Economic Optimism," *NYT*, 7 October 1985: 1 and 30.

Rodger, Ian. "Asia's Economic Tigers May Be Losing Their Teeth," *FT*, 24 May 1990: 6.

CHAPTER 15

Works Cited:

Franko, Lawrence G. *The Threat of Japanese Multinationals: How the West Can Respond.* New York: Wiley, 1983.

_____ . *World Market Share (WMS) Research Note No. 4, Corporate Performance and Geographical Location* (Ms.). London: J. Henry Schroder Wagg & Co. Ltd., Strategy Group, November, 1981.

Mason, Mark. "Foreign Direct Investment and Japanese Economic Development, 1899–1931." *Business and Economic History*, Second Series, Vol. 16, 1987: 93-107.

Moriya, Katsuhisa. "Urban Networks and Information Networks." Chapter 4 in *Tokugawa Japan: The Social and Economic Antecedents of Modern Japan*: 97-122. Edited by Chie Nakane and Shinzaburō Ōishi. Translation by Ronald P. Toby. Translation edited by Conrad Totman. Tokyo: University of Tokyo Press, 1990.

Ozawa, Terutomo. *Multinationalism, Japanese Style: The Political Economy of Outward Dependency.* Princeton, N.J.: Princeton University Press, 1979.

Sakudō, Yōtarō. "The Management Practices of Family Business." Chapter 6 in *Tokugawa Japan: The Social and Economic Antecedents of Modern Japan*: 147-66. Edited by Chie Nakane and Shinzaburō Ōishi. Translation by William B. Hauser. Translation edited by Conrad Totman. Tokyo: University of Tokyo Press, 1990.

Sanger, David E. "Unusual Path to the Top at Mitsubishi," *NYT*, 13 April 1992: C1 and

C3.
Scott, Bruce R., Rosenblum, John W., and Sproat, Audrey. *Case Studies in Political Economy: Japan, 1854–1977*. Boston: Divison of Research, Harvard Business School, 1980.
Tsurumi, Yoshi. *The Japanese Are Coming: A Multinational Interaction of Firms and Politics*. Cambridge, Mass.: Ballinger Publishing Co., 1976.

Works Consulted:

Abrahams, Paul. "Almost Untouched by Human Hand," *FT*, 21 April 1989: 24.
de Jonquières, Guy, and Dixon, Hugo. "The Emergence of a Global Company," *FT*, 2 October 1989: 18.
Econ, "The Multinational Eastern Style," 24 June 1989: 63-64; and "The Softer Samurai," 12 May 1990: 73.
FT, "Japanese Industry," 4 December 1989: special survey, section III: I-X; "Japanese Financial Markets," 15 March 1990: special survey, section III: I-XII.
Gannett, Nick, and Owen, Geoffrey. "Japanese Play a Mean Pin-Ball," *FT*, 18 January 1990: 19.
Jansen, Marius B., ed. *The Cambridge History of Japan*. Vol. 5: *The Nineteenth Century*. Cambridge, England: Cambridge University Press, 1989.
Sanger, David E. "Sony's Norio Ohga: Building Smaller, Buying Bigger," *The New York Times Magazine*, 18 February 1990: 22-25, 61-64, 68, and 70.

CHAPTER 16

Works Cited:

Associated Press, 1 December 1987.
Econ, 18 February 1989: 70.
NYT, Indian government brief quoted in 9 April 1985: 1 and 30; 23 March 1986: 1 and 7; 18 November 1987: 31; 4 October 1991: C4; 15 April 1992: C1 and C19.
United Nations Population Fund, 1990.

Work Consulted:

Frankel, Francine R. *India's Green Revolution: Economic Gains and Political Costs*. Princeton, N.J.: Princeton University Press, 1971.

CHAPTER 17

A significant part of this case study relies greatly on information presented in Ken McCormick, "China's Great Leap Forward: A Reappraisal," unpublished paper, Iowa State University, Spring 1980. I am deeply grateful to the author for permission to use his material.

Other Works Cited:

Ashbrook, Jr., Arthur G. "Main Lines of Chinese Communist Economic Policy." In *An Economic Profile of Mainland China*: 15-44. New York: Praeger, 1968.
_____ . "China: Economic Policy and Economic Results, 1949–1971." In *People's Republic of China, an Economic Assessment: A Compendium of Papers Submitted to the Joint Economic Committee, Congress of the United States*: 3-51. Washington, D.C.: U.S. Government Printing Office, 1972.
Delfs, Robert. "Collective Efforts Are Overwhelming State Enterprise." *The Far Eastern Economic Review*, 20 March 1986: 70, 75, 77-78.
Eckstein, Alexander. *China's Economic Revolution*. Cambridge, England: Cambridge University Press, 1977.
Econ, "Turning Grain into Pigs," 24 January 1987: 34.
FT, 13 March 1992: 1 and 4.
IHT, 23-24 February 1991: 12.
Ji, Bian. "A Programme for China's Reform of Economic Structure." *People's Republic of China Quarterly*, January 1985: 8-21.
King, Frank H. H. *A Concise Economic History of Modern China (1840–1961)*. New York: Praeger, 1969.
Magdoff, Harry. "China: Contrasts with the U.S.S.R." *Monthly Review*, Vol. 27, No.3 (July-August 1975): 12-57.
Shao-ch'i, Liu. *Report on the Work of the Central Committee*, delivered at Second Session of Eighth Congress of the Chinese Communist Party, 5 May 1958, quoted by Eckstein, *China's Economic Revolution* (Cambridge, England: Cambridge University Press, 1977): 56.
Sweezy, Paul. "Has China Lost the Road to Socialism?" Speech delivered at Iowa State University, 6 December 1979, reported by Ken McCormick.
Wheelright, E. L., and McFarlane, Bruce. *The Chinese Road to Socialism: Economics of the Cultural Revolution*. New York: Monthly Review Press, 1970.
Zedong, Mao. *Quotations From Chairman Mao Tsetung*. Peking: Foreign Languages Press, 1972.

Works Consulted:

Meyer, Tamara N. "Reform: Past the Midway Point with Deng Xiaoping." Unpublished paper, Iowa State University, Spring 1986.
O'Neill, Mark. Reuter article on Shanghai stock market, printed in the *Des Moines Register*, 3 October 1986: 5S and 8S.

CHAPTER 18

Works Cited:

FT, 29 January 1992: 7; 10 September 1992: 7.
IHT, 19 February 1991: 11; 23-24 February 1991: 23-24 (interview of Rafidah Aziz by Michael Richardson).

Works Consulted:

Bangkok Post, "Kaifu Puts ASEAN on Hold," 12 January 1991: 4.

Duthie, Stephen. "Singapore Supports Malaysian Trade Plan," *The Asian Wall Street Journal*, 14 January 1991: 1 and 5.

Keawkungwal, Sri-Ruen. *Buddhism and Existential Psychotherapy: An Introduction for Laymen.* Bangkok, Thailand: Editions Duang Kamol, 1989.

The Nation (Bangkok), "Economics to Dominate Talks in KL (Kuala Lumpur)," 14 January 1991: A3.

The author traveled around the world in 1990–91 and visited Thailand in January, 1991.

Index

Barbados, 134, 141
Bardi, 13, 14
Baring Brothers, 69
Bartlett, Christopher, 31
Bayer, 50
Behrman, Jack, 32
Belgium, 19, 21, 22, 26, 183; in
Africa, 25, 149, 200; EC and, 59,
60; ECSC and, 58; GATT and,
249; Latin Monetary Union and,
107
Belize, 141
Benci, Giovanni d'Amerigo, 12, 13, 15
Benin, 201
Bhopal disaster, 14, 211; case study
of, 227-33
Bian Ji, 246
Bienen, Henry, 191
Bismarck, Otto von, 26, 48, 53, 148
Black and Decker Manufacturing
Company, 186
Bolivia, 141-42
Boston Fruit Company, 85
Botswana, 159, 161, 184
Brazil, 100-101, 143, 222-24;
LAFTA and, 142; *mercosur* and,
141; Petrobras, 101
Britain, 8, 24, 32, 45-48, 50, 64, 65,
79, 102, 107, 218, 228-29, 250; in
Africa, 26, 39, 147-48, 150, 156,
158-66, 173-74, 181, 183, 185-86,
188, 189, 193, 194, 199-201; in
Asia, 26, 39, 206, 215, 228; in
the Caribbean, 39, 129-31,
133-35; comparative emergence
model in, 38-44; EC and, 59; in
North America, 39; Second
Industrial Revolution in, 43-44; in
South America, 104-6, 111. *See
also individual British companies*
British East Africa Company, 147
British Leyland, 54
British Peruvian Corporation, Ltd.,
112
British Petroleum, 33
British South Africa Company, 147

Broadbent, Ed, 93
Brunei, 249
Bulgaria, 60
Burkina Faso, 200
Burroughs, 223
Bush, George, 141, 142
Business culture, defined, 3-4
Buthelezi, Mangosuthu Gatsha, 153,
169

Caceras, Andres, 110
Cadbury Schweppes, 33
Cambridge University, 43
Cameron, Rondo, 58, 59
Cameroon, 194
Campbell, John, 33, 34
Canada, 130, 222; in Africa,
185-86; Free Trade Agreement
with U.S., 58, 65, 93-97, 141,
142, 145, 250; Liberal Party,
93-94; NAFTA with U.S. and
Mexico, 58, 97, 141-45, 224; New
Democratic Party, 93; Progressive
Conservative Party, 93, 96. *See
also individual Canadian
companies*
Cape Verde, 200
Capital, defined, 37
Carbocol (Colombian National Coal
Company), 121-26
Cardoso, Fernando, 100, 101
Caribbean Economic Community
(Caricom), 141
Carnavon, Lord, 162
Castillo Armas, Carlos, 90-92
Castro, Fidel, 83
Cavallis, Antonio de, 17
CEAO (Economic Community of
West Africa), 200-201
Centralization, defined, 3
Cerrejón Carboneras, Ltd., 119-22
Cerro Corporation, 66, 99, 150,
172; case study of, 103-15
Cerro de Pasco Tunnel Company,
112-14
Cetshwayo, 160

About the Author

DENNIS M. P. McCARTHY is Associate Professor of History at Iowa State University in Ames. His articles have appeared in publications such as *Humanities Magazine*, *The Journal of Economic History*, and *Business and Economic History*. He is the author of *Colonial Bureaucracy and Creating Underdevelopment* (1982).